The artist

&

the bicycle man

By Doris J. Paterson

Order this book online at www.trafford.com/08-0510
or email orders@trafford.com

Most Trafford titles are also available at major online book retailers.

Note for Librarians: A cataloguing record for this book is available from Library
and Archives Canada at www.collectionscanada.ca/amicus/index-e.html

Printed in Victoria, BC, Canada.

ISBN: 978-1-4251-7650-1

*We at Trafford believe that it is the responsibility of us all, as both individuals and corporations,
to make choices that are environmentally and socially sound. You, in turn, are supporting this
responsible conduct each time you purchase a Trafford book, or make use of our publishing services.
To find out how you are helping, please visit www.trafford.com/responsiblepublishing.html*

*Our mission is to efficiently provide the world's finest, most comprehensive book publishing
service, enabling every author to experience success. To find out how to publish your book, your
way, and have it available worldwide, visit us online at www.trafford.com/10510*

 **Trafford** PUBLISHING® www.trafford.com

North America & international
toll-free: 1 888 232 4444 (USA & Canada)
phone: 250 383 6864 ♦ fax: 250 383 6804 ♦ email: info@trafford.com

The United Kingdom & Europe
phone: +44 (0)1865 722 113 ♦ local rate: 0845 230 9601
facsimile: +44 (0)1865 722 868 ♦ email: info.uk@trafford.com

10 9 8 7 6 5 4 3 2 1

For Adrian Harper
who helps me achieve my goals

The drawings throughout this book
are from originals by the author

Front cover
Sir Willy to the Rescue, 1994
From *The Life Series,* acrylic on paper
22 x 30 inches / 55.9 x 76.2 cm

Coming together

Willy and the turkey

In the meat department I see this commotion going on down by the mound of turkeys. It's Willy. A group of women around him are tugging at his arm making pleading noises. With the look of a conquering hero, he comes toward me, arms above his head, holding a plump round turkey. This is all because my son wrote to say the only thing that kept him going when he was travelling was the thought of coming back to a home-cooked Christmas turkey.

Now, I should explain that since I've been living in the apartment building, I've been filling in as secretary for our strata council. The chairman is this fellow Willy. I type the minutes of the meetings and take them up to his apartment for his approval and signature. Well, I was telling him about having to get a turkey when he offered to help me get one that was advertised as the best buy. He seems to love the challenge of bargain hunting, so I agree. This man has been quite helpful during the past months. I have only to mention needing something, and he seems to make sure I get it.

Willy has taken this turkey project on as a personal crusade. We will get the best and cheapest fowl in Canada or the United States. He rifles through all the advertisements, then scans every local store window, reporting the latest find on the phone. It gets to the point where I'm in a state of high excitement at the thought of getting a turkey for two cents a pound less than usual. He phones.

"Sumas, across the border, has a great price on Butterballs. I can take you in my truck."

"Okay," I say, "we'll check it out." We drive across the border and go in the grocery store. Willy disappears.

Now, I should tell you about Willy. He is tall and thin, comes from Denmark and speaks in a hushed voice with an accent. He lowers his head so one can hardly hear what he says. This is a shame because his one-liners, combined with his original observations on life, make him very interesting to listen to. I don't know how old he is, but I know he's older than my sixty-five years. He says he knows my age because he saw my published journal article and pieced the years together. "It's better if you use a sneaky approach to that," he told me.

Well, here he is and he puts the bird in the shopping cart.

"It's the last Butterball," he beams, "they all want it, so you have to decide if this is the one."

"Yes," I tell him, "it's a beauty."

"Ice cream. You must have ice cream for dessert," Willy says, as he finds a sale product. There's a niggling feeling he is trying to manage my spending, however kindly it's meant.

"Yes, we'll take that and..." I see an extravagant box labeled Decadent Chocolate, "We'll take that too." Willy's face takes on a look of disbelief.

"But it's five dollars."

"I know," I say.

The line-up into Canada is long. It's going to take at least two hours to clear customs. Willy laughs like a little boy and, maneuvering around some houses, comes out ahead of the crowd. I can't bear to look at the faces of the drivers behind us and cower, red-faced, in my seat.

There's no room in my freezer. Willy tells me not to worry, his is empty. I don't believe it till I see it's true. Nothing. He finds an outside thermometer to put inside the freezer to be sure the bird will not spoil (he has read in the library the right temperature setting). On Christmas Eve day Willy comes down with the turkey, fretting about whether there will be enough time to thaw it out. I ask if he would like to join us for dinner tomorrow. "No thanks," he says, "I'll be in New Westminster."

"Well," I tell him, "I'll come to your apartment at five o'clock in case you don't go." On Christmas day I knock on the door as I said I would but he is not home. We have a good dinner. My son uses his culinary skills — and his appetite — with flourish.

The next day the children come to my place, so I go to invite Willy again. Yes, he will come. He is shy and the children don't really know what to say. I ask if he would like a drink but he says no. I ask why not and he says that he might get violent. From so inoffensive a person, this makes me laugh.

He never did go to New Westminster. He went for a walk so he wouldn't be home when I called Christmas day. He doesn't like to intrude.

2.

What's going on here?

Willy says I should have an art show in New Westminster's library.

"I can't take the paintings," I tell him, "I haven't got a car."

"Don't worry, I'll take you in my truck."

I take a long look at him. What is this man all about?

There's no worry about getting romantically involved. One just doesn't associate him with romance. We're just friends. I must admit though, it's wonderful to have him in the background. Mainly because I don't have a car anymore and anything connected to this art business requires transportation.

It has been four days since I've heard from Willy. Looking back over these past months, I realize that I have been seeing more and more of him. There's something funny going on here! Thinking about it more deeply, I see where he has unwittingly become part of my life. Now listen! This is not possible! I am being caught unaware.

Used to fending for myself, I've been leaning towards relying on him turning up all the time. Worse still, my senses are stirring and my sixty-five-year-old body is craving to be loved. Enough of that! All that is behind me. My figure has gone to pot. My varicose veins are a sight. I give out the message that I don't want to attract the opposite sex. So why this distraught state? Regardless, I miss him and decide to invite him to my apartment for dinner. I write a note and slip it under his door.

He phones and it's good to hear his throaty voice as he says, "I got your invitation and the answer is yes, yes, yes."

I'm nervous getting dinner ready but everything turns out just fine. After, he wants to go to the library so I go too. On the way home, the winds chill us through. I ask him in for a drink (I have some left over from Christmas) and we settle into chairs in the warm apartment. I feel I have to tell him that I care for him.

"I've missed you these past few days," I tell him.

He smiles and says, "Coming from such a lovely woman, that's a nice thing to hear."

I stumble on, "I care for you but I want you to know I'm not interested in having a sexual relationship."

He smiles and, like a torrent of rain, spills his thoughts out. "I'm going to tell you that I love you. I'm going to get you 'ringed-up.' I want to get you a dozen roses and a gold chain for your neck. I'm going to pay off your mortgage." That's when he said, "Give me another!"

This is earth-shattering. Here we sit, two older people. For at least ten years, we've both lived alone. And did I hear right? Pay off the mortgage? I thought he was poor! He does have a new truck but he didn't have a thing in his freezer.

We have another drink and colour blooms in his face. I suspect it's blooming in mine too.

"Don't think I'm saying this because of the liquor," he says, "1 always know what I'm doing and saying."

We laugh a lot over stupid things but in the back of my mind I am allowing doubts to crowd in. What about the stories of men who take older, single women for a ride, wooing them with romantic love. After wiping out their bank accounts, they take off. But wait a minute, you silly coo-coo, I tell myself, you haven't a cent in the bank and you wouldn't put your apartment in his name anyway.

I look across at this man who is grinning at me from ear to ear. Strange how his usual dour expression can light up so vividly when he smiles. His face becomes a maze of laugh lines and his eyes twinkle with mischievous humour. He comes over to sit next to me and, God, it feels good to rest my face against his shoulder. I look up and very slowly, tentatively, he kisses me.

Sometime later, I discover his jacket in my closet and set out my feelings in a poem.

3.

The jacket

It is morning and 1 open the closet.
Your jacket hangs there amongst my dresses.
Warmth floods through me
as I lift the rough woven sleeve to my breast.
Dear Willy.
Precious Willy,
it feels good to have part of you here.
How can it stir so many memories
when we've only known each other
so short a time?
How can we share so many jokes?
"Upstairs, downstairs."
"Don't ask questions."
"Check-mate."
How can you make me laugh so much?
How did you convince me that sex was beautiful?
How is it that someone like you really exists?
Did I dream you?
The Harris tweed is two tones of grey.
Harris tweed, my mother's coat that she
wore for twenty years,
the name of sturdiness and longevity.
Are you like that Willy?
It seems as if it's true.
But it doesn't matter if it isn't,

for 1 have known
the excruciating sweetness of you.
And I stroke the rugged jacket
and silently tell you 1 love you.

4.

Willy's bread

"I have to bake bread this morning," he tells me.

"Imagine! You make your own bread?"

"Well I don't know how good it is. It's just basic whole wheat bread. I figured if I could learn to make my own, I could live cheaply and healthy too."

"Did you learn from your mother?"

"*Chreest!* No. She wouldn't let me into the kitchen. But I went to the library and read through all the cookbooks. You know what, though? One author tells you one thing and another says the opposite. I just took what seemed to be right, mainly the parts with the least fuss. One person said it does nothing to let it rise in the bowl, so I just put the dough right in the pans. Another said there was no need to put the yeast in the water first, so I just threw it in with the flour. Then I put it in bread pans in an electric frying' pan with the lid on. I put it on low heat and let it rise. Trouble came when I looked at the switches on my oven. It gave the temperatures and Broil, but no Bake. I thought it would only broil things, so I changed all the wiring. No one tells you the numbers are for baking."

"Do you have failures?"

"Not really. One author said, 'if it turns out badly, just lump it out. No big thing."

Willy likes to act as a door-post in the mornings when I leave his apartment. In order to pass, I must hug him and kiss him. Well this morning, the door-post laughs at me for collecting loonies. "Look here Willy," I say, "you wanted me for what I am and collecting loonies is part of me. But now you are trying to change me."

"No, no, not change you," he says, "just make some modifications as I did with the stove."

5.

Boobs

Being thoroughly embarrassed by my make-do underwear, I go shopping for something more in line with a honeymoon. My brassiere size seems not to have been invented, unless it resembles a horse harness. I finally find one made of stretchy lace, a one-size-fits-all sort of thing.

Willy is interested in my purchases and I tell him I have found a soft, comfortable bra. Later that evening as we sit in my living room, he asks, "Are your boobs happy in their new bra?"

I nearly die! I blush when my youngsters use such language and here is a man talking about my... Well! "Willy, you must learn not to call them that," I admonish. I try to excuse him because English is his second language.

He is surprised. "What do you call them, then?" I'm flustered and try to think.

Actually, real ladies don't call them *anything*. One can refer to bosom or breast, but when one says breasts, one envisions the sisters clucking their tongues. And there is only one breast really, as in a man's breast. His eyes are still enquiring as I go make coffee, but I have to leave it as is.

Later in my apartment, he holds me there and says, "This is your booby-trap." I have to laugh, and I still don't know what to tell him to name them!

6.

Pork liver

He goes to kiss me and changes his mind. "Why?" I ask.

"I just had lunch and you would taste it from my mouth."

"Well that's all right."

"No."

"What was it?"

"Pork liver."

I draw back, visualizing the red, spongy, smelly stuff at the butcher's counter. He says, "You should really have some too, you know. It's thirty-six cents a pound. When it's on special you can get it cheaper, and it's good for you."

"Look Willy, you've got me eating at McDonald's and wearing running shoes but I draw the line at eating pork liver. It turns my insides to think about it. Don't even talk about it."

Our situation reminds me of Bernard Shaw's *Pygmalion* or the subsequent, *My Fair Lady*. But instead of a professor training a cockney flower girl to be a lady, Willy is busy showing a lady the common man!

We took the truck to the top of Mount Sumas the other day. The snow was piled high on the logging road and we got stuck. Willy put some cushions in the back of the truck and I had to sit there with as much dignity as I could muster, so he would have added weight and the tires would grip. Another first for me. As my daughter said in response, "Welcome to the real world, Mother."

We are supposed to go camping soon! I am game to try it but warn him, "There's no way I can pee in the bush."

"Why not?" he asks.

"Just my training, I guess. Just can't."

He smiles, and I know there's another lesson coming up. Now, when he wants to bring me in line, it's, "I'll feed you pork liver, Doris!"

7.

Sourdough

Willy mentions having made sourdough bread before.

"I love that stuff," I tell him.

"Okay, I'll see if the library has something on it."

When he returns, he tells me they only have something called Japanese sourdough bread and it takes sixteen days to get it together.

"Guess I'll have to remember how I did it before," Willy says.

He wracks his brain to recall how much flour and water, and how long to let it stand. He makes what he calls the *spong* and leaves it out on the kitchen counter. He gets me to watch as it "pukes up the bubbles."

"He's alive all right, he's not dead. He's a living, breathing thing." He adds flour at night and it sits till the next day when he puts more in to complete the process. He reserves another cup in the fridge and says, "The mother is being baked and says goodbye to her son who's doing his thing in the fridge."

My apartment is filled with the smell of baking sourdough bread. He comes to stand close to my typing chair. I turn and bury my face in his trim, firm stomach. For now, fears recede as I allow myself to think it just might be possible to live with someone again!

8.

Willy musings

It's rather a delicious feeling, this being loved by Willy. It also seems unreal as I watch the pleasure on his face as he gives me slices of his bread, coffee in the morning, or a gold chain for my neck.

I caught him once moving his large rubber tree from the light in the window to a place under fluorescent lights in his living room. He had to wrap both arms around the large pot just to carry it. The plant came to him long ago as a wiry, tiny item with two tiny leaves. Now it is five feet tall. The leaves seem to give out the same feeling that I have — knowing they are loved and cared for. Willy makes sure the pot stands just so, so that the top leaves are exactly two inches from the light. "That way it simulates the sun," he tells me. (He read this in the library.)

You would think he would want other plants if he cared so much for this one, but no, he says, "One plant, one painting and one girl. What more could you want?" It seems that Willy was made to give love, but didn't allow himself to do so while he was earning his living. He once loved a woman who died ten years ago. He loved his mother. He is passionately attached to his only brother and his wife, and their two daughters, all in Sweden. But he guards against any other encroachment to his feelings.

Even though Willy is kind and loving, at times I feel like I am his little Plasticine doll, being moulded and patted into the shape of his dreams, being decorated and dressed with wonder and delight. I worry a little about being the Plasticine doll. I do not want to lose my identity. But I'm still the same Plasticine and he doesn't want to change that.

Section 2.

Adjusting

1.

Commitments

I am afraid. Willy's going to pick up the diamond ring on Saturday. It's not an ordinary diamond. It's the most expensive in the store, or come to think of it, any store we've visited. Platinum with two small stones on either side of the large one.

As he's told me, there's no resale value for jewelery. If I change my mind about us and want to return it, we would not be able to recoup the money spent on it. In other words it would be like throwing all those dollars down the drain.

So I'd better be sure I want to keep it, right? Which brings to mind all the niggling thoughts that tell me I should be worried. He hasn't asked me to marry him so I ask myself, why is he giving me a ring? He had told me, "It's to *shew* you that I love you." My mind queries. Is it branding me, without commitment on his part? In other words, does he think, "She's mine, hands off, but I'm not prepared to make it legal as long as this will do the job!"

Are we trying too hard to fit into each other's thoroughly entrenched ways? What do we really want from each other? I know he finds it absolutely impossible to fathom why I would buy chili powder for $3.39 at the 7-Eleven when I could get the same amount for sixteen cents at Safeway, or why I would cut the speaker wires from my daughter's stereo when I couldn't figure out how to unplug them, or why I would buy a forty dollar amplifier that didn't even work. Now, on the other hand, he can't settle down to read a book, appraises women in a way that makes me feel uncomfortable, and bugs me to get up before our agreed time of 8 a.m.

Just as I kept an iron petticoat on my sexuality, he keeps an armor around his feelings. But, oh, how wonderful to catch him without it! Last night after a tiff, his heart shone through his eyes, vulnerable, just like me. But this morning, when I tried to tell him how afraid I am about the ring, he reacted with hostility.

"So, you don't want to wear my ring?"

Panic set in, "Yes I do," I told him, "but I wish it wasn't so expensive."
"Don't worry," he said, "if you lose it, you lose it."
I just can't explain and he'll never understand anyway.

2.

Getting ringed up

"Can you get up at seven tomorrow? I have coupons for Egg McMuffins at McDonald's. We'll have breakfast there and get free coffee for seniors."

"That's fine with me," I tell Willy.

"We'll go to New Westminster, pay the jewelers for the ring and get them to size it so we can pick it up on our return from Vancouver."

"What shoes will I wear?"

"Of course, you should wear your new running shoes. Everyone wears running shoes, even in Vancouver. Just to think, I've got you wearing running shoes and eating at McDonald's — how much lower can you get?"

We drive to New Westminster and once again I try on the ring. Then we catch the SkyTrain. Willy had told me he'd show me how to get tickets but he just punches them through.

"You said you'd show me how it works."

"Later, I'll *shew* you later. Now we've missed the train because you've fiddled around."

Prickles! But let it go, it could spoil the day.

"When we return, we'll take time to do it."

The SkyTrain gives me a sense of adventure. Willy tells me about the mountain that Vancouver people call the sleeping maiden. He points out all the interesting buildings and tells me stories about them. The sun is shining, the air is crisp, I hold his wonderful, large hand — tight, tight, tight. It's all too great to be true.

We have lunch on the sixth floor of the Bay — roast beef and Yorkshire pudding. A seagull sits on the window ledge. After lunch, Willy has to go to this trust company and that trust company. In one, a room is plexiglassed and highly secured.

"They're taking orders for stocks," says Willy. He takes me to the art gallery, and I didn't even ask! (On the way, I notice that not one woman downtown is wearing running shoes.) In the gallery, Jeff Hall is featured with large ad-type photographs. Innocent yet disturbing. He has staged some of them. He is there in person, talking to a group, asking them about their interpretations of his work. I move over and tell him he's great. There is one large photo, six by eight feet, of a young, nude man lying on a red chesterfield. Quite a bit of emphasis is given to his penis. Willy kids me that I am over-intrigued about this.

It's beautiful outside. We sit by the waterfalls and Willy points to the fourteenth floor of the Vancouver Hotel.

"We remodeled that floor," he says as he tells me about it. "E and I went dancing there afterwards." Oh, God help me take these references well. Help me to not show the jealousy that chokes my breath away. She's dead, poor soul, let him talk about their time together. But I want Willy to love only *me*.

We SkyTrain back to New Westminster and he does show me the ticket machine. We walk down the boardwalk, which is bordered by expensive townhouses. The sun glistens on the waves and everyone is enjoying the gorgeous spring. We go to pick up the ring and the saleslady laughs and shows her pleasure. It fits fine.

"May as well keep it on and get used to it," Willy says. I put it back in the box and hand it to him. He knows I want him to give it to me.

Going home, the traffic is heavy but he is patient. It could all be ruined if he were to get upset. He pulls into Earls where we often eat.

"This is a surprise," I say.

"You knew I would come here."

"No, I didn't."

"Well, your subconscious mind did then."

We order wine, and then skoal each other. He says, "I love you, and will you accept my ring?"

I say, "Yes," and kiss him. The waitress comes over and I tell her that she is the first to know that I have received this ring from Willy. She disappears and returns with two more glasses of wine and a card with a gift certificate from Earls for ten dollars.

"It's a good promotion," says Willy.

"It's a nice gesture and you've got to believe that there are nice things and nice people in this world."

"It's still a good promotion." He smiles when he says this and I know he is pleased.

The wine goes to my head and I flirt with him. When we get ready to leave, a table of customers calls us over. "We're very happy for you," they say as they admire the ring.

We return to my apartment and listen to the CD player while we finish off the rest of the famous Christmas brandy. I'm feeling very carefree as I climb the stairs to his apartment.

I want to spend the whole night showing him I love him.

Next morning he brings me coffee after I entice him back to bed. Halfway through drinking it, I see him standing in the doorway, looking at me.

"Are you happy?"

"Yes," I say, "I'm very happy."

"Good. Then keep lying there and being happy."

3.

A kept woman

Willy's apartment is on the third floor and mine is on the second. My solo life disappears as we become wrapped up in each other. He spoils me with buying anything that I casually mention I would like to own. He gives me space to do my writing and artwork, and uses the time to bicycle around the country on his extensive journeys of discoveries.

He bakes healthy bread. Carts my artwork to galleries, teaches me chess and loses constantly in Scrabble. He has given me a stereo and CD player so I can have unending music. Bought me new coats and a lovely gold chain that makes me feel feminine again. Warmth and love envelope us as we lie in bed together. He entertains me with his wit and funny stories. I read him a piece of my writing every night. In short: paradise.

Then why did I cry last night? Why would I want to change things when everything is working for me?

I have alimony from my former husband. Now I am faced with the fact that I am taking from two men at the same time. A decision will have to be made. If I choose to take from my new man, will it involve marrying him? But with all that marriage entails, will he be keen on the idea? After all, he's got everything now hasn't he? Everything but the knowledge that I could walk out on him anytime, not hindered by legality. If we had legality though, would it dull the senses? Right now, it adds a bit of spice when I put on his Vyella dressing gown and sneak down the hallway so the residents don't see me. But spice gets tinged with shame.

I've made myself terribly vulnerable and a feeling persists that there is something wrong. The sisters' teachings at the convent won't let me rest. Marry, marry, marry, they would say. But when you're not marrying to have a family, why marry? Marriage means taking for granted, locked in. Why should we marry? There's a heavy wadded chunk of something sitting on my stomach and it doesn't seem to go away. Why not? I'd keep my name if I married because it's connected to my art life and it's too late to change it now. Maybe marriage is a contract that you make together. Yes, that seems better. We could write an agreement stating what each of us expects from the other.

I was going to come down to my own bed last night but he said, "Never do that. Cry with me and we'll talk and sort it all out." I thought the honeymoon was over but he continued, "Now that we have been through that little down period, we know each other a little better and, who knows, our feelings may be stronger as we go through these times. Nothing stays on an even keel."

When you are our age, there's a lot of adjusting to do. He used to get up at six and eat a large meal at noon. I like to get up at nine-thirty and eat a large meal at night. We've compromised and get up at eight. We usually eat supper together, which is on the light side. I need to immerse myself in writing or reading papers, but he skips through them. I shop indiscriminately, he treats shopping as a sport to get the best values. So many other differences but most important, we *do* compromise and we're considerate of each other. When I told my friend that I felt like a kept woman, she replied, "Well, how do you feel when you're married anyway?" And it's true!

Suppose I had my own money. Yes, I would feel differently. I wouldn't need to be married. So what does that mean? It means I am nervous about what would happen to me if this paradise ceased to exist. I want assurance that there's going to be a roof over my head for the rest of my life. That doesn't mean a marriage contract, but it does mean a contract.

The wadded lump is easing now and I sure don't want to turn my back on the Garden of Eden. I would never have believed how wonderful it was. I won't reach for the apple yet.

4.

Doing his 't'ing'

I'm sitting by the side of a small road on an old wire chair that Willy found. He keeps it in the back of the truck for occasions like this. He makes the chair comfortable for me with a blanket and cushion, and then he's off to do his *t'ing*. His thing is this: Willy goes on these extensive walks and spies all kinds of goodies that people have thrown away. He makes small piles of these oddments. When he has need for two-by-fours or old pipes or wheels, he just goes to these piles and gathers them up.

He has noted that the small area behind the driver's seat is roomy enough for someone to sit, but there isn't a seat. So, today he's picking up an old kitchen chair. He will saw off the legs at a height so it will fit snugly in the spot behind the front seat.

Yesterday we picked up some heavy plywood from another pile for a shelf in his apartment. He's going to need more shelves because I'm moving excess items of mine into his cupboards. He has these large free-standing cupboards and there's nothing in them. "Why did you buy them?" I asked. "I don't know, for decoration, I guess," he answered.

To get back to these junkpiles, when he trashed his camper, he took all the pots and pans, TV, and camping stuff and hid them in Surrey bushes. The developers are closing in on his spot, but until they do, it's a treasure-trove for emergency needs.

The day is clear and sunny. One forgets one is sitting next to a junkpile. This man manages to live on practically nothing. His electricity bill is only seven dollars for two months. He has a fluorescent fixture rigged up in his living room for the one and only plant. He uses rabbit ears instead of a cable TV service. He doesn't run his fridge. He walks to the library to read the papers. Same with books. He cycles downtown for specials from grocery stores. He only uses his truck for carting my artwork or other heavy stuff or for going on excursions with me. Besides saving money by baking his own bread, he cooks porridge for breakfast, and makes use of broccoli stalks and other items that I'd throw out. Pork liver: thirty-six cents a pound. Eggs: seventy-four cents a dozen. His clothes are good quality and timeless really, he doesn't buy new ones.

I was reading my journal to him every night in bed but found the overhead light to be too bright. I told Willy and couldn't help laughing when he promptly rigged up a broom handle behind the headboard with a lightbulb dangling from it. He always finds answers to problems even if they are not routine!

5.

Bicycle brave

K brings me her bicycle. She wasn't able to sell it. I don't want to take it because I haven't been on a bike for forty years. Now, Willy's passion is bicycling. He cycles ten miles to Abbotsford to pay his telephone bill, saving forty-two cents in stamps, plus cheque charges and an *enveloop*. He has been hinting that I may enjoy cycling with him. But I hedge, saying:

"My back will hurt."

"My legs are too weak."

"I'll have trouble sitting on the saddle with my problems."

"I'm too old."

"Don't ask, I just can't do it."

But here's the bike. Nice looking one too. Sturdy. Bright.

"It's too high," I tell Willy.

"We'll accommodate it to you," he says.

K is concerned that I may fall. "Don't worry," Willy tells her, "there's a place I know that has a wide road like an airplane runway. I'll take her there."

We go to the wide road and Willy blows more air into the tires. He checks them for weaknesses and takes a spin to make sure the bike is okay. Then he holds it out to me. I get on and steady myself, then start rolling.

"Take it easy," he calls after me.

I'm off! The breeze caresses my face, the legs are on automatic and the fresh air seems keener. The years fall by the wayside and I am sixteen again, in England, in the spring. A boyfriend and I are cycling down quaint English roads and the Kent orchards whiz by. The smell of apple blossom is overpowering and songbirds are bursting with song. The wheels beneath are an extension of me. We are singing the song, "One day when we were young, one beautiful morning in May, you told me that you loved me, when we were young that day." All is one—spring, birds, bicycles, singing, and being in love. I now realize to be on a bike is as natural as breathing.

I suddenly notice that Willy has disappeared. Oh! There he is, going in and out of the bushes looking for junk. Maybe he'll find something for one of his treasure piles. He watches me draw close and his smile is the widest yet.

As I come into view,
his dreams are coming true.
This is something to really like,
Willy has Doris on a bike!

We're biking on a trail. A small bird is right in the path of my wheel. I have to swerve to avoid him because he just sits there. "Did you see that?" I ask Willy.

He says, "He hasn't read the manual."

"What manual?"

"The manual that's titled, 'How Not to be Run Over by a Bike.'"

Willy's mother

Willy drives me to the dentist—will pick me up in forty-five minutes. I look over to a nearby store thinking, if I get through early, I'll go and see what's there.

As if reading my mind, he says, "Don't go in any stores, stay right here."

"Why do you worry?"

"My mother wouldn't stay in the place I was to pick her up. She used to say I should know she would be in another department store."

W: "When I'd fly over to visit my mother, I'd fly for ten hours, then hit two cities for connections, without a chance to sleep, and then a train journey. But she got mad when I fell asleep on the chesterfield."

W: "It was the end of February when my mother died in Denmark. The winter had been hard and the therm-o-meter registered minus thirty degrees Celsius. We were standing around the grave and the sun came through and warmed the earth a few steps away and I saw there were clusters of snowdrops blooming there."

At Dorothy's one afternoon we have coffee and cookies. European cookies.

"They look like the ones my mother made." Willy says. "She'd take the dough and roll it flat. Then she'd take a round glass and stamp out big rounds. *Bam!* Like that. In between the rounds there'd be these shapes that we were allowed to have. And do you know what? They tasted better than the big ones."

7.

Sunny days and blue jeans

We are planning to go camping sometime soon and Willy says I should have a pair of jeans. Me, who didn't even wear pants until ten years ago. Jeans are for young people, aren't they? Not for sixty-five-year-olds.

"I can't wear jeans because none would fit me. I haven't got a waist."

Willy is not deterred. "Everyone has a waist," he says. He gets out his metal carpenter's tape and reaches it around my body, which is slumped in a chair. I won't even let salesladies measure me, let alone my new lover. Better we imagine what it may be rather than face the truth.

"Your waist is forty-two inches," he announces. The tape flicks round my bust.

"Boobies, forty-two inches," then, "hips, forty inches. You're almost square!"

I'm as mad as blazes. "You have no right to tease me. I hope you're satisfied, and as you can see, I can't wear jeans."

Willy is enjoying himself. Once more he has the advantage over me as he measures his waist at thirty-one inches.

"Never say never, we'll find a tailor or get designer jeans to fit you, wait and see."

I can't believe I'm really that large. When I get downstairs, on impulse, I find my dressmaker's tape. My waist is thirty-eight inches—the stinker!

He stands above me as I lie on the floor. Taunting, goading, pushing me to greater heights. But the *exerceeses* are good, I can tell. My back feels stronger and I walk with a spring in my step. Willy exercises three times a day and cycles ten miles or so, just for fun. His muscles are very obvious and his torso is that of a young man's. With my arm around him as we walk, I feel good and forget I'm in my sixties. It's like the other day when we were on the grassy riverbank. We lay back in each other's arms, soaking up the warm spring day, and the years just fell away. I found myself experiencing the deliciousness of being with a beau with the promise of summer around us—the smell of newly mown grass, the sounds of gentle waves lapping against rocks and young birds testing their vocal chords. Time becomes suspended when you know that you love and are loved. We're at the lake and Willy's brought a blanket so we can lie on the grass. Looking up we see the yellow-green leaves of spring against the blue sky and a Stellar jay flashing his peacock-blue wings. Willy draws me close to him. Goodness me! I love the way his arms encompass my body. I feel a young girl once more.

Sensing it, he says, "We should send a letter to the government. 'Dear Sir or Madam or whoever it may concern, please do not send any more Old Age Pension cheques to us. We are lying on the grass and feeling like sixteen-year-olds and don't think we should be considered seniors at this time. Yours very truly, Willy and Doris."

Adjusting
8.

A trip and a motel

We go away on our first trip together—a round trip in central B.C. Four days of being with each other constantly. No escape to our separate apartments. We start off the driving with having — what will I call it? Not an argument. He says something that sets my antennas quivering. I question again, do I know this man? I have to learn about him without expecting him to verbalize everything. But sometimes I conclude wrongly. An uncomfortable feeling creeps up my spine. I turn into a cold stone and am reminded of being with X. Hurt and afraid. Is it all worth it? Without a man, one doesn't try. One doesn't have to spend hours coaxing thinning hair into shape. One isn't afraid to face a glaring light, exposing the telltale signs of aging. One can let the stomach do its own thing without fear of being compared to a svelte, younger woman. And so it goes! Does he want sex tonight? Do I want sex tonight? Do I want more satisfaction from it? Does he? Well there's one thing about life with Willy. When you put the pluses against the minuses, the pluses always win. But right now, I can only think about the minuses.

Gradually though, the road goes on, and the words don't seem as bad any more. We find a budget motel and Willy asks me to sign the register. I understand this, as he is shy about his handwriting. But it hits me as I put my name down and his truck number that all of society is coming out of the woodwork in that small nondescript room and pointing a finger at me.

The next morning we go to the lake. To get a good view, we walk along a path on land that is up for sale. We reach an out-cropping where we look out upon the many shades of emerald and aqua shimmering on the lake's surface. The hills in the background are stubbly with dry grass and tumbleweed, and the Okanagan sunflowers spit out their golden-orange colour against the soft brown-greys of the earth. We lie back on the prickly grass and let the sun bathe us as we listen to the

28

songbirds.

"This is our little bit of heaven," I say drowsily, "maybe we could buy just enough to come here and renew our spirits whenever we need to."

Willy laughs, "First they will sell it for half-a-million dollars, then they will sub-divide, and your few square feet will cost you a fortune."

We were to get to a friend's place for two o'clock. Halfway there I said to Willy, "Pull off somewhere so I can get changed, please." Well, suddenly his temper flared and his face turned purple as he turned to berate me for leaving it so late that we might not arrive on time. Yes, but isn't that understandable when we are in strange territory and driving on unfamiliar roads?

So there it is again, the feeling that the honeymoon is over and the real person has started to materialize. It was all too good to last. I saw it in people's faces when they listened to me recount all my wonderful tales. I should have known. I'm old enough to know. But that makes it all so sad.

Back home again and, would you believe, Willy's temper flares once more. Okay, I'm going to have to re-evaluate this whole affair. I'm not prepared to be the subject of someone else's frustrations. After all, the only time on the trip I showed anger with him was when he took the toilet paper out of the motel bathroom when I needed it. "How can you take the toilet paper when you were annoyed at my suggestion that we take a couple of extra cream containers from the cafe?" I had spat at him. "There wasn't any when we came in last night, so I put in the roll that I brought with me," he had replied, horrified that I would think that about him.

It is time to walk and talk. He tells me that he feels our relationship is better than before. But I know it isn't. We walk on and I can't look at him. I pray I don't start bawling again. We talk about where my writing and art fit in and I say that I figure I don't really write good children's stories but that the Willy stories are good and, with the illustrations, it may be where I should be. But I say to Willy, "Maybe the stories won't be as funny anymore, maybe they'll be kind of sad."

The day after, I don't know what happened, but my Willy comes back to me. The one I thought I had just imagined. My hurt lifts. I feel vulnerable and giving as we spend the night together trying to tell each other, without words, that we belong together.

"This is our second honeymoon," he says, and it sure feels that way.

Adjusting

9.

Amusing musings

I wake up disconcerted and tell Willy, "I had this dream."

"Uh, huh."

"There was this large man with bulging muscles and he was trying to move some huge boulders. My car was in the way and he waved angrily for me to move it. I backed up and started sliding down the hill and realized the brakes had failed. I was pushing, pushing down hard on the brake pedal. I woke up to find I was pressing down on your leg with all my might."

He is laughing.

"What's so funny?"

"I was thinking it's a good thing you weren't trying to pull the emergency brake."

One of his annoying ways is that he avoids answering questions directly. Here are some examples.

D: "Where are you going?"

W: "I'll know when I get back."

D: "How many letters do you need for the answer to that crossword question?"

W: "As many as there are in rocks."

W: "We have to go to the Claim Centre."

D: "Where is it?"

W: "Everyone knows that."

D: "Where is it?"

W: "It will tell you in the phone book."

Sometimes he does answer directly.

D: "What will I call this painting?" I refer to a painting of white bald heads on a black background that is to be juried for a show. "Should I call it, 'The Visitors'?" I am thinking of spirits or ghosts reappearing.

W: "Call it 'Day of Reckoning,'" he says with a twisted smile, "that goes for you too when it goes before the judges."

I love the quaint way he describes things in translating from Danish to English. Instead of polar bear, it's ice bear. Instead of umbrella, it's parasol. It's not the stew smells good. It's I smell the fragrance of the stew. A cooling fan is a windmill, and comfortable is comfortABLE. Instead of exercises, it's *exerceeses*.

And talking about *exerceeses*, he does a series of them every day three times a day. He has these wire springs that he pulls in all directions. The sound of them stretching and relaxing is as familiar to me as the ticking of the clock. His stomach is as taut as a young man's.

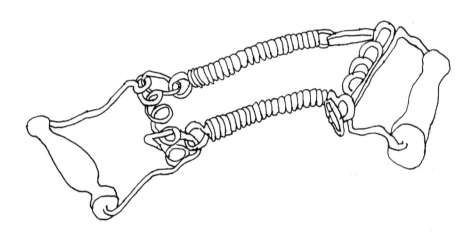

10.

A trip and a tent

The time has come. The time to prove that I can camp. I win an award that sponsors me to go to the Festival of Arts in Victoria. Willy figures that, afterwards, we might as well see some of the island and visit friends and relatives.

Willy spends a week organizing food and supplies. We buy a tent on sale at Woolco and practice setting it up in the living room. Hey, camping looks relatively simple. What's the fuss about, anyway? Like Topsy, the pile of supplies just grows and grows in one corner of the dining room. Willy contemplates the mound of stuff.

"I don't think we'll make the overweight on the ferry if we take all of this," he says. He'd like to take the bike K gave me and I'd like to take the waterproof air mattress she loaned us.

We load up in record time—thanks to Willy being used to things like that—and take off. When we arrive in Victoria, I register for the festival and then we drive to our motel. On the way, I think about the pre-registration phone call I had made:

"I'd like one double bed," I say.

"For one person?"

"Er. No. Two people."

"We must have the name of your companion. Is it male or female?"

"Well," I hesitate, glad they can't see my red face at this point, "you see it's like this. I'm sixty-five years of age. I met this man and he's sixty-nine. He's really very nice. And we have been going together. But we aren't married. Well, we will sleep in one bed. I mean we don't need two beds. Oh yes, and his name is Willy Smith." I remember that Smith is used for clandestine arrangements and quickly add, "It really *is* Willy Smith." Suppressed laughter comes over the line and I give up trying to sound nonchalant.

We go to the opening of the art show. It's a beautiful setting and my piece is hung to its best advantage.

"I'm proud of you," says Willy as he sees such impressive work around us. There's wine and cheese. Willy goes to the table and gets a kick out of watching the very merry bartender serving wine with a one-for-you-and-two-for-me performance.

A box has been set out so the general public can vote for their favourite painting.

"I don't know which one to choose," says a fellow artist. God! What's the matter with her? I vote for my own. After all, if you don't believe in your own work, who will?

After chatting with other artists, I spy Willy coming towards me. Holding about six voting forms.

"How do you like this for a work of art?" he says. He gleefully shows me how he's used different pens and different handwriting to make-believe other people have voted for my painting.

"You can't do that!" I admonish.

He smiles impishly and says, "We'll come back and I'll do some more."

I could just die. I mean what if my piece were chosen as the public's favourite! I could never accept the honour. I send up a silent prayer that it won't happen.

The following day I go for lunch at the mess hall, where they are feeding the delegates. A number of school children are participating in the festival and guards have been posted to see that the open cafeteria system isn't abused. Your hand is just about smacked if you reach for an extra. Just the same, I load up with as much as I dare, thinking I can take some food out to Willy. He waits outside in the truck, eating raw fish. He insisted on unloading the freezer when we left home and he doesn't want to start the camp stove for just one person. Honestly, that man! He may get sick. I finish my meal, stuff the extras in my big purse and go to walk out. One of the guards spreads his arms to stop me.

"Are you intending to leave?" he growls. My face burns. The goodies are weighing heavily. "The front door is blocked. Would you please use the rear exit," he adds, impassively.

When I get outside, I tell Willy all about it.

"It was awful," I say, "I felt so wicked."

Willy takes off with his imagination: "When she is going to the gallows for punishment of her crimes, they will say, 'and it all started when she sneaked extra food for Willy at the Arts Festival. Then she stole more and more till she was holding up banks and now she is a hardened criminal'."

The next day the sun is up and the wind whips from the ocean. The tourists start to pour in. They look like they have come from another planet, all dressed alike in white pants and wind breakers, wearing sunglasses, all carrying their cameras. I ride my bike while Willy runs alongside me. We cover a lot of Victoria, and tour Beacon Hill Park.

The following day, we take the truck to Oak Bay but find the road is blocked. We park on a nearby street so we can walk along the beach. After scrambling over jagged rocks and up a hill, we find ourselves on the grounds of the Royal Victoria Yacht Club. Willy is nervous, and says they prosecute people who trespass. We see a sign near the clubhouse, No unauthorized person can enter.

"But we are leaving, not entering," Willy points out to me. We have a good laugh and Willy goes on about how he can tell everyone he took me to the yacht club, so he can't be the stingy person he's made out to be.

We go to visit an old friend of mine. It's raining and I'm concerned about the cushions in the back of the truck. We pass a 7-Eleven. I know Willy would have a fit if I suggested we buy some garbage bags so I suggest instead that we could ask my friend to give us one.

Willy flares, "Don't ask anyone for anything!" I tell myself that if we are ever able to live together, the agreement must be that I have my own money to spend as I want, without quibbling.

The rain turns to hail. Willy calls them stone drops. We go to Mount Douglas. As is his wont, Willy disappears behind a rock. He looks back and sees I have my camera aimed at him. He squats so I can only see his head and, with wrenching devilishness, he raises his hat like a vaudevillian finishing his act. I kid him that the camera caught more than that flourish!

The trip goes on at a peaceful pace. We call on friends in Nanaimo and then trek out to Long Beach. There, in the early evening, great mists roll in off the ocean. Trees emerge and submerge, as the sound of waves roar in to shore.

We set up the tent and realize we forgot the foam for sleeping. K's mattress doesn't give enough support to stop my back from aching. I wrap up in one cocoon and Willy in another. I miss the comfort of his body weaving in unison with mine. I hear awful noises outside the tent and am stiff with fear. What if a bear's claw rips through the tent on my side? I won't have the presence of mind to unzip the opening. I need a knife to cut myself out. I jab Willy hard.

"Please see if there's a bear out there," I plead.

He mumbles and turns his back to me, "There's no way I'm going out in the cold to see if I can find a nonexistent animal."

Well, he's not much of a gentleman! At three in the morning Willy gets up to pee and comes back talking his head off, just like a little boy.

"Be quiet," I say. "Stop it." But no—jabber, jabber, jabber, until I explode.

"Shut up already!"

After more talking and laughing, he finally settles down, but now, of course, I can't get back to sleep.

In the morning I find that the washroom, heaven be praised, is heated and there is hot water for washing. I never thought that a heated washroom would be so coveted. Willy's thermal long underwear was the source of much amusement when he said that I should bring them along. Now I hang on to them like a life-support system.

The next evening the rain seeps into the pocket inserts of the tent. Willy holds up our massive brown blanket, which is dripping a stream of water, and says, "It really isn't wet, you know." Dampness penetrates into my bones. I try to be entertained by the pitter-patter of the drops of rain on the tent. I spend endless minutes watching the rivulets of moisture run in twisted channels down the roof. It is important to Willy that I camp out. I must put a good face on it. I'm also determined to spend enough nights in the tent to make up for the eighteen dollars worth of foam I bought in Tofino.

When we eat out in a restaurant in Tofino (our only option since the rain is now coming down with a vengeance) I see in a mirror that my eyes are bloodshot and my hair has lost every trace of curl. Willy sees this too and decides that it's time to leave and go back to civilization and motel life if the weather doesn't let up.

One more night of tenting in Parksville and I am surprised that a person gradually adapts to camping. Willy makes a crackling good fire and we sit down on our famous wire chairs. Mosquitoes make an appearance and Willy is very bothered by them. As he's worked outside so much of his life, I'm surprised.

"Aren't you immune to the bites?" I ask.

"May as well say you can get immune from wolf bites. No, they give me a bad time," he replies.

Willy buys some bagels and puts them in the back of the truck for just a few minutes. He's also found some chocolate cookies. We go for a walk on the beach and when we return, we see that ravens have feasted and left a mess all over the truck. At Long Beach, Willy had fed a Stellar jay some porridge and peanut butter. It was funny to see the bird put his head to one side, as he tried to make out what strange food it was. Then his mate screamed at him when he delivered some to her. It must have got stuck in her beak.

Back home again. It's peaceful and orderly in the apartment.

"Did you like the rain forest?" I ask Willy.

"No."

Well I didn't expect that answer.

"Why not?" I push.

"The trees are sick."

"Well, of course they're sick. They're left there so we can see how nature works—how they decay and form food for new growth."

"There isn't new growth. And the reason is that the old trees are sick and still standing and they shut out the sun."

"Well, it's interesting to see what happens when nature is left to its own devices."

"Would you say it's interesting to see what nature will do to a sick old man? Should sick old men be put on display for people to look at. Shouldn't they be tended by doctors? Well, by the same token, these trees should be cut down to make way for another planting. Look at these trees at home, they stand straight and tall and proud because they have access to the sun. No. I don't think we should keep rain forests like that."

Section 3.

Letting in my art life

Willy and the deer

*There's a meadow next to our
apartment block.
Wild daisies, bearded grasses and
waist-high weeds.
A deer has been seen there.
Someone phoned me and said,
"I looked out the window
and saw Willy in the field.
The deer came close to him
and they walked together.*

2.

Trial togetherness

I watch him gather my art supplies and other personal things to move to his apartment upstairs. Fear curls its fingers round my chest and pulls hard. Friends have sold their house and need a place to stay for three weeks. It seems logical to offer them my apartment because I can stay with Willy if he agrees. Willy says it's fine, that it's about time we experience being together for twenty-four hours a day.

He is the opposite of me in many ways. I knew that when I first went into his apartment and saw three vacuum cleaners, standing like sentries in a row. Plugged into different outlets so he never had to lug the cleaner to a different spot. Each its radius to clean. Now to me, all machines must be out of sight because they disrupt my train of thought. I can't think peace with a cleaning apparatus sitting in front of me!

His furniture is placed in straight lines. Mine is at angles. I have dainty figurines and vases around. He has an ashtray from Mexico of a bikini-clad woman lying on a Mexican hat. Shivers!

And how can I feel romantic when, instead of a pajama top, he wears to bed a T-shirt with a life-sized face of Trudeau with a big red mark through it. I mean, one just can't concentrate on anything else.

He enters into the spirit of the thing, moving his fluorescent light to a place where I can work and cleaning out closets and cupboards to accommodate my things. It will be a good test for us. It really is crazy to run two residences. But with each small load that is removed from my place, freedom seems to ride on its back.

I don't know how I managed to clean out my bedroom studio. It contains piles of mat-boards, empty frames, art paper. Unfinished paintings, unsorted slides, masterpieces, articles on how to be a millionaire artist, articles on how easy it is to sell your paintings. Mixed paint that I can't bear to throw out. Letters to be answered. Clothes that have to be altered to fit a slimmer me. With all the piles removed, the room loses my personality and stares back at me with a coldness that sits heavy on my heart.

That night we go to bed in Willy's apartment and. heavens! start an argument. I feel like running down to my place in a huff when I realize I can't do that now. I have no haven to run to! I swallow hard and talk myself out of luxuriating in annoyance. Grow up, I tell myself, learn to compromise. Stop taking offence so quickly. But it's hard when you haven't had to compromise for so long, and you really do think you have a grievance.

3.

Modest moments

The heat is sweltering and the water looks inviting. Willy and I are at the lake to test camping in decent weather. I remember the enjoyment I used to get from swimming. Willy ogles the females, checking their sizes, seeing if they're in good shape, seeing how white or brown they are. He says that in Acapulco the Mexicans look at tourists' skin colour to figure out how much they might buy. The white ones will be suckers to sell to. Next come the red-skinned ones who've been there long enough to at least get sunburned. The ones who are tanned have bought all their souvenirs and tell the sellers to buzz off.

I dip my feet in the lake, regretting that swimming belongs to my past. The water is warm so I pluck up my courage and say to Willy, "Would you still love me if you saw me in a bathing suit?"

"Ya! Ya!" he says, impatiently.

He has given me birthday money and I decide I will use it to get a bathing suit, so we drive to town. He doesn't want me to buy one at my favourite department store and quotes the stores that have better buys.

"It's my money," I blurt out, "and I want to buy where I want to buy." We go to the store of my choice, and what do you know, the suits don't look too bad—if you pretend I don't have any legs. Willy asks that I get bright colours so he can keep track of me in the water. Keeping that in mind I choose the one that best hides my defects.

Back at the tent, I change into the suit with the nervousness of a bride getting set for the altar. As Willy comes back from the toilet, I decide to get it over with and meet him in the lane. His face is soft and actually lights up when he sees me. He stops in his tracks and kisses me, saying, "You look very lovely."

I try to avoid looking at the fluorescent bikinis on young, trim figures, lying on the beach. We get to the water's edge and, by jingo! it's colder than I thought. My shoulders slide under the water and my legs automatically pump into swimming position. The buoyancy and freshness bring so much pleasure. Memories of English beaches and Hong Kong seas that were so much part of my life, come pouring back as I peacefully breaststroke away. Willy stands on the beach, grimacing with cold. Clutching his arms to his chest he tries to avoid the razor-sharp stones as he dips himself in long enough to say he's been swimming.

"Well, you've got more padding than me," he shouts across the water and leaves me to the watery caresses.

I rest in my lawn chair. I've been back in the water five times and no longer attempt to cover my figure. What the heck, so I'm sixty-six, it's good to feel the sun and breeze on my skin. I try not to care about what Willy or anyone else thinks.

4.

The old and the new

"Wah, wah, I can't go!" I bawl my head off. I had finally got my nerve up to go for my repair operation, only to find I couldn't pee once they removed the catheter. They gaily inserted another and sent me home from the hospital, an uncomfortable mess.

My daughter is getting married in Vancouver tomorrow and here I sit bleeding. Willy tries to calm me down and I phone the doctor for help. We arrive at the emergency, and sure enough, the bleeding stops and I feel better. After checking, the doctor reassures, "These things happen, there's no obvious cause."

"Would I be risking it, driving to my daughter's wedding tomorrow?" I ask.

"No," he reassures me, "and have a glass of champagne for good measure."

My dress doesn't cover the catheter bag. Willy takes me to the mall and I struggle to try on a long dress that I spied on a previous shopping trip. It is a beautiful dress of georgette material. Flowers in an all-over pattern, black taffeta lining, and a full skirt that could hide six chickens, let alone a catheter bag.

Willy has padded the seat in the truck with foam cushions and a comforter. Straddling my legs, I sprawl in a very unladylike fashion across the seat. Holding my breath most of the time, I make it to the site of the wedding, a great Tudor-style house on Jericho Beach. I stay in the truck while Willy paces around. He is getting geared up to meet X, my former husband. I see X in the distance and he is doing his pacing, moving chairs around and going in and out of the building.

From this position I look at the two men. They are different from each other but have striking similarities. Are we always attracted to the traits that we seem to want to get away from?

X sees us and comes over. There's an embarrassing moment. Do we shake hands, or what? He reaches through the window of the truck and I open the door at the same time, accidentally hitting him with it. He handles things well though, grasps my hands and holds them tight. I feel his eyes search mine but I can't deal with that and call Willy over to introduce him. Whew! That's over with.

The commissioner who will officiate is dressed in a royal blue university-type gown. She waits for some sort of order to appear. My sons come to help steer me to a chair and Willy brings cushions and a coat. The guests are at last appearing and someone murmurs that the bride is coming. Sure hope she beats the rain that threatens to douse us at any minute. It's cold by the ocean.

I turn my head to see my older daughter in peach chiffon. Her long golden hair, just curled for forty dollars, is now blowing straight and carefree after driving in an open convertible. My granddaughter is in her princess dress and lace parasol, and the bride arrives in a Cinderella gown. She was supposed to wear an old cream-coloured dress but found this one in a SallyAnn store and decided to fix it to suit her. It cost forty-five dollars. The sleeves had to be enlarged and stains had to be taken out. The girls sewed pearls into the bodice and made a matching veil and headdress. They took the dress to the cleaners and were quoted a price of ninety-five dollars to clean it. In tears, my daughter brought it home and in spite of the label *do not wash,* she washed it by hand, hung it out to dry, and sat down to pray. Well, the stains did come out and she patiently ironed the many lace frills until they stood out in splendour. So here she is, my youngest daughter, the little rebel, the unhappy teenager, now grown up with two children. Such a good mother, wife and sister.

The ceremony is brief with one *akward* moment (as Willy says). The commissioner wants her money halfway through the service so everything comes to a halt while someone scrambles to find the envelope. Willy remains in the background and disappears when I go to talk to X and his wife.

"Your girls are so romantic," his new wife says, "they fell in love with the bathroom here, so decided this building was the place for the wedding."

I laugh. "Guess I'm guilty in that regard."

She smiles. "I sort of guessed that."

We are contrasts. She dark and tailored, in a black and white printed dress. Me, flouncey, flowery, blonde and too soft for my own good.

Hastily taking the opportunity when X is next to me, I say, "Thanks for understanding about Willy and me and for keeping the alimony coming until I make a decision about moving in with him."

We sit down for a wonderful meal. When dinner's over, it's all I can do to thank God as I get up from the chair. I go to say goodbye to the bride and groom and all of a sudden X is there and he gives me a hug. I turn towards Willy who patiently waits to take my arm and lead me home.

5.

Artful dodging

A friend said, "Beware my dear, before committing yourself to life with another man. You've been your own person for a long time. Small irritations now will feel like impossible hurdles later. You can't escape them, and he will not change because he's been his own person for a long time." Well, have we got a small irritation here, or an impossible hurdle'

The opening of my one-person show is on Sunday. We are to deliver forty-one pieces of work, thirty-five miles away. He has an open truck, so don't you think it's logical to suggest that we buy a tarp to cover the stack of paintings that will travel in the back? Ah! But I said the word *buy*. Now Willy can say that word whenever he wants, but when I say it, he becomes incensed.

I have years of work invested in this load and any moisture that gets between the frames and the glass will ruin the art. Biting my lip and trying to think minor irritation I calmly say to Willy, "What do you propose to do if it rains?"

"I'll figure it out."

"Why can't we buy a tarp? We could use it when we go tenting."

"For Christ's sake. We don't buy anything we don't need. It will have to be stored like that foam you bought in Tofino."

Rage! He still doesn't know how sore my back gets if I don't have foam to lie on. With great effort, I decide I'll leave it to him and if the ruddy things get wet, I will deal with that and him later.

Now, in his bedroom Willy has this huge, old seaman's trunk. He throws all kinds of things in there. Old lampshades, rug-hooked hangings, old sheets and so on.

"We'll pack some of your work in that," he informs me.

"You'll never get it up on the bed of the truck." After all, he'll be seventy in

December—doesn't he know that?

"I'll *shew* you!"

So we pack the work. The trunk must weigh a ton. I shrug my shoulders and lift my eyes to heaven in hopelessness. Later in bed I can't sleep. I toss and turn, certain that I don't want to cuddle up to such a contrary person. Resisting the urge to look out of the window to see if it's cloudy, I watch the clock's hands, willing the hours to pass.

Seven o'clock comes. He's no longer in bed. I get up and part the curtains. I knew it! Low-hanging clouds and grey, grey, grey, everywhere. He brings me coffee and grins.

"It's all set." Sure enough, when I go down, the crazy thing is up there and he has the tent alongside so he can use that as a tarp, if necessary.

Off we go. We do not converse for miles. Mist dampens the windshield when we go to the highest point on the trip, but not enough to penetrate the wrapped paintings.

"How many seconds will it take to hang each painting?" he asks.

"I don't know. You don't figure it out that way."

"Why not?"

"Well you have to stack the work around the walls and figure out how the pictures will make the best arrangement. It's not a question of time."

"I figure if you can eliminate a couple of seconds from each picture you hang, you'll have a half an hour more to go inner tubing."

"Oh! You'll never understand!" I am tense as I watch the pregnant clouds come close to delivery. But we arrive at the gallery unscathed by rain. Willy unloads in record time.

Seeing the work leaning against the walls, I am seized with the dread of exposure. All of it looks faded and naked. Well, nothing to be done about it. The curator leads me to understand she doesn't wish me to stay to help. She knows the space well and I can leave the hanging to her. I say adieu to my creations sitting there forlornly around the floor. I will see them on Sunday, hopefully in happier circumstances.

When Sunday finally comes, S and B arrive from Kelowna. They drive Willy and me to the opening. I wear the flouncey dress that I wore to the wedding. The air is hot and because the gallery is on the lakefront, bathers have taken every parking spot. We are early but S says, "Let's go in."

"No, no, not yet." I say. Five more minutes go by.

"Time now." She gently nudges me.

I don't want to go in, having to hear, 'my aunt paints too' over and over. So much palaver. I have visions of standing there, knowing my work falls short. But of course, we do go in. S takes a quick look around. The curator tells us that a girl upstairs had a fire in a chair and doused it with water so now there's no water for coffee or for flushing the toilet. S discovers that the book depicting my art life is soaked and dripping with water. She dries off the book while I go to each room assessing how the show looks. My immediate reaction is that everything looks smaller than when it was in my place. Stark white walls are not good to present my work. The plumber arrives and starts the water going. The coffee begins to perk and, one after another, my friends and previous customers pour through the door. And what do you know? I remember names and introduce everyone okay. Family comes and my patron arrives with an armload of beautiful flowers. Compliments are received. My ears perk up to register the pieces that my peers see as superior. I will learn through these remarks.

It gets warm inside, but it also feels warm to me because of the support I receive from these human beings who care about what I try to do. All of a sudden, the lonely hours of struggle and disappointments that come so often in an artist's life are forgotten. I feel I have touched a chord in this group of people. Having a one-person show has been worth the effort—even if we never did buy a tarp.

6.

Closing the show

We're on our way to fetch the work from the show. It's a bright sunny day, so there's no worry about the rain this time. Chattering away, halfway there, I see a large garage sale by a gas station.

"Maybe we can stop in there on our way back," I say to Willy. "There may be some good stuff, as it isn't near civilization."

"Bunch of junk, we won't stop there," he retorts in that spitting tone of voice that sends the acid rushing from my stomach to my throat. I fight to stay quiet, but it's no good.

"Why is it," my voice cracks as I ask, "why is it, that when I suggest anything it's never any good?"

"The stuff's been sitting there all night, so obviously it's just junk." He has dismissed the idea, and me at the same time.

The sun still shines but my insides are heavy black clouds. Funny how I never noticed at the beginning this peculiarity of his—the fact that everything has to be his idea, or it doesn't amount to anything. Maybe it's because he's being more himself now than he was eight months ago.

Good Lord! Has it really been eight months? I remember the first week. Every day seemed to be a century long. We made so many decisions in those first few days. But stop thinking about those times and start thinking about what is happening. If this continues, I will have no life of my own. Every matter will be dealt with his way, whether I approve or not. And here we are, travelling in his truck, getting ready for him to pack and lug all my work again. He truly wants to be a help and he wants the best for me but I am so troubled. There seems to be something in human nature that dictates if the freedom to make decisions is taken away, it is worse than being a prisoner. The miles slip by and, as I know by now, it is his way to keep quiet until I have argued with myself long enough to stew myself out, so to speak.

We arrive early so sit in the truck while he produces a cup of coffee from the thermos. The curator comes and my heart is heavy as I see my paintings on the walls, waiting to be boxed up and taken home again. All that work. Does anyone care? Is it really, as Willy says, a waste of time? I look at the sales book and see that at least three small prints have sold, and. hallelujah, one lady bought the woodcut of the iris and a painting of a carousel. Remarks in the guest book say the routine things, except for one: "Doris, you have the key." This is in reference to a note in my art journal about looking for the key in art.

The curator has lots to say, including that she doesn't know why more pieces didn't sell. Meanwhile, methodically, Willy stacks and packs and carts to the truck. He never stops to talk to anyone when he has a job to do. Nothing slows him down. When he was a foreman, he knew that if you wanted to get a job done, you kept your concentration going only in that direction. Makes me wonder how on earth I accomplish my tasks as I'm always talking to someone. Not only do I talk to them, but my mind visualizes everything they talk about too and emotions get all tangled up. I can't help at this point, warming up to Willy, as he bends to put cardboard around yet another piece of work.

I had borrowed a yellow water lily painting from a precious customer and we are to return it on our way home. They live on a farm, midway between the show-place and home. It's too early to go yet so we sit by the lake while Willy produces hard-boiled eggs, cheese, bread and muffins. Other people are sitting in outdoor cafes under colourful umbrellas, choosing from the menu. Why do I want to join them? Is it rebellion I'm feeling? We surely go out to dinner often enough. I think it's because the lake and nearby hotels create a festive mood and you feel you want to indulge. And of course, that's what Willy avoids like the plague. Tourist traps, he says, are the scourge of the earth. He will not even buy a cup of coffee in one.

"I'm glad you sold a few things," he says, "so it wasn't all for nothing." The tears sting behind my eyes, but I manage to control them. I feel like I'm losing confidence in myself as an artist.

We return to the truck and drive to my friend's farm. She waves from the gate of her house. Willy looks for her painting while I step into the foyer. A feeling of tranquility slowly encompasses my body as I stand there. These people come from Holland. The husband grew up in Indonesia where the family had a tea plantation. They have many paintings, one of which belonged to the husband's family and which they inherited. It is so large they had to build an addition on to their house to accommodate it.

The foyer is bathed in sunlight, which washes over the black and white tile floor. Reminds me of Matisse's chapel. On a small antique table there is a royal blue vase that holds a delicate spray of Dutch iris. Oil paintings are shown to their advantage around the walls. The foyer is the size of a living room. There is a large wooden chest on the floor to the right. Heavy metal engraved bands reinforce it.

R sees my gaze and says, "It's the kind of chest that people used to move from one place to the other in the old days. It could survive sea journeys and carriage bumps."

To the left, a staircase winds to the next floor. The light on the wall highlights a lovely little watercolour of Mount Baker. With a pleasant jolt, I realize it's my work.

We are taken to a room that houses the large, inherited piece. A feeling of restfulness and good taste prevails. The oil painting is massive: old sailing ships at sea. R fetches iced tea and talks about the other work in the room. Willy hands her the water lily painting and she undoes the wrappings, then props it up on a chair by the window. I look at this thing, conscious of another oil painting behind it, and am stunned. Here I have been worrying about not being contemporary enough and, in this context, the thing shrieks modern. The marbled texture and the design quality combine with the pure translucent colours to make the work sing as it sits there. My confidence returns as I know I am looking at a good piece of work.

R takes us to a spot where her son is bunching iris to be sold at an auction in Vancouver. He gives me an armful to take home. She remembers I love potatoes from the garden and brings me some, along with some lettuce and plums. We return to the house and R shows me where my other work is hanging. It looks good too.

On our way home Willy pulls into the garage sale, saying, "It's a bunch of junk, but if you want to look at it, it's all right with me." I am determined to buy something and find a book by P.G. Woodhouse.

"How much is it?" I ask the girl sitting there.

"You are welcome to have it for nothing," she tells me. "We really only want to find a home for things."

"How much was it?" asks Willy.

"I got it for free," I say, smiling, and I feel so much better, both about the garage sale and my artwork.

Coutdown to 70th birthday party

1.

The wonderful world of innertubing

We often park near a bridge that goes over a creek and then connects to a larger beach. When we walk on the bridge, we watch youngsters below us, lying on air mattresses and inner tubes, letting the current whiz them down the creek until a bed of stones stops their movement. They climb up the bank, run back to the source and experience the thrill again and again.

"Looks like fun," I tell Willy.

"Then why don't you try it?"

"I knew it would come in handy one day," Willy says. He's talking about the spare inner tube he bought for his Volkswagen twenty-three years ago and never got around to using.

"I'll blow it up and you can have fun with it in the water." His face lights up with pleasure. "It's just the right size for one."

So here we are and I follow the small fry and, stepping into the cool water, arrange my bottom so I won't scrape my new bathing suit in the shallow places. Splat! I'm sitting on the ring of rubber and without even a chance to get readied, the current swirls me on my way. The water is so clear I can see all the coloured stones. One gets a fish's-eye view of the bulrushes on the bank. What a light-hearted feeling. I think of the Lady of Shalott (not that I resemble her in my inner tube, mind you) floating down the river, borne by the tide, long golden hair trailing on the water, flowers on her brow...but here's the bridge already and Willy is watching for me. I think he is going to burst with glee as he catches sight of me. It was all *his* idea, you see.

Disappointed when the stones stop more progress, I understand a little better why my sons loved rafting so much. And I was always telling them not to do it.

Coming up the bank, Willy holds a towel for me to dry off. He says, "I was just counting the number of sixty-six-year-olds floating down the creek in Volkswagen inner tubes, but I only counted one."

After a few more trips down the creek I venture into the lake. Lying on my stomach, I watch the underwater life. It is a peaceful feeling, the sun is warm and I forget all about time. When I turn towards shore, I see Willy standing at the edge of the water, beckoning madly with his arms for me to come back. I see now that I have drifted far out. I have to laugh though, for he looks like one of those over-protective mothers, calling her child out of danger.

"Well, you can get cramps or something," he mutters when I reach him.

The next day Willy looks out the window and proclaims that it's inner tube weather again. We go to Ruskin Lake, a pond really, a short drive from town. We clamber over a fence and pass a huge 'no trespassing' sign.

There is hardly a ripple on the lake. From my inner tube I look out on what looks like a field of forget-me-nots at the edge of the water but it turns out to be hundreds of peacock blue dragonflies. Lazily I watch as they gracefully fly to and fro and mate in a ballet-like performance. A male, curving in an arc, clings to a female as she lights upon a waterlily leaf, laying her eggs. A fish jumps through the surface and the eggs disappear.

A frog hops close by. My reverie is broken as an underwater weed curls around my leg. Ugh, it is clammy and clinging. I kick free of it and work my way back to the starting point. A young girl offers to swap me her beach ball for the tube. I agree and play with it for a while. Time is getting on, Willy will be calling me in. Forty-five minutes he figures is enough before I will get cold. Claiming the tube back and paddling towards shore, I smile as I think about this period of my life. Trying the new and rediscovering the pleasure of the old things, simple things. And all because of meeting Willy.

2.

Designer Willy

I am inner tubing in our favourite spot. Looking up, I see my man clambering down the stony entrance to the lake. What on earth is he wearing? I haven't seen him in anything that jazzy before. I manoeuvre close to where he is stepping into the water and see that the swimming trunks are black cotton with columns of bold patterns down the sides. In large letters, the word Gucci proclaims the designer's name.

"Where on earth did you get those?" I ask.

"I found them floating on the water."

It takes a while for me to get used to him upstaging me with his attire, but I laugh a little as, once again, he has made use of someone else's discard or loss.

"Come and hang onto the inner tube," I call out. "I'll paddle around and you can have a ride."

Willy lunges towards me and makes a grab for the slippery rubber. He loses his grip and, my God! I can't see him. He's under the water. I try to work myself free from the tube but am stuck and it seems he is caught under me. I frantically beat my arms around, trying to get hold of some part of him but the tube is in the way. It seems like hours before his dear head breaks through the surface. I foolishly fish his hat off a wave as he puffs and groans to reach a point where he can stand. All this time I haven't been able to free myself to help and now anxiously watch as he struggles to get his breath back. Then we laugh! It doesn't seem we will ever stop. It now seems hilariously funny. But I will remember. In those few minutes, he could have drowned.

3.

Designer Doris

We go to Cultus Lake. While cycling, Willy finds a pair of thong-type shoes in the middle of the road. The soles are shaped in a scoop form and there are braids of green, royal blue. red and yellow across the toes. There are small red leather oval patches on the outsides of the braids. On the inside of the soles there is a stamp with some wording.

"What does it say?" I ask Willy.

"It says Shore Patrol," he says, and repeats the name delighting in the picture of me and Shore Patrol shoes in the inner tube. I wear them to step over the stones on the beach and into the water. Sitting in the tube, I take them off and use them for paddles. Goodness! I can whip along like anything. It's every bit as good as being on a boat. Steering is easy and it's great fun whizzing around in circles. Everyone around me smiles and has something to say. Willy is on the shore, pointing out to people what a good time I'm able to have, and we haven't spent any money to do so. He makes up stories about me being found in the Pacific Ocean, on my way to Japan. He has not a worry in the world with me in my inner tube and Shore Patrols.

4.

The price of vanity

Does everyone lose earrings like I do? Do other women find it hard to get beautiful ones that are clip-ons? When they do find them, do they suffer during a dinner date, and not concentrate on what their partner is saying because it feels as if a couple of parrots have their beaks locked onto their earlobes? Well, I'm tired of it.

"I should get my ears pierced," I say to Willy.

"Why?"

"Because I want to look nice in some of those lovely earrings."

"Well have it done then."

"Not right now. Some other time. I think it will hurt. I might get infections. It costs money. Anyway, I've always said it was barbaric. Maybe later."

The next morning Willy shows me an advertisement, 'Ears pierced, three dollars. Seniors' day, ten percent off everything.'

"Let's go," says Willy.

"It's too hot. It's not the time. Sounds too cheap." But we get in the truck and drive to the place. He actually propels my elbow to the earring counter.

"Does it hurt?" I ask the girl. "How do you do it? Do other seniors have it done?"

She smiles, "We shoot it in, so it's not painful. And we have a disinfectant to stop infections if you're worried about that."

"All right, let's get on with it." I figure, now or never. I sign a form saying I won't hold them responsible for any problems I might have. I sit on a stool, hang on to the counter and hold my breath.

Whack!

One ear now has a pale blue stud shot through it.

Whack!

And there we are, may God help me.

Willy appears. "Is it okay?" he asks.

"I think so," I reply, hardly able to believe it, as I gently touch my ears.

"I think in all women there's a sixteen-year-old waiting to get out," says Willy.

"Well, in this case, I think it's a gypsy," I retort.

The girl told me to turn the earrings twice a day. I find it hard to do so, and Willy takes on the job.

"I wonder what other seniors are doing." he says. "We are so busy with turning earrings and all the other things."

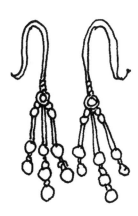

5.

A little off the top please

I watch in amazement as Willy goes onto my veranda for the fifth time to report on the three tomato plants. These things have had their soil changed, stones brought up for their drainage, fertilizer, watering every day, pots turned and new sprouts tied...and tomatoes are selling in Super Store right now for thirty-eight cents a pound! It's the urge, I think. Something very basic in human nature.

Willy's rubber tree is now seven feet high. The upper leaves are in danger of touching the ceiling and he is in a quandary, not knowing what to do about it.

"Well, I know what I would do," I say to him in an exasperated tone.

"What would you do?"

"I'd lop its top off."

His face shows disbelief and he says sadly, "I'll forgive you just this once for saying that. How would you like it if someone lopped your top off."

Now, when I think something isn't working right, he tells me to lop its top off.

6.

Falling into the future with Willy

Willy and I have bought a house. It all started when we decided to go out for a drive one day.

"There's an open house on this street. Let's go in and see what it's like." Mind you, this is out of the blue, me not having any idea this was in the offing. We go in the front door and right away I can tell it used to be a small two-room house that a handyman has added on to. The supposed suite downstairs has only enough room for one of Snow White's dwarfs. We look around the yard and Willy's eyes light up like a kid's. "It has rhubarb in the garden!"

I have dismissed the place already and can hardly wait to leave. I go back into the house and make for an exit through the front door, turning to see if Willy is following me. No, he's talking to the real estate agent and, get this, he's saying, "Of course, it will be cash!" Frantically, I move my eyebrows up and down, trying to give the message to stop everything. He catches on at last and we walk out to the truck.

Spluttering, I say, "What on earth were you telling that man? That house isn't any good."

He's quiet for a minute, and then says, "Well, it had rhubarb in the garden."

Then and there, sitting in the front seat of the truck by the side of the road, I figure I'd better speak up.

"If you are buying for an investment, I have no business in the matter. But if you are intending to share a house with me, we'd better iron out a thing or three. In the first place, we should discuss the whole matter. For instance, what will happen to my apartment? In the second place, I will not live where I am not able to do my artwork. In that house, there wasn't any light or room to paint. The whole atmosphere was depressing and I wouldn't want to live there even if there was enough room."

"How come?"

"How come? I don't know how come. I just couldn't."

"That doesn't make sense to me."

"Well, that's the way it is. I need a view. A place to work and store my things, a good feel about the place and..."I may as well spit it out, "I want my own bathroom."

He sits, digesting this bit of outlandish news. I mean, this is the man who won't use a pillow for fear of getting used to an easy life!

"Regardless," I continue, "we should not buy a house just because it has rhubarb in the garden." He puts the truck into gear and we head for McDonald's to have hot raspberry pie and free coffee for seniors. He seems to be able to think better in this atmosphere.

"Maybe I would like to live in Hatzic," I tell him as I imagine being surrounded by mountains, a lake and ducks and birds.

"We'll look out there then," he replies with a look of relief now that he has some guidelines. Mark you! He hasn't asked me if I *want* to live with him, but let that pass. I'm now warming to the idea of having our own little parcel of land in the world. Memories of sitting out in my own backyard bring a smile to my face. Especially when I think of living with someone who will do all the work!

This turns out to be the beginning to weeks and weeks of sorting out exactly what we want. Willy is not keen on asking real estate people to do the work for us. He lives in dread of being taken by someone. We are reduced to looking in the local real estate weekly for open houses. These, he doesn't mind investigating.

What do you know, we find one that fits *our* requirements and I promptly fall in love with it. I say it fits our requirements, but actually Willy objects to the wasted space in the basement that would have to be heated. He also thinks the price is too high. Thinks the owners are greedy. We continue to visit other open houses together, walking and cycling around possible streets. My heart sinks lower and lower as Willy bides his time on the one house, figuring the owners might get anxious and settle for the ten-thousand less that he indicated he would be prepared to pay.

My dreams at night are all the same. I see him sitting in the living room or tending the neat garden. I see me working in the front bedroom and the great old-fashioned kitchen. It's all as clear as day. I have to leave on a trip to Australia for a few weeks. Surely, if he really loves me, he will get this house.

When I am away he phones often. Biting my tongue, I don't want to harass him with the question. I put down the receiver with that stupid old heart crying out to hear that we have a new home. A couple of phone calls later, and his voice is so apologetic, "I'm sorry, honey, the house has been sold. I'm truly sorry." Take hold of yourself Doris, there's no good in bemoaning the fact. It's not fair to give him a hard time. After all, it's his money, not yours. But that cold hard lump sits on my chest and there's nothing to do about it.

When he meets me at the airport, it feels good to have his arms around me. And do you know what I'm thinking? I'm thinking he's going to tell me he just wanted to surprise me and he bought the house after all, and we'll pull into the driveway of our new home and he will have moved all the stuff from our apartments and everything will be waiting like I knew it should be when I first went into that house. But of course, it isn't so and the house is gone.

We go back to looking again. After experiencing semi-country living in southwest Australia for those few weeks, hearing the dogs bark at the 'roos and the foxes, I decide that country life is not for me. Living in town, a little farther from the main street wouldn't be so bad, as long as we were on a bus route. That gives us a little more option. We go into places that are built of cement blocks, run down and smelling of mould. Willy eyes one structure and figures he could rebuild. I get panicky.

He's almost seventy and I am sixty-six. I don't want to spend these years surrounded with brick dust and half-finished walls. I hang in for a house with a view but these are few and far between. Some have wonderful views but not much house. Others have too much property to keep up. And so it goes.

It's Sunday again and we are on the familiar trek of going through open houses. This one looks just as disappointing — my spirit still half-lives in the first place I liked. Going in the front door, I am surprised to see that the lobby is pleasant. Stairs lead to the living area; there is a bricked area to one side with plants and a window—great place for Willy's rubber tree. A balcony leads to the living room — everything bright. bright, bright. There's a skylight and windows everywhere. A bricked surround for the wood-burning stove. A view that encompasses the whole valley and Mount Baker, a skylight in the master bedroom!

"You can work in here," says Willy. The backyard is private, backing into a hill that is wooded. Gives you a personal feeling.

I am quite encouraged and say, "Maybe we should consider it."

Back in the apartment building, Willy is thinking about it. I am imagining working in that light and seeing Willy clipping cedar trees. Willy loved the oversized bathtub. He breaks the silence by saying, "I can't wait to see how the grandson would love to swim in that thing." But the days tick by and I don't know what is to happen. I leave the real estate lady's card in full view. It is getting harder to find anything that would fit us as well as this.

Hallelujah! He phones her. She comes over and he makes an offer. She already knows how much they will accept and we sign the contract.

I am trying to recall what we have bought. We did not re-examine the place. At the time, we didn't make the decision to buy so we weren't that thorough in looking at it. By chance we pass the real estate office and our agent is there. I ask her if we can have some photos of the house and place.

"I know you haven't had a good look at the place," she says, "why don't we go up there right now so you can see what you've bought." Oh, I could have kissed her!

We drive up to the street and park, and she walks ahead and turns the key in the lock. There are two large mirrors in the hall. Nice.

Willy checks out the bathroom and calls out, "Look at this. A solid oak toilet seat. They cost $29.95, on sale."

"I think it's $39.95," the real estate lady smiles. We see the charming ceiling fan, the good wallpaper, the drapes that are to be left with us. We see more closets than we remembered and, always, the surprises are happy ones. We get excited and start to call to one another to look at this and look at that.

Willy keeps saying, "Imagine, a solid oak toilet seat." For the while, he has forgotten there isn't any rhubarb in the garden!

7.

Reality

I am standing in the middle of my apartment. This is the place that I thought I would stay in until I die. Now it's as if I've been caught in a centrifugal force, whirling round and round a gaping cylinder, being dragged ever nearer to the bottom. But there doesn't seem to be a bottom. It's black below and doesn't seem to have an end at all. Am I being melodramatic? Who knows? I only know that all my good intentions to remain my own person, all the definite proclamations made to keep my apartment, all the talk of not giving up my art time, have come tumbling down with me into that cylinder.

Now I must make the effort to sort through my things. Art supplies that have been carted from Winnipeg and haven't been used in all that time. Must find a deserving recipient. I take down the jars of powdered pigments that I used for Japanese woodcuts. No use looking at the prices still labeled on them. I remember how hard it was to find money to afford them. I could use them for making my own watercolour paint, but it's a tedious process and they would have to be ground so fine that it would take me ages. No, no, get on with it. Put them in the cardboard box.

It's almost lunchtime and Willy will be putting his nose around the door soon, telling me I must be hungry. Stop pussyfooting around, make decisions, Doris. I know what I'll do, I'll empty drawers in the bedroom and take the dresser up to Willy's. I need some drawers to put my underwear in. I dump the contents of the first drawer on the floor. Why on earth have I kept all these bits of paper. Perhaps because good water-colour paper is so expensive. Well, let it sit on the floor until I can make *that* decision. The second drawer holds an assortment of failed paintings and, what is this? A red silk drawstring bag from Japan. Something in it. My stars! What am I to do with this? It's my old dentures. Once again, kept, just in case. Can

I brace myself to throw them away? What if I lose my new ones? I'm not solving anything here. Ah, well, I have two piles of junk on the floor. That's a start. I get a damp cloth and wipe out the drawers, standing one near the door, ready to take upstairs. I have already moved some clothes and artwork to Willy's but this is the first piece of furniture that will be transferred. Somehow it has more weight — excuse the pun.

This isn't something that can be hurried. I want to acknowledge my feelings with every move, so I can be sure of what is happening. My phone is to be disconnected on Friday. It will go upstairs under my name and Willy will give up his phone. He has cleared out some cupboards for me, and the fridge is at last working and bulging with food. How lucky can I be? But human nature doesn't allow for one to just enjoy luck. You always have to fret about something or other. At least I do.

I take the elevator up to his place and open the door.

"What have you got there?" Willy asks me. He sees that it is a drawer from my dresser and, leaning against his muscled chest, I tell him it feels strange to bring my furniture here. He wraps his arms around me and, as always, things seem better.

8.

Letting go

Willy is getting my apartment ready for renting it out.

I feel the way one does when you are about to be married. It seems like such a major step, and somehow you feel like you're locking yourself into something that won't be easy to escape. The caterpillar named fear is squirming again, but this time he is edged with excitement.

Willy asks me to pick out the colour I want for re-painting the walls. All those nail holes, millions of nail holes where I have randomly hung paintings over the past two years. Systematically, Willy works like a robot, filling in gouges, sanding and preparing the place.

I start to fill boxes with my belongings and pack paintings and art materials. Can I bear to give up these precious art books? Can I be brave and turf these ornaments? Stupid things I've kept. Pretty ribbons. Craft magazines. All the cards my children have given me over the years. Why must I keep everything. I need someone to hit me over the head and say, "You're sixty-six. Stop hoarding non-essentials. It will be too much for someone to have to sort out if you die. What the dickens will anyone do with such things?" Willy appears and I tell him this.

"Don't throw anything away," he says, "you don't have to. There's lots of room where we're going." Relieved, I pitch it all in boxes, essential or not, mark it, Oddments, Etc. and forget about it.

I partially moved out when my friends borrowed my apartment for a short time but my paintings were left on the walls. Now they are packed and there is a sense of loss. Willy plods on, ignoring me sitting on the bedroom floor. Patch and sand, scrub and paint, he goes on and on even though people come and talk and meal times are overdue. Take out light fixtures and wall sockets, unhitch curtains, patch and sand, scrub and paint.

I've dumped the contents of another drawer on the rug. I summon my brain to decide what to do with such a varied display. What do I do with a letter that was returned address unknown. Can I let this friend go? Could I trace the address? I think of this friend and how great he was. His mother died a while ago. We enjoyed our times together, his mother and I. She was a truly original artist. This was the letter I wrote to tell him how I missed her and to let him know how sorry I was and here it lays on the floor and he never knew that I wrote and will think I didn't care. I used to love getting his letters, there was always an enclosure about an art-related incident of interest to me. It's no use. I'll leave everything till I can make quicker decisions.

It isn't long before that guy of mine is finished. Quite shocking to see how bright the apartment looks with the lighter paint. Other than being too sterile for my liking, it has a spanking new look. Willy happens to see the manager and mentions that I'd like to rent my place out. Bless me, within an hour of him saying so, the manager brings prospective tenants through the place. With horrors, my mess still where I left it. And the place is rented. They are to take possession in three days.

Willy is back. We package up the rest of my stuff and clean cupboards and shelves. Willy brings down his power vacuum cleaner and cleans the carpets.

I am now — lock, stock and barrel — in Willy's place and I want to fight someone. Anyone. Don't ask me why, I don't know why. I just want a fight. I'm mixed up inside. I start to go through the boxes, wrapping tape around them with a vengeance, and writing in large letters with a big marking pen what the contents are —on four sides and on top of each box. Willy stands over me, foreman-style, and says, "You don't need to do that."

I grit my teeth, "I *do* need to do that so I can see what's what at the other end."

He snorts, "I'd say that was overkill."

I could lunge at his throat but fortunately he's on his way to the door to go for a walk. On his way out he mumbles, "Maybe you'll cool down soon." It would be nice if I could cry, but I can't.

9.

A plan is in the works

Awake, I make stretching and yawning noises in the bedroom, my signal that I'm ready for a wake-up coffee. When Willy doesn't come, I call him. He arrives with a pencil stuck behind his ear and in his hands, a brown paper bag with some scribbles on it.

"I am writing my literary masterpiece," he says and recites what he has put down. "This is fiction-writing at its best. They're going to come all the way from Texas in answer to this ad. They're going to fight tooth and nail to rent this place. They're going to be lined up all down the street and I will have to be firm. I will have to say, No, no, I want to take this *brightle* old lady as a tenant. Calm down now."

Fourteen days to go before we move into our new house. We drive up to it to savour it from a distance. There's a truck outside and people are bustling back and forth.

"They're moving out," I say.

"Either that, or someone's moving in," replies Willy. I try to laugh that thought off.

Willy will be turning seventy about the time we move, so to celebrate and, at the same time, to share our pleasure in the new house, we decide to have a house-warming party. Everywhere I go, I jabber on and on about the place and ask people to be sure to come. After some time has gone by, it occurs to me that I may just have invited over a hundred people.

Willy starts to show worry lines and has taken to muttering to himself.

"It's not the move I'm worried about," he reassures me, "I'm panicky about the whole town of Mission appearing and then running out of food and drink. Another thing is, I, myself, haven't asked one person, do you realize that?"

"Oh God!" I say, "I guess that's true!"

Three people ask me whether we're having Danish food, seeing that Willy comes from Denmark. I hadn't thought about it, but it might be kind of fun. Problem is, what is Danish food, anyway? A Danish lady lives in our apartment building so I ask her if she can give me some suggestions.

"I'll give it some thought and you can call on me in a couple of days," she tells me.

The next evening the door knocker sounds and the Danish lady enters with a pad of paper and pen.

"Let's get this thing organized," she says and directs Willy to write down all the items needed for a typical party from Denmark.

"One eel."

"What do you do with an eel?" I interject.

"Well, you peel it and treat it — not to be concerned, I will do that," she says, moving to the next item on the pad.

"Smoked herring," she nods toward Willy.

"How do you serve that?" I ask.

"No worry, I will see to it." She checks something off her list.

"Red cabbage."

Well at this point I venture, "Can you show me how to make that dish?"

She looks at me with disbelief. "You can't make that. Even a Dane has to have years of experience to make it the right way. No, no, I will look after that."

"Well, that's kind of you, but how are we going to work all this out?

"Simple. Willy will get all the stuff and I will come to your place early in the morning and set the whole thing up." Goodness knows how I am to repay her.

The days tick by and all the little matters start to resolve themselves. Willy is nervous. He's wondering if he can carry me over the *threshold,* and he's found out that eel costs twenty-three dollars a pound!

On the day of our move Willy opens the door and somehow gathers me in his arms to carry me over the threshold. We stumble and lurch into the hallway of our new home.

Willy puts himself into gear and unloads the truck over and over, lifting heavy furniture against protests.

"What are you worried about?" he asks in an exasperated way.

"Well, you forget your age. You shouldn't be hauling that stuff around."

"I know what I'm doing. It's only when you don't know what you're doing that you have cause to worry. Now leave me in peace."

What do you do with someone who doesn't want you to worry over him? I see now that this has been one of my ways of expressing caring for a person. I feel somehow rejected and not needed and, to tell the truth, I'm not.

Boxes keep coming and coming. How did we have all this in our apartments?

My paintings and art stuff are never ending. We collapse on the bed in the evening and I feel there's something wrong somewhere

"You know what it is?" I say to Willy. "It's quiet. No trucks charging up the hill. No road noises. No dogs barking."

In the morning Willy brings me coffee in bed and draws back the drapes. Stellar jays and finches are flitting in and out of the trees in the backyard. An orange-coloured bird pecks about the brown, mottled leaves on the ground. It feels strange to walk around a house. Our house. I don't think I'll ever get used to the view. A whole panorama with Mount Baker in the front and wooded hills in the back.

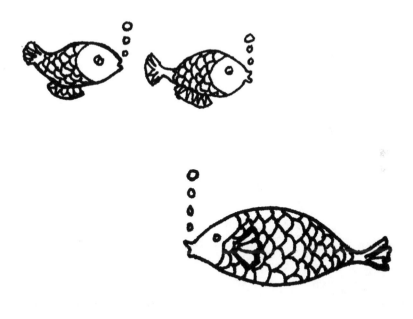

Countdown

The 18th of December — on this day, a year ago, he drove me to the dentist's and, as it was lunchtime, I suggested we go to a Greek restaurant and I would pay for the meal. He accepted and told me it was his birthday and so he considered the lunch to be a birthday present. This year, I give him a *bearometer,* which is the only thing in the world I have ever heard him say he wanted. He loves it and finds a good spot on the paneled wall to display it. We go to lunch, sitting in the same booth as we were in a year ago. I tell the waitress that it's Willy's birthday, and she brings a slice of carrot cake with icing and a candle. Two other waitresses sing Happy Birthday to a red-faced Willy.

The 22nd of December — the day of the housewarming party. Willy has spent much of the week scurrying around to get items on the Danish party list. He is frantic that we won't have enough food for everyone, and we haven't a clue how many people we've invited. He keeps buying more and more goodies as back-up. Willy is to pick up the lady at nine. She arrives with her own pots and knives. She is a senior but by no means frail. She has been cooking and catering all her life. Since coming to Canada she's cooked at various lumber camps and oil rig sites, catering to hundreds of men at one time. Often she was the only woman. When asked if men tried to get fresh with her she was aghast.

"No way," she said, "it's a known fact that the cook is off limits." She tells me that she was known for her terrific coffee. Laughing, she says, "When it was cold and men dropped in from other camps, I always put some aquavit in. They spread the word that no one could make coffee as good as me."

The wooden spoon stirs the pork and veal, and small pieces are dropped into the fat to cook. The red cabbage is combined with red currant juice to make a wonderful salad. The eel is skinned and treated, ready for squares of Danish rye bread. The herring has been marinated in onions and vinegar. One daughter prepares the platters and decorates them with parsley. Another daughter arrives with Willy's birthday cake, a large rectangle of carrot cake adorned with tall thin candles. She also brings Nanaimo bars, shortbread, and cookies. Everything is so festive...but where is Willy? We find him looking out the window, sadly saying, "No one is coming." But the doorbell chimes and many friends come. It is a warm and wonderful party, even without the fire burning. The Danish refreshments are praised to the skies and Willy gets another birthday song.

December 25th — Christmas day and we joke together. We have had so much going on that neither of us gave much thought to Christmas gifts for each other. Willy got me to choose a pair of earrings in the store, and I found a pair of gloves for him. The main thing was that I was buying a used chain saw for Willy. I don't know if he would be mad or not, he's so proud of his $5.95 cross saw that he got from Canadian Tire. He used it the other day to start to cut down some trees in our backyard, but it's not an easy job. "I never thought I would be logging on my very own property," he said to me with a grin.

I'm getting used to being in my new surroundings. Caught the bus at the end of the street and it's very handy. The town looked so pretty during the ride and everyone on the bus was so chatty. I smiled to myself when I passed Holiday Street for the first time. There are still a few things amiss, like the leak from the roof, when conditions are bad. But Willy doesn't freak out. He expects these things to happen and he just goes about fixing them.

He didn't like the chain saw. Ridiculed me for thinking such a small one would be any use at all. I am subjected to stories of people not knowing the difference between real machines and toys.

He has a drawer where all presents to him land up — his souvenir drawer.

It's really very wonderful to be living here with Willy, even though when he tells people about the threshold ceremony, he always remarks, "I never thought 120 pounds weighed so heavy!"

Willy tells me a story about one Christmas Eve in New Westminster. He saw this woman (about forty-five years of age) struggling to carry a boxed, artificial tree up the hill to her apartment. The street was icy and it was snowing. She asked if he would carry it for her. Willy tells me it seemed the decent thing to do. It did occur to him that she should have thought about the awkwardness of it before she bought it. The wind was cold and the apartment beautifully warm as she unlocked the door. It was an elegant place. Two large windows of the dining room overlooked the river. The table was set for dinner for two, complete with wine glasses and candles. Willy started to get nervous and went to put the Christmas tree in the coat closet. Inside were *three more boxed Christmas trees.*

He ran out of there.

Section 5.

New experiences

1.

Our first anniversary

I am spitting mad at him again. I twist my head so my burning eyes fasten on the white icy fields flashing by as we drive towards Sumas. We are driving to Sumas to celebrate the anniversary of the day when I told him I cared for him. How sweet of him to want to recall the day. He's given me one hundred dollars to buy some sweats too. Sweets, he calls them. I've never worn sweats before but I asked my daughter what other women wear in the house to keep warm. She said, "Mother, everyone wears sweats. Fleece-lined soft pants and tops — they're casual and cosy."

So why am I mad? Would you believe we are fighting for the second time over my making the simple remark the other day of, "Look Willy, how the snow is falling off the roof." Now how on earth can you have an argument over that? We had been walking and I pointed out to him some snow gathered into a mass that hung precariously over the rim of a roof, which was about to come crashing down to the ground. His face had turned beet red and his voice took on an angry tone as he berated me for saying the snow was falling off the roof. He hissed, "People like you say stupid things like that without thinking. I go out every day and I watch the way nature works and it is not snow on the roof but snow that was caught up by the wind and whipped around until it built up to the roof." Well, after I gave up trying to explain my position, we came home and I had a cry about his forever contradicting me. We smoothed things over yet another time.

Driving along today I see a farm with the ruddy snow about to fall off the roof and before I can stop my tongue I say, jokingly, "There's more snow falling off the roof." Well, as he is fond of saying, that is when the u-know-what hits the fan. He goes on a tirade all over again. And we're supposed to be celebrating.

We go into the Lone Jack Saloon as we did a year ago and order the house wine. He gets me laughing again and while he talks, my subconscious thoughts surface and I ask myself how I really feel about having been with this man for a year now.

2.

Questions and answers

What is the matter with me? Why am I like this? Surely I need a good shaking up or something. If anyone has an ideal existence, I have it right now. But that knowledge doesn't help. I'm having a hard time from keeping tears spurting from my eyes and lifting that stone from my chest. We were finally reaching such a warm state, Willy and I. It always seems that when we do, that is when the hurting remarks come.

I am eating my last mouthful of peanut butter for breakfast, when he leans over to kiss me.

"No," he changes his mind, "I don't want a peanut butter kiss."

"Well," I tell him smartly, "If that puts you off, maybe you won't get one at all."

So he goes on about sending a letter to Ann Landers asking her to mediate about whether or not he should have to settle for a peanut butter kiss.

"Bet she's never had a letter on that topic," he says, pleased with himself. "She will let me know if I've wasted the last year of my life or not."

Up to now it was amusing but what a thing to say! Of course I retaliate.

"And she would want to know what the heck you did before that wasted year!" All the underlying meaning in that sentence, let me tell you, was pushed home. A life the *dead-opposight* of mine. No phone calls or visitors. No books. No business with members of boards or clubs. No absorbing passion but to be with nature, walking, cycling outside. Well maybe the stock market is his passion, but it's a solitary one.

Okay, so we survive that bit of swordplay and it's dinnertime, and I'm vocally working out how much I have to pay in income taxes with my quarterly installments. He works it out to be so and so. I am bothered by the fact that I have to declare the income from the rental of my apartment on my form when that income goes to Willy. I want to bring my income down and this doesn't help matters. So that I can truthfully say the house is half mine, why can't I sign my apartment over to him? But he says no.

In looking over the income tax forms I see where one can transfer money or property to a spouse without capital gain. For purposes of accuracy, a common-law relationship is designated as spousal after one year of living together. During the conversation, he adds that common-law as regards inheriting the other's money is specified as at least two years of cohabitation. What the heck is he bringing up inheriting money for? It's as if I was hinting that I am now entitled to inherit the ruddy stuff because we've been together more than a year. My cheeks are flaming red and I can't face the yogurt in front of me because my chest becomes tight with anger and humiliation. Damn his money. There I've said it. But I am surrounded by this house, which is the result of that damned money. I've got to have time to think but not without somehow asserting myself, and my voice is strangled as I say, "Another thing I want to do is sign a legal document to say that if you die, I do not want any claim on what you may have." Let him leave it to his brother and his brother's children.

I think of my friend the artist who couldn't understand why his wife left him "when I gave her everything — did everything for her." Relationships are more than that, surely. It's giving of yourself, but that's the part this friend fought against. If he gave of himself, then he felt he had to commit himself. A person who knew my friend said of him, "He draws you to him and smothers you with warmth, then, without warning, he withdraws and gives you to understand he prefers to be on his own."

Pride — how it gets in the way. By the way, I caught Willy using the chain saw the other day.

This week I read Secrets about Men that Women Should Know. Perhaps it will help me to understand some of the misses in communication between Willy and me.

We are back to normal again and he's making a concentrated effort to control his tongue. It makes him less him though, and there we go, I'm trying to change him. But then again, doesn't he try to change me? One thing is certain, he doesn't ever, ever want me to control anything in our relationship.

We must learn to allow for each other's differences, and the key is to focus on the good things. For instance, Willy loves the outdoors and so do I. He likes to spend evenings at home He is gentle and steady. He always makes me laugh. He fixes everything—therefore nothing is a disaster. He takes pride in his home. He cooks and does housework. Only on my insistence do I cook dinner at night. Hmm!

A month goes by and I haven't been mad at Willy at all. I think this is the longest period I've gone without wondering if I've made the right decision. This afternoon he rigs up a fluorescent light in my gallery. It is a terrible job but he keeps at it even though the wiring has to be redone and we don't have a stepladder to reach up high. I would have bought the lights at the regular price but he waited for sales and saved me twenty dollars.

At night he holds me in bed until his arms go numb. I remember back to the beginning of our togetherness. He thought it was awful to hug or kiss me during the daytime, figuring everything has to have a time slot, and daytime was not for smooching. He sure has changed in that direction and in many other ways too. I guess we are slowly learning about each other.

3.

Inventory

It's been fifteen months since we have been "an item" as the saying goes. How have we fared, Willy and I? At first I stayed only the nights in his apartment. Then the days and the nights. We had the flu, one after the other. I knew we cared for each other when I made him rice-water for his diarrhea. And when he sprang out of bed to catch me falling in a faint. Sat by me on the floor for thirty minutes, covering me with a blanket until I recovered. I had lain there, vomiting and letting off wind, absolutely giving up hope I could ever be a romantic figure to him again.

He nursed me after the repair operation and gradually my stuff was moved from my apartment to his. We've lived in the house for four months now. Everyone thinks I'm lucky. I said to my daughter the other day, "I have a room for matting and storage, a room as a gallery, a skylight studio and, you know what, I've just moved the word processor into our bedroom."

"What part of the house belongs to Willy?" she asked.

"He has the garage." I said. I'm fooling of course. He has a room too. A room I try not to look in to. He has string crisscrossing the walls so he can dry his washing. (He doesn't like to use the dryer.) He has geranium cuttings growing in various stages. Tools. Potatoes in storage and all that. So you see, I'd rather not know.

He's cut down twenty-five trees from the backyard and the split woodpile is now twelve feet high. We watched *Field of Dreams* last night where the main character has a dream to build a baseball field on his farm, and Willy said to me in the morning, "I dreamed I built a woodpile to the moon and everyone came to see it." There's a gleam in his eye when he looks at all the timber in the backyard. It's scary because it seems to give him a high to cut the trees down with his trusty $5.95 saw. We have a willow tree that I like to look at from the bedroom window as I lie in bed having my morning coffee. I revel in the glowing delicacy of its branches, the dewdrops on the leaves reflecting rainbows in the morning sun. It gives hope of spring, even in January, as its tendrils take on fluorescent gold colours. Willy wanted to take it down but doing some quick thinking, I named it Doris and told him if he did, I would haunt him.

He's dug up a six-by-eight-foot patch in the front yard (the only place to grow anything here) for rhubarb. He climbed a nearby mountain to get some rich earth for the soil. He then added a pail of fish that he found by the roadside and, for good measure, some steer manure. Friends brought over some roots of rhubarb to plant. When anyone visits, Willy shows off with pride, the lovely alizarin stalks and curly spring-green leaves. Every night we have a fire in our wood stove. Willy only uses wood that doesn't cost. His journeys on the bike allow him to find discarded boards, broken pallets and free wood offered by local lumber companies. He collects it from everywhere and puts what he finds into stockpiles to be loaded up later with his truck. When he needs to, he uses the wood from the trees he has felled in the backyard.

D: "The backyard looks lovely, Willy, with everything blooming."

W: "Yes, especially the dandelions. Those fellows poke their heads up no matter what. Even when you *moo* them down with the weed-eater, they take no offense and pop right back up."

The tomato plants have been soaked with last night's rain. Their leaves are curled and turned away from us. Willy feels sorry for them and says, "They look as though they have sinned and are covering themselves with shame."

The bottle trees

Willy knows
where wood is for our fireplace.
We go in the truck, behind the industrial site.
1 get out to walk
where cars have worn down a rough road
amongst the brush.
It's late winter cold and
trash is everywhere.
1 shiver
and am repulsed, not wanting to know
the why of it.
The track widens
and suddenly it is a fantasy route
and I smile. Branches are boasting
hundreds of up-ended, sea-green wine bottles.
Late afternoon sun brings out the
emerald colour; they look like lanterns.
Looking closely at one,
1 see it acts like a terrarium,
a leaf has sprouted in its small greenhouse.

Willy says
this is where the drunks come at night
to drown reality.
Even so, 1 think, they leave their mark.
Like Christo the artist, who wraps part of nature
so we will be more aware of it,
the wine drinkers have made their artistic statement.
And the green bottles sway in their
lonely gallery.

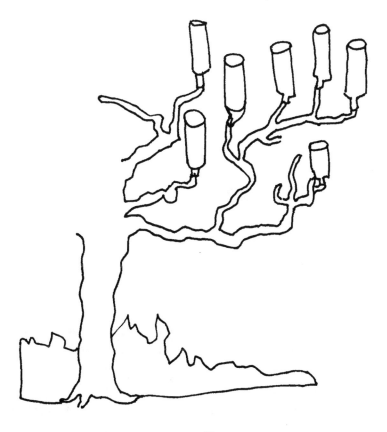

New experiences

5.

Census

The yellow form lies on the coffee table. "Count yourself in" it says on the cover. Willy has a dread of filling out forms and it will have to be me who completes the thing. We must do it together though because he has to agree with the answers I put on the census description. Pulling at his sleeve so he will sit next to me on the chesterfield, I read out the questions.

Question 1. Who is making out this form?

I write in Doris Paterson. Reading on, I see it says this is Person # 1.

Question 2. Name other people living in this house.

I write in Willy Smith. Call this person, Person #2, I read aloud.

"I knew it! You are Person # 1 and I am only Person # 2," he says.

Oh, boy, he's going to be difficult.

"Would you like to be Person # 1? That's fine with me. I don't want to be living the rest of my life apologizing for writing that I'm Person # 1."

"No, no, keep it as it is. I know my place!"

Gritting my teeth, we go on.

Question 3. What relationship are you to this person?

Pen is poised mid-air.

"Well?" My eyes are on his face.

"What choice have we got?"

"Married or common-law."

"Maybe there's a loophole somewhere."

The dirty dog. He knows he's being cornered and he hates being tied down or labeled. My pen stays poised and he senses the frost descending.

"Put common-law," he says, and the corner of his mouth shows he's trying to hide a smile.

So he has finally mouthed those words. Pretty ugly words really, at least to a person from England. "Common" means bad taste, unacceptable in civilized company, vulgar. "Law" conjures up court cases and those who are outside of decent living. I have used all the other terms appropriate to our situation — male-partner, my man — but I think it's time to call him my husband. Of course, he has no idea that this thought is churning through my mind as we fill in the rest of the blanks. Our house is in joint tenancy which means we both own "a whole of the half" and if either one dies, the house automatically goes to the other. Otherwise we have never pledged our lives to each other and we have never, yes that's it, we have never had a *ritual* declaring our status. Strange how rituals are so important. I don't want the marriage ritual but I want to know what I am involved in. Needless to say, he doesn't give a damn. He would probably say, what good did all those rituals (wedding vows) do to the thousands who are now with other partners? Live the best you can and if it gets so you can't hack it, leave, without letting the lawyers benefit financially.

Other than his constant jokes about me being Person # 1, we finish the census project and he goes off to talk to his spinach plants, from which, by the way, we've already had two meals. That's not enough for him because he paid four dollars for all the seeds and he's deducting the cost per meal, and it hasn't warranted the price of the seeds and steer manure yet! God, what a man. You can't even enjoy a spinach dinner with him without a lesson in economics!

I'm thinking about all this as I go to work in my studio, and think that it's time I made a decision about my X too. I don't take much alimony from him but it's still a link with him. In spite of receiving advice from every source, and I mean every source, I am a one-track Person # 1 and decide that it's time to put this financial connection to bed.

Phoning X, I blurt out — I always seem to blurt out when I talk long-distance to him — "I have decided not to take any more money from you. Thank you for being good about it all these years, but this is the end. I will manage with my old age pension. You are now free!" I don't want to add, "And so am I."

X responds with, "Whatever you want is fine with me too."

"Do you want me to return the cheques or shall I burn them?" I ask.

"You can destroy them," he says, and that is that.

I've had a shower, it's ten o'clock and time for our glass of wine. Willy suggested that we wait until now to burn the cheques. Rituals again. I pick them up and open the glass door of the stove. A finger of fire catches the side of the slips of paper. I see his signature dissolve under the charcoal base of the flame. For a fleeting moment, I feel like dragging them out again and my eyes are filling with tears. I go back to the chesterfield and Willy puts his arms around me. He hugs me hard. He understands. As we clink our amber-coloured glasses together, the bell tones sound loud and clear.

6.

Roughin' it again

I wake to the "plop" sound of something dropping on my chest and struggle to open my eyes. The green glow of the nylon tent is a reminder that Willy and I are camping. I see a letter sitting on my chest. Willy peeks his face through the zipper opening and calls out, "Mailman, mailman, special delivery!"

Bleary-eyed, I find the wrist with the watch on it. Yipes, it's 6:30 a.m. I thought we were on holiday. Falling back to sleep, I figure I'll deal with it later.

He's a bit more cautious, an hour afterwards, as he calls out "mailman" again. Groaning, I realize it's my sixty-seventh birthday. I find the envelope. It's addressed to "the one and only." Inside is a card with piano keys and a single red rose on the front. A note at the bottom states, "Your present is tickets for *Phantom of the Opera*." I notice a drawing of a tiny mask. Willy waits for my reaction and when I grin, he comes into the tent for a hug. This is a bit difficult because I am lying on my newly purchased air mattress.

He doesn't like my air mattress, of course. Says I bought it unnecessarily. Before I bought it, he would take two levels of foam with us from our double bed. It would take up so much room on the truck that I thought it would ease the situation if I got an air mattress. Since only single ones were available, I now lie higher than him. He may take it as a sign of distancing, who knows? I'll have to be prepared for many years of snide remarks about why I would waste good money when he had it all figured out.

So I'm sixty-seven and am camping in the Olympic Peninsula. I have often asked people why they like to camp. My daughter said to me, "Mother, it's because you can hug a tree." I am learning not to convey these gems to Willy because now, when there's a lull in our life in the wilds, he will say, "Why don't you go and hug a tree?" Titter, titter. So what is the consensus of the why of camping. Some say, to get away from the phone and the TV. Well our phone hardly ever rings and we seldom watch TV. Others say, to get away from the noise and job stress. We don't have job stress and there's more noise in the wild than at home. The snuffling and moving of animals at night scares the pants off me, and the thumping music of teenage campers jangles my nerves. One thing though, out of necessity, I learned to pee in the bush.

I thought the Olympic Peninsula would be rugged rocks and beaches but most of it is endless green trees. Of course it's a national forest too. An artist-friend and I go painting together at times. Once I told her that I felt like giving the trees a good kick. She asked me why I felt that way and I replied, "Tree after tree — standing ram-rod straight and green, green, green. No chance for a painter to put her brush to orange or red." No. It's an exercise in how many greens you can fabricate and what compositions you can come up with, looking at nonstop sameness.

Well, we continue on the road and come to a beach with some atmosphere, a lodge and log cabins. I sit and paint in disheartened fashion, conscious of Willy having nothing to do. Stopping midway, we have lunch, and I leave my bulky equipment outside. We ask for a table that looks out on the area so I can keep an eye on it.

"No," the waitress says, "we don't want to use that side." Willy is annoyed.

"Government run!" he grumbles. It's as if he's got ants running all over him when he's in places like this and I can tell he's unhappy. As we enjoy a delicious lunch of salmon soup, cheese on a croissant, and white wine, he remembers my birthday.

"If you want, we could stay in a log cabin."

Well, I do want, but visions of a similar situation frighten me out of my wants. I think back to a time when X and I were in Calgary. He was on business and we needed to find a hotel for the night. He had just made a phone call to his office and was told that two-thirds of his division were to be let go, so the timing wasn't great for making a special request. But from the time I left England, I had dreamed of going to the Banff Springs Hotel. Canada is personified by posters overseas of this wonderful place, and I had thought of it often.

"It'll cost too much," he said, red in the face.

"I'll phone and ask," I persisted and found out it was about twenty dollars more than a good hotel in Calgary. But the price included ballroom dancing and use of the spa. In Calgary we could easily spend that on extra entertainment. He was livid, but I stuck to my guns. We got in the car and he rammed his foot on the gas as hard as he could. We sped down the highway and I wished the police would catch us as I was petrified. He jammed on the brakes and I could smell the rubber burning. A display of anger because I asked for such a thing.

Of course, we ended up having a good time in the hotel with the spa and dancing, but you'd better believe the incident is burned on my brain and I'm not about to try the same thing with Willy. So my birthday fizzles out with driving through small towns. Dirty, discouraged small towns. We look for motels off the highway and finally find one in the middle of faceless gas stations and the steel-barred windows of gun stores, pawn shops and liquor stores. We go for a walk and I try to stay pleasant. It was me who asked to go around the peninsula, but I can hardly wait to go home.

The next morning we drive to Seattle and I get scared when I see the winding arms of different highways, like an octopus waiting to trap you. Willy finds my darling art store without trouble and patiently waits while I go nuts looking at all the goodies I can buy for my work.

Coming back to the truck I suddenly feel tired and jaded.

There haven't been any motifs to paint and I'm weary of the driving. Willy wheels into a discount mall. Packs of people but nothing interests me. Too many racks with the same merchandise. Too many aggressive salespeople, obviously suspecting shoplifting, a man in a cage high above the floor reminding me of Big Brother. Ugh! Let me out of here. On to Bellingham and into the public art gallery. What a relief to stand amongst real paintings. Back to Mission and routine life. Another trip over with and getting used to being older.

7.

The Christmas gift

Was it four years ago that we were in K's living room, reading the pieces for Christmas? Our stories seemed raw and hurting. My piece was about the opal ring that I had always longed for. One of my daughters saved her money and bought me one with tiny stones. It was dear to me but I thought that if X had bought it, it might have been a sign that our marriage was not doomed. That Christmas I faced the fact that it was.

The Christmas after K's party, I had written about grudgingly accepting my changed status from being the loved wife and needed mother of a large family in Christmases past, to being a woman alone.

Then Willy came along and we bought our wonderful home. A room for framing, one for painting and one for showing my art. How great to have skylights. We watch the moon through them and, when it's clear and dark, the sprinkling of stars. Even the rain sounds soothing on the glass. The house always seems full of light. How good to have rhubarb, veggies and a small secluded forest in our backyard. Then there's the fireplace. Willy starts a fire at four every day and oh, it reminds me of the fireplaces of my homeland.

I was all geared up to think that such comforts were never to be again. I accepted this fact, yes, but still my heart was heavy. These past few years have seen many changes in my life.

I tell Willy that I want him to make me a bird feeder for Christmas.

"No," he says, "you can buy them cheap enough."

I tell him, "I want a personal one."

Well, build it he does, after collecting the necessary materials from his stockpiles in the bush. The result is personal all right. It stands five feet tall on a moving pole and measures about thirty inches square. "Enough room for the cat too!" he says. I don't voice my doubts but wonder if the birds will have any idea what it's for, as it doesn't resemble anything I've seen before.

A few days later Willy says to me, "I have decided what your present will be. I know something you have always wanted."

I thought my Christmas present from him was the bird feeder. But I say to him, "What?" as I rack my brains to think what it might be.

"An opal ring of your choice."

He must remember the story, as I have read it to him too. "All right," I say, "that sounds good, but you'd better put a ceiling price on it."

"No," he says, "find the one you want and we'll get that."

We look for one everywhere in the area and they're either too dark or too light, too small or too unevenly shaped.

He takes me to Vancouver. We go to Birks first. The doors are massive and glass with huge brass ring handles. I push on one slowly and the opulence of the store is revealed to me. It reminds me of *Breakfast at Tiffany's*. In the centre aisle, a musician in a tuxedo plays Christmas songs on a black grand piano. Marbled pillars and mirrors are everywhere. Recessed lighting gives a hushed elegance and helps accent the gleaming glass cases housing diamonds, pearls and gold. Willy is wearing his "Truckers Union" hat that he found in a ditch and I, too, am wearing a man's hat that was also one of his finds. I expect the assistant to dismiss us as unlikely customers but she doesn't. I say in an authoritative voice, "I would like to see a good quality opal ring." She leads us to the appropriate case and doesn't hesitate for a second in extracting one from its velvet base.

"This is the best in the store," she purrs.

It's not what I had in mind, but its voluptuousness dazzles. It is a large rounded opal surrounded by diamonds. The setting is raised so that the peach-coloured lights glow through. As she turns the ring, different fires and colours dance in front of me. I fall in love with it. It seems she has too, as she displays it on her slim tapered finger, then allows me to hold it. Willy asks the price. It is in the thousands. Reluctantly I push it back across the counter. The other rings now look as if they've come out of the Salvation Army giveaways. We tell her we may come back later.

As we leave Birks we come across a nicely dressed middle-aged man standing against the wall. "Please can you spare some change." Guilt brings a flush to my face. A little farther along, a young fellow asks, "Can you give me some change for food for my pet goldfish?" Willy looks at him and says he has to feed his goldfish too. He seems to be a phoney. I feel better as we start our trek up and down the streets of Vancouver looking for jewellery stores that may have something not quite so extravagant. We go through cases and cases of rings, but the Birks' opal sits squarely in front of my eyes. I cannot shake it.

Willy sees it's no good and says, "Let's go back. I know that is the one for you."

My relief and, at the same time, horror, are profound. Here is a chance to prove to him that I don't want the very best and I'm not trying to get as much as I can from him. The ring costs far more that I anticipated. By the same token, it is beautiful.

We return to Birks and the saleslady recognizes us. I wonder if she is thinking we can't afford it. Willy finds it hard to talk with her over the background noise of the Christmas music. He writes out a cheque for so much. The lady doesn't understand. It isn't the full amount. Then he brings out his ratty wallet and, for a seemingly endless time, drags out hundred dollar bills. We both watch this display with fascination. The lady works out on paper and calculator how much cash he's supposed to add and, of course, Willy is right, to the cent.

"Can I have your credit card for ID?" she asks.

"I don't have such a thing," Willy replies, "but here is my driver's license."

"Your Care Card?" she asks.

"I don't subscribe to the medical plan," he replies, "but here is my social security card."

I am thinking to myself, if she makes him feel the tiniest bit uncomfortable, we will leave without the ring. I start to feel bristly, in preparation, but she is okay, even though a veneer of hardness has settled on her voice as she makes sure of the business end. Of course she has to phone for a bank credit rating before she sizes the ring, so Willy makes phone calls outside while I wait in the store. Slowly, walking around the glass cases, knowing the security guard is keeping his eye on me, I feel like Audrey Hepburn. Then I pretend I'm the duchess, ordering a diamond and a ruby necklace. I see one that boasts a hundred stones. I say to myself, "We won't take that one, no, no, it is definitely too tacky, my dear."

Willy returns and tells me we have time for a cup of coffee before getting the ring. Off we go down the street. I can never get over the fact that he knows Vancouver so well. We go to McDonald's for a cup of seniors special coffee. What a contrast to Birks. Small crowded space, bodies jammed together, noise and clutter.

Back at the jewelry store again, we find the saleslady with the ring already enlarged to fit my finger. I put it on and revel in the wonder of it. She gives me a velvet box and a tiny silver and blue Birks bag. Then a catalogue for future purchases, and her card so I can ask her if I have any needs. My feet hardly touch the ground as we go out through the big glass doors onto the main street. I see that the "walk" light is about to change so I call out to Willy, "Let's run and beat the light," and I race across the road. The traffic is angry and ready to go. The drivers are not amused that I skim through when they want to get moving. Willy waits on the other side till the light changes. When he reaches me he wags his finger and says, "Don't ever try anything like that in Vancouver again. Even if you are carrying a Birks shopping bag."

The next morning, Willy bursts through the door of our bedroom. "I have such good news!" he says, with a grin that lights up his entire dour face.

"What is it?"

"The birds! The birds have come and accepted my bird feeder. Come and see!"

Crawling out of bed, I pull the comforter around me. His arm pulls me close and we look out the bedroom window together. Four black chickadees are enjoying the fruits of Christmas time too!

The night we came home from getting the ring, we watched a news program that said that Birks was in trouble financially and was closing one of its stores. Two days later, as we sit in the truck, I am thinking about this. I say to Willy, "Too bad that a place like Birks is going downhill."

He answers, "It's only because of people like you that it's in business in the first place."

Wham! I want to make sure I haven't misunderstood him. "What did you say?"

"It's just women like you who are always wishing for luxury jewelry that allows Birks to exist in the first place."

My throat contracts. Will I throw the ring at him? Will I scream and yell? Will I hate him forever because he has destroyed any romance of him giving it to me? What? What? But none of that happens. I sit there once again, with my stupid hot tears and I silently vow never, ever again, to accept a gift from him. No, other than flowers, he can keep what he has in mind to give me.

Never again!

Two weeks later, Willy decides we will go to the States and that he will give me two hundred dollars to spend on art supplies or whatever I want. And what do I say? "Thank you very much."

Takes all kinds

1.

What makes a Dane a Dane

Peter called round this morning. A Dane who Willy knows. I told him to come in to wait and have a cup of coffee as Willy was out on his bike. He was investigating buying a piece of property near Mission. I showed him through the house. We went in the garden where the wood pile was and the rhubarb in the front lawn.

"I don't know Willy well," Peter said, "but I'm a Dane, like him."

What makes a Dane a Dane? Can one generalize? A visit to Vancouver Island is an example.

While on the Island, we called into an area on the shore before the town of Duncan. Eventually, we found the house Willy was looking for. Eric used to own cottages and acreage but now has a small house and a cottage to rent. Willy hasn't seen him in ten years.

When we came into the driveway, Eric was walking to the house, carrying some wood.

As we stepped out of the truck, Eric, displaying no surprise said, "Hello 'Villy'."

I was introduced and knew I was being evaluated for reports to be relayed in the tribal, drum message rapidity to other Danes.

"Haven't had news about you for years *'Villy'*," he said. "It seemed you had disappeared."

I knew this was like being a traitor to other Danes.

Eric took us for a walk down a slippery, knotty path to the shore. Willy lagged behind, taking notes of his residences and how much they were worth and having a pee in the bush.

I spied a seal smiling at us from the water. Eric laughed at my delight as I watched the seal dive and reappear.

I saw large logs tied up to a tree on the beach and asked him what they were for.

He looked sheepish when he told me, "The logs wash up on the sand. I tie them until they dry, then carry them up to my place so I can have firewood."

Remembering the steep, awkward path, I couldn't see how he could carry them. He was eighty-two years old.

"I'll show you what I do," he said.

We call to Willy, "We're going back to the house," and with me panting, we climbed the pathway.

Eric took us to a wood pile, twenty feet long, six feet wide and eight feet high. We were impressed. Then he showed us another with the same dimensions.

'You'll never use all that wood," I said.

But he still hadn't finished. He took us to another, another and yet another stack of split wood. We looked at him in disbelief.

"I guess it's my hobby," he said. "I just can't seem to stop splitting wood. I started out thinking I needed some reserve but it sort of got out of hand. I have a compulsion to accumulate more and more."

He took us into his house.

"You have everything so neat Eric," I said.

Blue and white Danish plates hung on the wall. Photos meticulously arranged on the window sill. A small Danish flag and map of Denmark on the corner wall.

"Schnapps?" Eric asked as he brought out three shot-sized glasses from the sideboard.

While the men talked in their native language, I looked around that orderly room.

His wife died ten years ago. He doesn't consider marrying again. This was his life, a continuation of what was and the reassurance he will never run out of wood.

Willy asked him about his family, what they were doing and where they were living. Information collected about all the Danes known to one, to be passed onto the next Dane who calls. I don't know if another Dane was in trouble, the others would do anything about it. It's enough they are *Danes* and must keep track.

I looked at the photos of happier times. Visits to relatives in Denmark. The wife. How stern these older Danish women look. It seems they have known a frugal and a hard life. A lack of romance.

We said goodbye and climbed in the truck. Eric noted the year, condition and value of the truck. Memorizing all to tell the next Dane who came.

2.

Chestnuts

When I see on TV the mountain goats battering their heads together, it reminds me of the verbal battles I have with Willy. There's no backing down or softening. Bang! Bang! Bang! The reverberations surround us. Sometimes I feel ground down. Sometimes I feel ungrateful, guilty and confused. How will I deal with these feelings?

It follows a pattern. A lovely day, everything going fine, then, *wham!* one single sentence from him ruins it all. Take, for example, the chestnuts. We bought some at Wong's, the local vegetable people, after I told Willy about England and the tradition of buying them hot there.

Oh, yes, that's another time. I once told him you could get good buys at Wong's and I was subjected to a half an hour tirade of "yuppie ideas, no good buys, can't compete with the chain stores, etc. etc." until I felt like screaming. Now, where do we zoom off to for fresh veggies and discarded apples at fifty cents a box? Yes, Wong's!

This evening, Willy took me to eat at the Bamboo Palace. He had sweet and sour with two kinds of noodles and I had bean hot-pot. He ate his and half of mine. His fortune cookie read, "He loves you as much as he can."

Back at home it's chestnut time. I absently think about the first time Willy tried to roast the chestnuts. He put them on the stove and we forgot all about them. A few minutes later I saw something suddenly run across the living room chair and thought we had mice in our new house. It was a chestnut exploding and ricocheting across the room.

Well, this evening, sitting on the couch, I say to Willy, "Not going to offer me chestnuts tonight?" And do you know what he says?

"I would think you've had enough to eat and you wouldn't want more," in a disapproving voice.

Silence

He ventures, "Do you really want some chestnuts?"

Well, tell me if I'm wrong but my chest gets dry and my veins begin to throb. Who is he to tell me if I've had enough or not. I answer in a voice that crackles with ice, "After that remark — no way."

He gets two nuts, balances them on the stove, times each side and when they're done, brings them to me on a plate. I put them on the coffee table and they sit there. We go to bed and they sit there. In the morning I put them in a small jar and put them on the kitchen window sill. Exhibit A. I will not move the jar. It stays there as a reminder to him not to treat me as a mindless teenager.

Weeks later, Willy asks if I'm going to eat the rest of the nuts. I look in the brown bag and see that they are rotten. I notice too that the bottled ones are gone. I figure he got the message.

3.

Curiosity kills the tastebuds

I am standing in front of his open sock drawer in a state of shock. Peeking out from the different coloured specimens is a bottle of Scotch! Now, I know I promised him that I wouldn't pry into his closets or drawers, but I honestly thought he had cleaned this one out as it's part of my chest of drawers, and he didn't want to use it. Hearing the front door open, I know he is home and that we have to have this out. After all, I don't know his background, do I? I know most of his stories have taken place in beer parlours and are about people he met there. That seems natural enough because what else does a single man do for company? He has a different outlook on liquor than I do, but then so does half the population. He has made remarks such as, "If I'm going to have a glass of something, I'd rather have something that has a kick with it. This tastes like Kool-Aid!"

Liquor. That old bugbear! My life would have been different if it had not intruded with such a vengeance. Is it going to come back and haunt me again?

I don't even wait for him to get to the top of the stairs. "Willy, I found the bottle of booze in your drawer. I have to know, are you a secret drinker?"

He grins and doesn't ask what I was doing looking in his things. "I put it there when your son visited. I didn't want him finding it and drinking it. I had it in my room where he slept."

Does it sound logical? Yes. I'll accept the explanation but I wish it wasn't necessary to deal with this in the first place.

He goes on, "I'm not a secret drinker, but if I feel like a drink, then I don't see why I shouldn't have one. And it's not often that I do feel like it."

We hug and wipe away the tears that blur my eyes. Memories of tears before for the same reasons.

No further episodes for the next few months. Then today. I go to put the iron in his bathroom cupboard, which is empty and which he told me to store things in. What do I see, out in the open as plain as day? A bottle with what looks like vodka in it. My insides churn up to my throat and a sack of iron sits on my heart. Now wait a minute, don't jump to conclusions, it may be something else. I pour some into my hand so I can smell it. No smell at all! But didn't he say something about vodka being undetectable? I swig a mouthful and swish it around in my mouth to get a taste. Well, there's a burning sensation all right but it doesn't taste like alcohol. At this point I notice that my hand is sticky. I put it under hot water, but still it's like honey. Now, my false teeth feel tacky and my tongue feel strangely furry. I run to get my glasses to see what's on the torn label of the bottle. My dear soul! It's liquid floor polish!

I run hot water through my mouth. I start to panic! Think, think. What will counteract liquid floor polish? My heart beats fast. I feel sick to my stomach. The phone rings. It's my son. Keep calm, act normal, don't let him know. How could I possibly tell anyone that a sixty-seven year old has swallowed floor polish, they will want to know why...Oh, the shame of it all. I hear him talk about his upcoming wedding and I come in with the uh-huhs until I can stand it no longer and interrupt him to say, "Oh! I've just done such a silly thing."

He gets his sister on the phone, a nurse.

"Take milk," she says, "then put your finger down your throat to induce vomiting." I hang up and drink some milk, right from the jug. Ugh! I feel worse. I get the bottle again and try to make out the ingredients. Acrylic is one. I dash to my artist's acrylic mediums to see if there's an antidote. Oh please don't make me have to go to emergency to explain all this. The story will be all around Mission in an instant. "Acrylic," it says, "can be removed with alcohol." Alcohol? Alcohol! There's half a bottle of wine in the fridge. I swish it around my mouth. I clean my teeth, which are gleaming as never before. Then, with my stomach full of milk, wine and liquid floor polish — I wait.

Willy comes in and I try to drag him to the bedroom explaining that I've got to tell him something important.

"Maybe you should wait until tomorrow to tell me," he says. But I've got to tell him now, that I was still suspicious of him, and that I am ashamed and frightened. He listens to my story then tries to make out how much floor polish I ingested. He figures it will be all right and says, "It's okay to be suspicious, but for goodness sake, don't carry it to that length again."

4.

San Francisco

Mendocino is a long way from anywhere. I guess that's what makes it so precious. The ride to Santa Rosa is unending. We snake through vineyards, redwood forests and hills until we believe we have gone through every curve on the earth. My back hurts and the gas tank registers empty when we finally come to the freeway. We join the madding crowd on the way to San Francisco and I'm sorry I said I ever wanted to see the place. The traffic is horrendous and the rain pelts down. Whoever said that California was warm? I'll never make it. My back is ready to break in two. I just know we'll have an accident.

After spending the night in Santa Rosa, we take off down the road and I see the scenery change. Before you know it we're on the Golden Gate Bridge. Quite the achievement to have built this. Coming off the bridge we see a motel, advertising rooms for thirty-four dollars.

"Take it," I tell Willy, and he does. As we open the door, we're hit by a smell of mustiness, peeling paint and general disrepair. On closer inspection, we find the heater doesn't work either, but I'm relieved just to find a place to park the truck. Willy has given me the heebie-jeebies with his mutterings that "we won't be able to park anywhere" and "hotels charge about eighty dollars extra for parking."

Seniors' bus tickets are only fifteen cents and we can have transfers, so off we go to Fisherman's Wharf. We pass the senior centre and an elderly Chinese man ushers us in to have lunch. We sit around a table with other seniors and eat lamb stew. One fellow says he was a seaman for many years. His laugh is as gnarly as his face. He says, "I never visit places if I have to go by road. I only know how to travel by ship. If I can't go to a place by sea, I stay home." Leaving the centre we find crowds of tourists on the wharf.

I look round to find restaurants galore on the wharf and loads of boats in the harbour. I see seals with steady bored gazes holding their sleek charcoal heads above the water. They open their mouths whenever food is dropped from above. We take a tour on a mock "cable-car" bus. The black driver keeps up a barrage of information and we cover most of the highlights of the city. We pass a building with a Moore-like sculpture and I yell out, "Who did that piece?" Poor guy. No one had ever asked him that before. He stops the bus and rummages through all his information.

"I will make it a point to find out," he tells me, kindly.

A ride on an authentic cable car is next, but we find there is quite a line-up. Everyone asks everyone else, "Where do you come from?" There's a couple of buskers playing their guitars and a woman with what looks like a snake winding round a stick held in her hand. After a while I can see it's made of paper. She has orange hair, so closely cropped that you can see the scalp show through. Her complexion is sallow-grey and she has eyes that match. She wears a dark wool cape and in a mincing way calls out, "Only a dollar, only a dollar."

My film runs out and after rummaging in my bag for the next one, I decide to sit down to find another one. On a public bench nearby there is a suitcase and what looks like a mile of orange knitting. No one is sitting next to it, so I make myself comfortable and start taking out everything from my bag. Something tells me to look up and I see the snake-lady, eyes afire, cape flapping, making straight for me. Before I can gather my wits, she swivels her hip into firing position and thumps into my side, sending me flying off the seat. She breaks into a storm of yelling and screaming. Thank heavens this is interrupted when another woman accuses her of being drunk. As I am left standing there, without dignity, I slink away to join the line-up. Willy says he didn't see a thing but one person interjects, "It wouldn't pay to argue with her."

Trying to get back to normal I shrug, "Well, I wanted to experience San Francisco, so I guess I have." The snake-lady is back, weaving up and down the line as if nothing happened. "Only a dollar, only a dollar," she calls out.

The ride is an experience and we get a further idea as to what the city is all about. Next is the Museum of Modern Art. Giant white buildings face each other in a square. Library. Symphony. Theatre. Congress. So much walking in between. Willy says he will be back in an hour. I don't dare think of what I would do if something happened to him. He has no health insurance and I just found out that my credit card has expired. Anyway, I pay my dues and go up in the elevator in that massive building with innumerable floors. And what are the rooms filled with? Photographs. Yes, I know photography is an art form but these public galleries are carrying things too far.

I realize insurance is out of sight for travelling shows but the galleries can't cop out that much. We must see paintings too.

I stay to watch some videos and some audience participation computer animations. But I am surprised to see that I long for something more stationary, something that goes beyond mechanical images. In other words, a painting with a visible artist's expression. I expected more from San Francisco. The galleries at Fisherman's Wharf boast the same productions, ad nauseam. The museum had just acquired one of Matisse's green ladies. They couldn't wait to have thousands of posters made from it. The museums are our worst enemies.

Willy is back on time and we walk away from the cold looming buildings that resemble something from ancient Rome. We wander into a part of town that shows us the seedy life. Mainly black men, strangely not thin, dragging all their belongings in grocery carts or sitting helplessly in doorways. Their eyes seem to bore into mine and I feel shame.

The rain pelts down so we step into a Japanese Restaurant to eat. The food is authentic and good. Back to the motel by bus. We've managed to travel for five hours on our fifteen-cent tickets!

No heat in the motel room and the guy next door has his TV going non-stop. I can't sleep and I've been getting mad at some of Willy's remarks. My back hurts and I'm going to cry. Willy buys a small hot plate and leaves it on overnight to warm up the room. Well, with me and fire danger, I now double-can't sleep. And him? He just looks over and says, "Too bad others can't be like me. I can sleep on hard or soft beds, in ditches or anywhere." He's such a pain sometimes!

Next morning with bleary eyes, I don't know what to make of my misery.

"Do you want to stay another night?" he asks.

"I don't know," I mutter.

"Well it's up to you."

The thought of another hot plate warming and TV thumping curls my insides.

"You decide," I say.

"You take the easy way out," he tells me, and I want to cry. But he goes to get another motel room next door and, mercy me, it's warm and quiet and, at last, my back seems a little better.

5.

Home

It looks as though we will always be together now. We've knocked the corners off the humps, as Willy puts it. We're more natural now. I've gained back the weight I lost. I have an exercise bike and try to look nice in spite of it all. I have a good supply of earrings and a few pretty dresses. Still can't find a pair of jeans to fit me though. I understand him better now and in the things that I don't, am more inclined to shrug my shoulders.

He doesn't say Christ or God damn anymore. He's stopped spitting when he walks in town and he doesn't hurt me as much with that turnabout viciousness of his. He can tolerate Classic Theatre and Masterpiece Theatre on television even though he dreads them continuing for a two-hour stretch. At long last he's applied for Medicare after being without it for ten years.

He's still so righteous about his good health and weight it makes me want to throw up! It's not fair that people like him manage to sail through life without getting a good dose of flu to make them more humble and understanding. You'd think he would get sick. Out in all weather every day of his life.

He rejoices in berry time, having little feasts on berries and cherries from May till October. He tried to share the experience with me, but when I saw the number of worms the salmon-berries had in them, I gagged. Blackberries are okay, but he gets picky about when you should harvest them. He knows, of course, that berries turn sweet when the seeds are ready to be taken by the birds. They're bitter before that time to discourage eating too early. He stews the blackberries until the 'sap,' as he calls it, is thick, then he separates the 'rocks,' meaning seeds. At first he didn't want to waste these and chastised me for not wanting the extra fibre. He intended to eat this lump of seeds, but then, even he found it hard going and threw them out.

When we first got together, Willy was always saying, "We're on the home stretch" and "No use thinking years ahead, we may not be here." Now he's a bit more positive.

Our government figures a life span is possible until ninety-seven years of age. If Willy can collect pension from the government up to that time, you'd better believe he's going to survive until then!

He can work in forty degrees below zero weather and forty degrees above and — it's always the same — if he has a job to do, then it's pound, pound, pound, saw and nail. Chop and carry, on and on until it's done. People try to talk to him but he never stops. Pound, pound, saw and saw. Seems inhuman sometimes, after all he's seventy-one now.

People ask what have we got in common, Willy and me. Well, we enjoy cycling, walking, cryptic crosswords, quiet, simple living.

I'm grateful for having him in spite of our differences, and you now have an insight as to why I wrote these stories.

6.

The Spartan

A seventy-year-old fellow
with arms of steel
and legs like machines
pumping bicycle pedals
twenty miles without tiring.
A Spartan.
He reminds me of a Spartan.
They took pride in cutting out
anything that smacked of comfort,
like cosy beds, pillows
or food which wasn't basic.
No hot water.
No languishing.
They became feared
because they could endure
what others could not.
And they had disdain
for weaker mortals,
those who didn't train minds and bodies
to be immune from feeling.

New work
(Differences, chapter 6, page 120)

Differences

1.

Out of the past

One picks up the phone automatically when it rings. You don't expect the voice on the other end to be from your past. Throat constricts as I recognize it is X, my former husband. Our family is torn apart and he wants to discuss the situation with me.

"Willy!" I call out, "Jim is on his way to take me for lunch. We have to talk about the family situation."

Poor Willy! He runs to his electric razor and *Brrr... Brrr,* the shaky old thing vibrates with only small success. He cleans it out, then runs downstairs to find a better pair of pants. He digs out his gold cuff links and watch.

"He won't be here for ages," I say. But I am jittery too.

We've met on many occasions since the divorce, but always surrounded by others. This will be the first time alone. I put a dab of rouge on my cheeks. My opal ring. Yes, it's okay to wear it. I sort through my blouses. This one's too tailored and that one's too flouncey. I settle for the pale blue, rose flowered cotton. A cross between serious and frilly. I start pacing, I don't know why, I just have to.

His Budget rental car pulls up and I go out to meet him. Funny how one expects other people to stay looking the same. His hair is shockingly white, but his eyes are still sapphire blue. His smile is how I remember it, but seems forced. He looks tired and worn behind the laugh lines. I jabber away as I always do when I see him. I take him through the house.

"This is Willy's dog house," I say.

Oh! Oh! I bite my tongue. I've made it sound as if he sleeps there; it's only a joke. "This is my gallery."

He takes a step back, eyes flitting over the forty or so paintings. He sees my biography and awards on the wall. I don't think he really sees the painting.

"There's a lot of work here," he says. He seems impressed.

He likes the way the stairs lead to an open area where Willy's Jade tree stands. He admires Mount Baker from the living room window. We always pray that the mountain shows itself when we have visitors.

Willy appears and shakes hands with him. Two good men. Willy respects Jim for the enormous job it took to raise and support our large family.

I show him the bedroom. Does he feel uneasy?

"And here's my studio," I say. "It was supposed to be the master bedroom, but it is a good space to work."

He notes the skylight, then the painting: a mother with two children looking after the figure of a man with a suitcase walking out the door.

"That's you and that's me," I want to say but for once, am quiet.

"There's something about her," he says. My spine prickles. I tug at his sleeve to go.

Willy says, "Phone me when you're through and I will come and get you." We get in the car to go to the restaurant.

It wasn't easy to bring up our large family. We could not give undivided attention to each child. We did what we thought was right, but now there is resentment from the children. Jim has just heard about this.

"Can we find a way to sort things out?" he asks.

"Maybe we'll have to take one step at a time."

He doesn't wallow in helplessness as I do. He has calmed me somewhat.

He orders more toast; his ulcers are acting up. Mine would too, if I had any.

Our talking is getting agitated and I'm waving my arms around saying, "Can you believe this?" and the waitress appears.

"How is everything?" she asks with a set smile.

We look at each other dumbfounded. Doesn't she realize we are lost in our worry?

I remember the cafe table when I asked him for a divorce. He was in the process of saying "yes" when the waiter asked, "Are you enjoying your meal?"

Common courtesy forces you to say "yes, thank you." You had forgotten life goes on for others while you sit drowning in your unhappiness.

He has to get back to Vancouver.

"I'm glad you're well looked after," he says.

He hugs me goodbye and takes off in the Budget car. I go to find a phone booth.

Willy comes in his blue Nissan truck, grinning his special grin.

"They have specials on chicken legs today," he says and we go into the grocery store to buy some.

2.

Communication

Eight months, nine months, we've chugged along without flare-ups from him or tears from me. But it hit me yesterday. He doesn't communicate enough!

I chatter away like a magpie while he sits in his green armchair in silence.

"Willy, I wish you would share your life with me."

"What do you want me to do?" he asks.

"I go downtown and come home with all these stories, but it's as if you go into outer space. You don't share your experiences. You go on your morning bike rides, but never tell me where you go. For example, tell me what you saw this morning."

"Blackberries."

"Where were the blackberries?"

"On the thorns."

"Where were the thorns?"

"By the road."

"Which road?"

"Near the river."

"North or south of the river?"

This is our conversation. He blames this evasion business on the Nazis. When the Germans took over Denmark, the Danes never answered their questions directly. This way they would not contribute to their getting ahead.

He also avoids small talk with people.

I asked why and he said, "Such a waste of time and energy with 'How are you? I'm fine. Isn't it a nice day?' and on and on."

"When he first came from Denmark and didn't speak much English, this fellow told us, 'There are funny customs over here. When you meet someone, you shake their hand and say, How do you do?' Do what? We wanted to know."

Once, when he was in a hotel room, Willy heard someone knock on the next door and call "Are you decent?" He thought they were asking if the people were good citizens or something.

3.

Hawaii

Willy holds up a pair of valentine-red satin shorts.

"They will come in handy on my walks," he says.

I make a mental note not to be with him if he wears this latest find.

Willy has decided we will vacation in Hawaii, even if only people without brains go there. What can we possibly do in the evenings? Everything will be expensive. We'll have to watch out we don't get sunburned and what about *tieves*? We mustn't leave our clothes on the beach when we go in the water because the *tieves* will take everything.

But he gets an idea.

He found these Gucci bathing trunks. He will sew up the inside pocket, all but an inch. He will stuff his hundred dollar bills in a condom, tie a knot in the end and squeeze it in this small opening.

Presto! A waterproof safe!

Willy is quite bald. When we come to departure morning, he tells me, "It should be warm when we get off the plane, but if my head turns blue, you'll know it's because I've taken off my long underwear."

He has packed peanut butter, jam, granola, decaffeinated and regular coffee, the small percolator, spoons, knives, dish washing soap, bagels and cheese for a snack.

We go through the house before leaving. I follow him and move up the temperature so we don't come home to a frozen house. We go out the door but he about-turns; he's going in to recheck and move the thermostat down again.

It's 1:15 p.m. and we barrel along the highway.

"Think I'll take the back route," he says.

Back route! Oh! No! But eventually we get to the terminal and park the truck.

He hands over the keys.

"Wonder if we'll have a truck when we get back," he says.

We line up for boarding passes and go through a gate. A red haired lady sits in a cubicle and, waving her hands, beckons us to hurry.

We have two hours. Will there be shops or toilets once we go through the gate? We debate what to do. The lady goes red in the face, accelerating her hand movements.

"Come along, come along," she calls out.

"We're not sure, we don't know what's behind you," I say.

"Planes!" she replies in great exasperation.

I give her the eagle eye and we turn around to wait in the main area and eat the *baagles* that Willy brought. He has coffee too. Someone has left newspapers on the seat, so we read those. I study the painted murals facing us. It makes me proud to be in Vancouver. Skiing, mountains, lakes, whales, swimming, sailing: all in one temperate zone.

The red haired lady is gone and we go on to customs. I find a vacant seat in the boarding lounge, while Willy mosies around. A lady from Nova Scotia sits next to me and we're soon chatting easily.

Time to board. We're seated in the middle aisle and my back is starting to act up. The movie comes on. It is awful. I read my book on creativity which I've been meaning to get to for ages. It's nice travelling with Willy. He carries heavy stuff like this book because my wrists torture me. I don't think those movie people have read a book on creativity.

Funny how one gets lulled on a plane trip. It's even fascinating to watch people come down the aisle. There's mostly seniors on board.

As someone said, "Youngsters can't afford it like we can."

We hit turbulence.

Pilot says, "Stay in your seats and do up your seat belts."

Willy has just gone to the toilet. I envision him bumping around.

The plane trip was hard on my back, made worse by standing around waiting for the "lei" lady. Willy had paid extra to be met by luscious Hawaiian girls who were supposed to put a lei around your neck and give you a kiss. Other people were being met like this, but not us. Willy refused to budge. Enough was enough! I took off for the baggage carousel, a disgruntled Willy in tow.

Here is the "lei" lady, but she's an American, large, with white hair, wearing a red patterned muumuu, red shoes and a boater straw hat. A petite Asian lady appears in a sarong dress and when the Red Muumuu calls out our names, the small one drapes our necks with a purple orchid lei.

The Red Muummuu herds us to the baggage, giving instructions as to hotels and buses. I just want to lie down.

I think we're all tired, with puffy ankles and stiff limbs.

"Does she mean for us to go there?" we ask.

Someone says, "Yes," and we all move.

"No! This way!" the Red Muumuu calls loudly. Like sheep we all go to where she's pointing.

The mini bus is loaded. At last it won't be too long before we get to the hotel. The Red Queen counts us, she finds we have an extra person. A passenger owns up. She has brought a friend and will pay for her later. Finally! The mini bus has its motor going and we're off.

It's raining, but through the windows it looks like Vancouver with Palm trees.

We're the only ones to get off at this hotel. Is it second rate?

At the registration desk, the young man tells me I have to sign a separate form because "You have a different name from Mr. Smith!"

Willy pays fifty dollars deposit for the keys.

We look for our room, 1203, but there's no twelfth floor on the elevator panel. Willy returns to the office. I hear a moaning song from the bar, clinking glasses and the forced gaiety of drinking men. What kind of a place is this?

Willy comes back.

"The twelfth floor is marked PD," he says, and we press the button.

Our room is basic, but good. I test the bed. I never know if I'll be a cripple by morning. I've brought my small quilt for extra comfort. We untuck the bed covers and push the twin beds together so we will be able to touch each other.

This is our first *real* vacation. A vacation when there are no driving worries, or socializing. We are just going to enjoy!

It's morning and we go to the other hotel for an orientation breakfast. The buffet is fine but we have to endure an hour's promotion talk.

Willy sneaks out and signs up for the Polynesian Village.

"One hundred and forty-two smackers," he says.

We set off in the mini bus to the garment factory. The rides are free.

The factory houses millions of muumuus and every gold chain imaginable. All types of gizmos, like plastic gold fish swimming in black plastic boxes.

A man is looking at them in fascination and I say, "At least you don't have to feed them." Then realize, one has to feed them batteries.

On and on there are stalls and dresses hanging from above. My head swims like gold fish and my senses go numb. Material is printed in every subject, design and colour. I feel I'm inside a Kaleidoscope. I try on a burgundy slip dress and buy it. Outside the air is caressingly warm. We take a bus to Maui Divers. After seeing a movie on how the coral is harvested, we come to a room displaying finished jewellery pieces. On a counter, there is a container with oysters. The lady behind the counter guarantees I will get a pearl. The oysters cost ten dollars. I choose an oyster. I follow her lead to tap three times, then sing loudly with her "aloha." She clangs a brass bell to attract more customers. Inside the shell there is a silver black pearl.

"She's lucky," she tells the audience, then pressures me to have it encased in gold. I decline, but stay to watch what the others get. I like to see the pearl appear and hear "aloha."

A free shuttle takes us to the Dole Pineapple cannery.

Stores and boutiques crowd what used to be the cannery. We see a film about the start of the pineapple industry. There's a line-up for free pineapple juice. Willy gets his, then goes to the end of the line to get another. Hawaii doesn't export pineapple any more. Vietnam has taken over the job.

I order stuffed eggplant for my lunch in the restaurant. It's large, so Willy eats half.

We return to the hotel room for a rest. I haven't recovered from the flight and my back is telling me to take it easy.

Afterwards, we walk to the beachfront of Waikiki. The air is balmy and stress slips away as we cover the boardwalk, the waves lapping the sands.

This is the day for the Polynesian Village...

As we travel, the rain stops and I see spiritual mountains with their steep ruts of lava rock, the white mists speeding over their apexes as in a fast-motion film.

We reach the centre and the bus driver wants to be our guide. Willy is interested in the facts, but I sneak away to where a young man carves spears.

I rejoin the group.

The bus driver says, "Except for one third, who are professionals, all who work here are students of the Mormon University."

The Samoan exhibit has a well-built young man, dark skinned and curly hair and impish face. He shows us how to crack a coconut.

The driver leads us to a shed with fruits and vegetables of the South Pacific. He shows us how the taro root is used to make poi, which is a staple food in Hawaii. It tastes exactly like library paste glue!

Dinner isn't that great and Willy's stomach reacts to the pork cubes.

Everyone has raved about the show, but there sure is a lot of noise and jumping around. Willy likes the hula dancers. Overall, it's been a good day and we head for the bus.

The soft rain comes and goes every day and the wind blows, but it's warm. I cling to my jacket and my hair looks like pula pula, the brown ragged hair of the coconut. Willy puts his longjohns on.

He has figured out all the buses. We board one going to Sea World. What a ride! White sand beaches with surfers and palm trees.

"We've seen it all in the movies," Willy says.

At the aquarium, we watch dolphins, false whales, penguins and seals. We see albatross, known as gooney birds, and another bird with a six foot wing span.

Frommer's says one must experience "shave ice," unique to Hawaii. Shaved ice doused with flavoured syrup.

Sitting on the bleachers, waiting for the whale show to start, I tell Willy, "I think they might have some shave ice there."

So he goes to get some. He comes back with a cone topped with a tennis-ball-sized, pink-fluorescent glob. The ice resembles fractured broken glass of a windshield. I taste it. It is god-awful! I hand it to Willy.

"How much was it?" I ask.

"One dollar and seventy-five cents."

I wipe my syrup stained mouth.

"You'll have to eat it, I can't."

He pulls a face, but keeps at it; he can't bear to waste anything.

Meanwhile, the seats have filled up with Japanese tourists. They notice Willy's treat, it starts a chain reaction. I'm killing myself laughing. Everyone in the bleachers is now sucking on a ball of shaved ice!

The show starts and the commentator tells an old folk story about a princess on an island. One could easily believe in fairy tales here.

After breakfast we catch the bus. Eighty-five cents for seniors. We get off at the Pearl Harbour Memorial.

We are taken by pilot boat to the modern structure that straddles a sunken ship.

The ship entombs one thousand, one hundred servicemen. A wall lists the names of the men who died.

"There are a lot of Smiths there," I tell Willy.

He smiles, "But they didn't get this one."

A large wreath on an easel in front of the wall. A sign reads, "From Japan."

I lean over the railing. Coral is growing from the hull of the rusting vessel. Striped black and gold fish skirt in and out of it. Life from Death.

On the way back to shore, people throw lei tributes into the sea. The flowers float gently out to the ocean.

Circles of absolution.

A beautiful building, Honolulu State Library. What I like about Hawaii is you are always aware you are in this country because buildings like this have courtyards with tropical plants, waterfalls and paving in patterns. Cutout designs of their flora and fauna are incorporated everywhere. Modern structures. McDonald's has plate glass partitions etched with Hawaiian motifs. The library has a great selection of art books. Willy leaves me to devour this banquet. Two hours later, I wait in the front hall for his return. Outside, people are sitting on the grass under the long shadows of the umbrella trees. No, it's not grass, it is weeds, mowed to appear as grass.

We go to the Honolulu State Art Gallery; it is celebrating Japanese culture.

Dancers have painted white faces.

I run out of film. Everywhere I turn, I want to record something. I ask Willy to track down more film.

He says, "I'll find some, meanwhile you have lunch in the courtyard restaurant. I will go around the corner for a ninety-nine-cent Whopper."

The courtyard has a waterfall. There are plants, trees and sculptures. I order soup and half sandwich for six dollars. Good coffee. The sandwich is zucchini, crookneck squash, avocado, pickled onion, coriander mint spread on buckwheat walnut focaccia bread, served with green salad. The soup has beans and vegetables with a gingery taste. Willy can keep his Whopper!

Good selection of contemporary art. There's a stand of slender iron rods with tops like bull rushes. Sign says, "Touch Lightly." They sway against each other, setting off bell sounds.

Three small oils by Georgia O'Keefe. She was asked to come for a month, paint what appealed to her and they would purchase some. Interesting. I connect with the primitive art of gods and goddesses made of wood and clay. I linger, feel the spirit, let it encompass and fill me.

We get the bus through Chinatown. This is the other side of life. The prostitutes from Waikiki have come here. My antenna is jerking. Our hotel room is feeling like home. I can relax on the bed without back problems. Willy goes to make coffee, emptying the grounds in the toilet, flushing them down and realizing the stem of the percolator has gone down too! Happily, it doesn't plug up and Willy heats water in the pot, puts some grounds in the basket and strains water through to a cup.

Tonight we take a sunset cruise on a catamaran with 1,000 other people. There's dancing, dinner entertainment and five free alcoholic drinks each. What state will Willy be in after ten free drinks? Ten, because I am not drinking alcohol.

We sit opposite a couple from Alberta. The men have a hard time getting the waitress's attention. Ron gets up to dance and asks Willy to get him a drink when a waitress comes. Willy gives her two tickets but she brings a double for Willy.

"You'd better give some of that to Ron," I say.

He pours half into Ron's glass and takes a swig of his. His face lights up.

"All the rum is at the bottom," he says.

Willy doesn't dance. He said if I really wanted, he'd take dancing lessons, but I don't think he feels rhythm. Mind you, if he had his full quota of drinks...

The lights of Waikiki glitter and the catamaran turns back to shore.

Today we line up for the trolley. We come to Bishop Museum. Willy goes off looking at things which interest him and I go to where the princess's heirlooms are housed. The building has polished redwood stairs and banisters. I go to an open area where they will have Hawaiian entertainment. Willy surprises me when I see him already sitting there and he has a space for me next to him.

Some men and older women work on Hawaiian quilting. The oldest one they call "Aunt" designs original patterns.

I ask one lady, "What do you mean by Hawaiian quilting?"

"When the missionaries came, they taught Hawaiians to take scraps of material and piece them together to make quilts. Hawaiians didn't have extra scraps because they used all of their material for their muumuus. One day, *"Aunt"* had a sheet laying on the grass to dry. She saw the pattern made by the shadow of the bread-fruit tree. She folded some cloth, like you fold paper for snowflakes and cut out a design. This is appliquéd onto a cushion cover or quilt. All designs are based on our plant motifs."

We walk along the sea walk again and hearing the sounds of bands, join the crowd at the side of the road. It's a parade for the Hula Bowl, whatever that is. There are many marching bands, even a bagpipe band, about three hundred dancers who are here for a competition. Cheerleaders somersaulting and shouting out their calls. Everyone catches the festive mood and it's fun.

It's clean in Waikiki. Street venders keep to the side and don't coerce you to buy. No prostitutes because the police made a point some years ago to follow them, step by step, until they went elsewhere.

The beach doesn't have seaweed and junk washed up because there's hardly any tide in Hawaii. Roads are alongside the sand without danger of flooding.

There aren't any coconuts on the palm trees lining the beach. A woman was hit on the head with one and her husband sued the city.

We go to see Fosters Botanical Gardens. The price of one dollar admission hasn't changed since twenty years ago. Countries from all over the world have donated different species.

Willy examines each tree and reads all the labels. The chicle tree which gives the principle ingredient for chewing gum (Chiclets?), the wax palm which has carnauba for furniture polish. I leave Willy to find more specimens while I sit in front of an orchid display painting. What gorgeous concoctions. How graceful the curves of their stems. In the middle of Honolulu, for the price of a dollar, I can sit in this natural wonder for as long as I like.

Willy finds me writing and shows me two mosquito bites on his arm. "You must enter that I had two stings," he says.

4.

The book

He's figured out the hours involved in writing, getting an editor, checking and rechecking and paying for the printer. Works out to be ten dollars a book, which is what it's sold for. That's how stupid he thinks it was to publish *The Willy Stories*.

He comes in from the garden with a handful of beans for supper. Here's my chance...

"Beans are selling for thirty-nine cents a pound downtown," I say.

He looked shocked.

"You bought the seeds for two dollars. You trucked in mushroom manure for sixty dollars. You spent twenty hours weeding, tying them up, making stakes, and harvesting. Those beans in your hands cost at least ten dollars."

He grins sheepishly. I've hit where it hurts.

"I just want you to understand how it is with writing," I say. "I enjoy it. I want to share my experiences with others. You love being outdoors and being one with nature. These things count far more than money."

He looks at the beans.

"There'll be another crop tomorrow," he says.

5.

Willy goes to Sweden

He asked me to go with him but I said "no," so I'll have to get used to being on my own. I'll do some visiting, catch up on my painting and won't bother cooking or anything. That's what I thought before he left.

I was afraid at night. Left the bedside light on. Tossed and turned for hours. In the evening, I lit a fire, curled up on the chesterfield and overdosed on television. I knitted a bit but art and writing were ignored.

It takes a long time to get into another gear. Every night I tumbled into bed later. I counted the days for his return. I remembered how it was to be alone and appreciated him more.

I was at a meeting when he returned home. After travelling for twenty-four hours, he'd gone straight to sleep.

I didn't even take my coat off. Ran up the stairs, knelt by his side, and pulled the comforter from his face.

"Welcome home, Willy!"

His large hands drag me close and he strokes my back and shoulders. He jabbers away, all the time while stroking. We kiss.

"There are gifts on the living room table," he says. "Snip the string and see what is there.

"The small box is from me," he says. "The store wrapped it and they took this narrow ribbon and pulled it into all those curly-cues."

Inside was a pair of dangling twisted silver earrings. I go back and kiss him. He starts telling me all about his trip.

"I had four hours to wait in Copenhagen after midnight. Instead of going to a hotel, I slept on the railway station bench. It wasn't too bad. Everything costs three times as much there. When I got to my *brudder's* place, I was walking up the street and a man came up to me, thinking I was my *brudder*. I guess we look alike. We went to the resort which is owned by my *brudder's* daughter. Everything is high class there. We looked through a photo album and I saw when I was a little kid."

I had forgotten it's easier to sleep alone. His elbow jabs my shoulder blade.

"Willy, your elbow hurts. You are too boney," I tell him.

"I'm sorry dear. Tomorrow, I'll go to the doctor and get deboned."

I laugh. I'm so glad to have him home.

6.

New work

Willy thinks of the greatest birthday gifts. He paid for me to visit my sister in England. Then he paid for me to take a week-long painting workshop in the States with Carole Barnes.

I learned to use acrylics with a searching, finding process, allowing erasing and adding until subjects appeared.

Stone figures loomed out of my work. A nude bride appeared, legs apart, the Virgin Mary behind her. It shocked me. I couldn't believe it had come from me and figured it was the end of clients buying my work.

Arriving home, I told Willy of the new development and he said, "Don't show me the work! In six months, you'll be back to normal again."

The following morning, four young people came to see my paintings.

"What did you do in the workshop?" they asked.

"I haven't unpacked yet and you may be offended by what is there."

"We can take it," they said, "let us see."

Out came the bride and other works. The men were apprehensive but the women were moved by them, feeling the pieces had underlying tenderness and power.

One bought the bride and the other woman, a singing lady. The husband was embarrassed with the bride's legs apart.

"She needs something across that area," he said.

"You have my permission to do that," I told him.

"But you haven't got mine," said his wife.

After they leave, I show Willy the cheques. He says, "It's beyond me!"

It was hard to believe people *could* relate to that kind of painting yet it's good to know I wouldn't be alone after all.

7.

The mattress

"I need more room in bed," I told Willy.

It might have something to do with age, but I twist and turn at night. If I roll over one way, he rolls over as well; to reverse the procedure is impossible. He cocoons inside the sheet and no amount of struggle will free it.

We have slept on his bed-chesterfield for the past three years. I don't want him to think I'm always wanting something better. However, I think a firmer mattress might help the situation, so I broach the subject.

"I will look in the second hand stores," he says.

End of discussion.

I think the *real* solution would be for me to have my own bed, close to him of course, but I wouldn't know how to tackle that one.

He saw a mattress at a second hand store.

They quoted one hundred and thirty dollars.

We went down to examine it, me nervous because I hadn't tried it out. Would my back go out of whack?

But I said, "It's fine. We'll take it."

The saleslady discovered if we wanted the mattress, we'd have to take the whole bedroom set. I was sure the wood was veneered cardboard and I recoiled at living with such tacky stuff.

"We don't have room for extra furniture," I said. That was that.

Willy became a primeval hunter. Where to find a mattress with the best quality and price? While I was at an art function, he went up and down the streets, pricing and comparing. On his way back from Vancouver, he checked in Budget Furniture and The Brick. Every day is mattress hunt day.

He left me in Eaton's while he went to buy cheap gas and goodness knows what, across the border. I look in the furniture department and there are these rows of beds with labels and explanations on them. "Okay," I thought, "might as well get to know something about what we will be buying."

Like Goldilocks, I tried one, read the label, and went to the next. No salesperson was around, so I took my time. The further up the aisle I went, the better they got. The prices got higher too. It was inevitable of course; the last one was the best. The price was one thousand, one hundred dollars.

Willy returned and a salesman materialized, sensing a sale.

Willy greets him, "We're looking at mattresses. It's not because of me, I can sleep anywhere, in the ditch, on a piece of plywood or anything. It's for her."

My adrenaline soared. I bit my lip and stood there accused. We left to go to dinner and I made up my mind to have the whole thing out in the open.

At Earl's over wine, I said, "I'd like to discuss the mattress."

"Okay," he smiled, happy with himself.

"If you can sleep in a ditch or on plywood, it remains only me who requires a new bed. I can buy my own bed and you can bring up the old one from the basement for you."

"I don't think that's a good idea," he said.

I came in for the kill. "That way I won't have to be subjected to you telling salespeople it's only because I am *fussy* that we have to buy a mattress."

So here we are in yet another furniture place, with me sprawled out on a mattress. Willy and the salesman looking down on me.

"Well?" the salesman asks.

And Willy says, "We're only buying a mattress because she wants one. I can sleep on anything, in a ditch or anywhere. I've slept on hundreds of different mattresses in my time and slept well on all of them."

It was just too much! I can't let it go.

Still in my undignified position, I say to the salesman, "Yes, this man is a miracle man. He can sleep on anything. He can eat anything. He asks for nothing. He has created this crowning halo for his head so the world will know he is superior to all other mortals."

The words come out with spitting force and the salesman is as red as the Danish flag. Poor soul! I used him to humiliate Willy.

Willy smiles broadly and hasn't taken any offence. Getting up with as much dignity as I can gather, I give up!

As we leave the store, I say, "I think I'd sleep better in my own bed."

"There isn't space for two beds in that room," he says.

"I'll move the studio and we can have the larger room."

"The light in the skylight would bother you."

"I'll block it out."

We skirt around each other, I think he senses danger. I realize it goes deeper than these surface arguments, so I back off.

"Perhaps a queen sized bed would give me more elbow room," I say. He breathes a sigh of relief.

Another week has passed and we're still investigating but without him showing off. The salespeople are pressing the fact that there's a thirty-year guarantee on the good mattresses, when it is us that need the guarantee!

The best ones are the single pocket springs with foam padding on top. Tomorrow we go to Chilliwack and then we'll decide. I've already decided but whether the "halo man" will agree or not, remains to be seen.

He's made the decision. He will buy the single pocket spring unit but the double, not the queen size.

"How much is the under frame with wheels?" Willy asks.

"Fifty-nine-fifty," is the reply.

We are in the town's finest furniture store.

"Will you throw that in if I give you cash?" Willy asks.

"No."

Willy goes to the counter and measures out his money. One thousand, one hundred dollars and eighty-six cents, plus tax. They will deliver on Friday.

Once home, he takes his free two-by-fours from Lumberland and makes a frame for the bed.

Friday.... Two young men bring the set to the bedroom.

"Try it out," says Willy.

I lay down and bounce up and down.

"It's very good," I say, "come and try it too."

He comes next to me, there's no doubt it is roomier. He puts his arm around me and we lay there, getting used to it. It's comfy and he's warm and throwing his time slot routines to the wind.... "Oh! No!"

It's the doorbell. My patron lady calls out from the bottom of the stairs. I've told her not to stand waiting downstairs, but to go up as she often has arm loads of flowers or rhubarb. I rush out hoping Willy will pick up my underpants and have got himself zippered.

She comes in to see the new mattress.

"What on earth is that lumber underneath it?" she asks.

The thrift store has a brown plastic, padded headboard. He checks with me if we should buy it. "It's only $15," he says.

When he goes to pick it up, the volunteer ladies feel sorry for him and say, "You can have it for $5."

We now have a thousand dollar mattress sitting on a home-made wooden frame, backed by a $5 headboard!

8.

Differences

"Why do you spend so much time writing and painting for so little financial return?" he asks.

To be truthful, I don't know. The agonies of juried art shows and publishers' rejections are part of my life.

Willy's major concern is getting products at the lowest cost possible. I get embroiled in people situations. Willy isn't close enough to anyone to be hurt by them.

He does love his plants though. The other day a leaf had fallen from his jade plant into a patch of dirt outside. When he picked it up, he saw it had hair-like roots. This is his baby now. He gives daily reports.

"Look how my stickling is growing. I gave him his own little pot. He's as happy as a small child getting his first bed."

He has dozens of small plants in different stages of development. I bite my tongue when I look at our elegant window ledge cluttered with starting pots, some covered with plastic bags. He's used our loaf pans for seed germination and all our small plates are gone, used to catch water overflow.

I think it's sweet when he tends to these plants, but when will it stop?

Section 8.

The car

1.

Oregon

We have returned from a trip down the Oregon coast. We even had one night in a motel on the shore, walking until evening and having the beach to ourselves.

We saw whale spouts, called into the sea lion caves, and went to Newport Aquarium. We had to pay admittance to the last two. Willy must be mellowing.

To get to the Sea Lion Caves, you descend in an elevator. The caves were lit, giving everything a surreal look. The large sounds of those massive creatures rebounded against the rock walls filling the place with a bass symphony.

At the aquarium, a seal behind glass took a liking to a man in the audience. When the man moved his hand or arm, the seal responded in like manner. We tried the same thing but the seal snapped at us. When the man twirled his fingers, the seal spun his head. When the man turned to leave, the seal's eyes were pleading for him to come back. I couldn't tear myself away. I didn't know seals were so intelligent.

Peach coloured jelly fish, with their pulsing, transparent umbrellas and their silk tendrils, performed a ballet in a cylindrical glass enclosure in the lobby. My camera wasn't working so I haven't got a record of that exquisite beauty.

I painted a couple of Oregon coast landscapes. Even though they are tiny, five by seven inches, it took me about two and a half hours each. A five year old, serious-faced girl sat beside me for the whole time I was doing one. Her mother said she was interested in art and of course, I knew.

She never spoke, only watched. Towards the end, I gave her some paper, pencil, a brush, and the palette with my extra paint.

I got a bit of a sun burn, even though I thought I was being careful,

Willy's potatoes are ready to be unearthed and we have spinach for dinner. Flowers and plants respond to him as the seal did to the man in the aquarium.

2.

April fools

Willy has brought my morning coffee and I lay in bed listening to the radio. The announcer says there's a huge pileup on the roads going into Vancouver. He mentions that today is April Fool's day.

I remember jokes I've played and wondered if anyone has ever played one on Willy. I'm sure he knows about it.

I go into the studio. I'm going to pretend there is a big spider. I don't mind killing small ones but some in B.C. are positive monsters, so I always call Willy to dispose of them. He wraps a cloth around them and throws them outside.

"Willy!" I yell. "Come quickly and get this huge spider. Hurry! Hurry! He's so big!"

He runs in, cloth in hand.

"Where is it?"

"April Fools," I say with glee.

His face goes red and for a minute I worry. Maybe he won't like this joke. But he puts his arm around me and laughs and laughs. I laugh too.

He's going on his morning cycle trip and calls in the studio to say goodbye. He never used to do this; he'd just disappear. It was disconcerting. Today I'm smiling. It's kind of nice to be in your late sixties and find laughter in such a simple thing as April Fools.

3.

Halloween

Three hundred small chocolate bars lie in four containers on a table covered with a red, embroidered Scandinavian cloth. On the side, there are ten, one-pound bars. Willy wants to keep up the Danish tradition of good eating.

It is Halloween and Willy has never experienced this part of it. He was either up north on building sites or in apartments where Halloween ghosts fear to tread.

Coming from England, I have felt uncomfortable with this festival. We had Guy Fawkes Day on November fifth. It was pretty gruesome, but at the time, only fun.

Since we're in a house now, I hand the matter over to Willy, who has taken it on with a flying tackle.

He brought home some cheap candies, which he got for a dollar off.

"The kids don't like those hard things," I tell him.

"What do they like then?"

"Kit-Kat, Crispy Crunch, that sort of thing."

So, every time he comes back from downtown, he has another supply of goodies. Because I am a diabetic, I ask him to hide them.

"Come see if you approve," he calls from downstairs, and there is this display.

"Why on earth do you have those one pound bars?" I ask. "Don't you realize our house is only one stop out of fifty? Think of the mothers! Think of dental bills!"

"I don't want the neighbours to think we're stingy," he says. "The big ones are for the kids who live near us."

It's six o'clock. The door bell rings. I'm upstairs but I can hear what goes on.

"Hi," says Willy.

It must be the neighbour's children. I hear rustle, rustle and then, "Thank you

Willy!" There go the one-pound bars!

The doorbell goes again and again. No conversation, just "Hi", rustle, rustle and "Thank you!" I hear a boy outside.

"Look what we got. Let's go back later!"

The pace slows and the table is still loaded. At least he didn't face the humiliation of running out of stuff.

"Did you have Halloween in Denmark?" I ask when he comes up.

"No. We had a day at the end of February when we'd go to the neighbours for money."

"Did you get much?"

"Yes, actually we did, sometimes ten dollars at a time when a day's wages were a dollar."

"What did you do with the money?"

"I don't remember."

Fireworks are popping off down the street.

He settles down next to the fire with a smile on his face. He did a good job and I'm sure the kids think so too. But now to unload those chocolates!

4.

1993

When Willy and I first came together, my adrenalin rocketed. We walked every-day, not noticing the distance; just being together was great. My blood sugar de-creased and I lost weight. Too bad those initial months couldn't last.

I'm sitting in the waiting room of the doctor's office, contemplating my rising blood sugar and the medication that is losing its effectiveness. Will it mean insulin needles? I sure haven't felt good.

I get afraid sometimes. Afraid of the years catching up with me. I know I have been lax about enough exercise and have settled into lazy routines. Comfortable things, routines. But they can get unvaried and become so many squares of netting. When there are enough, you will be caught and have become a dull individual.

My alarm wakes me at eight-thirty and I make noises to let Willy know I am awake. He brings in coffee and reports on the birds and the weather.

My breakfast never changes. He has doled out my porridge, which I heat in the micro. Two minutes. One tablespoon peanut butter and a teaspoon diet jam. No bread. Go to the exercise bike, picking up reading material and pump my legs until the computer reads 120 calories.

I then work at whatever I feel driven to do while semi-listening to the radio. I must hear human voices. Willy lives in a cocoon really, is happy with silence. For me, I don't like a vacuum.

Lunch is about one p.m. and Willy will be home from his bicycle trip. He will cut me two slices of his bread for my lunch and I have some cheese to go with it.

In the afternoon, we will go for a walk. Once a week he takes me to Abbotsford. He drops me off at the mall while he goes across the border for good deals there. When he picks me up, we will have an early dinner out. Eating out isn't a treat for me. I worked one day a week in a restaurant for a short time, just for the experience of knowing what life was like outside of the home. I found out nearly all the food was packaged frozen and since that time, most restaurant meals are tasteless for me.

I told Willy today, "I started to write this morning and the thing just took off and wrote itself."

"It would be *really* good if it would *publish* itself," he said.

To get back to routines. I make supper. Willy washes the dishes, dishwashers are a no-no, and I play the keyboard for a while. I read to him out loud. We've run out of short stories, so we read books like "Moby Dick," a bit every time.

"We must be the only ones who have read all the measurements in entirety," says Willy.

The doctor has given me some pills. No insulin yet; I have a reprieve. It was a virus that made me feel sore and achy. Maybe it's all right to have a routine life when you get older. Maybe I shouldn't worry about being stuck in our habits.

5.

The accident

Brakes! A crash! Silence and then sirens. I heard them all with the familiar lurching of the chest, knowing someone's hurt — or worse.

The doorbell rings and yes, Willy has been hit by a car while biking home. The neighbour says she will drive me to the hospital.

What will I find when I get there? Is he going to live? How bad is it? What would I have to do to keep the house going if he was disabled? I couldn't do it.

I'm sitting outside the emergency room. Willy is screaming in Danish. Six nurses and orderlies are trying to hold him down.

The doctor puts his hand on my arm.

"It's mainly the quiet ones we worry about," he assures me.

Now Willy is swearing in English and yelling.

"Take these things off of me!"

He means the neck brace, oxygen mask and intravenous. For someone who mumbles, he's sure making a lot of noise.

He wants to go to the toilet. He'll be humiliated when he realizes that he's got a catheter. He won't know what that's all about.

"Get me the *Hell* out of here!" he shouts over and over. I go in to see if I can reassure him. The doctor brings me close to his bed. "Do you know who this person is?" he asks Willy. And praise be, Willy says, "Yes, that is my wife!"

His eyes and head are bleeding. The car was going eighty kilometers an hour when it hit him. His head bashed the windshield and he rebounded onto the road.

He's shivering now, but has calmed a bit since they gave him Valium. A nurse brings me his wallet and broken glasses. They have his medical card and I am to sign an admittance form. The receptionist calls me Mrs. Smith, but I go into my usual spiel about not being married but living common-law.

"That's fine," she says, "but if he needs an operation, you're not allowed to sign permission."

Again, I have it that society still has not accepted our living arrangements.

I'm sitting on the wooden bench outside of emergency. Waiting for results of his x-rays. I'm trying to collect order in my thoughts.

The doctor comes to sit beside me.

"Willy is feeling nauseous," he says. "We'll keep him overnight."

I tell the doctor I'm relieved.

"I don't think I could handle him the way he is," I say.

"He made me nervous too!" the doctor says.

We go back to see how he's doing. The machines are beep...beep...beeping and red lights blinking.

"Wiggle your toes please, Willy," the doctor says. No response.

"English is his second language," I interrupt, "maybe he doesn't know the word wiggle."

"Move your toes, Willy," he says.

The toes go back and forth, a good sign.

They are starting to clean him up, swabbing the blood from his eyes and the front of the shoulders. I pace up and down outside. How awful for this to happen to Willy! Will it mean he can't bicycle anymore? No broken bones, but they can't get a good picture of his neck.

I phone my daughter.

"No," I tell her, "nothing you can do. I just wanted someone to know."

I go to the waiting room. Lots of drama going on here.

"What has happened to bring you here?" a young fellow asks me.

A semi-trailer went over him when he was on his bike two years ago. Legs shattered. Another fellow is brought in by ambulance. I can only see his chest, it's as grey as ashes. A small girl recovering from heart surgery is crying in pain.

It's now eight-thirty p.m.

"How about this God? Are you going to give us a bad time? I send up an express call.

I look to the peach and cerulean sky. A young eagle glides in the dreamy way eagles do. He lets out a child-like call. Is that God telling me that it will be okay? Seems to be. I've never heard an eagle cry.

I hear Willy vomiting. He struggles to sit up. Now I can see the mess on the back of his head and shoulders. How bad is it? When will we know?

"They're taking him to intensive care," the nurse tells me, "come back tomorrow."

The house seems alien in the dark without Willy there. Will I sleep? I relive events in the emergency room. They asked him questions.

"Where do you live?"

"Cherry Street."

"Do you remember your accident?"

"What accident?"

"You were struck by a car, Willy."

"Who said that?"

He doesn't remember. Will he ever remember? Will he be mentally unbalanced? Will I cope? But I know the answer to that one. If I have to deal with something, I get on with it. It's the dread of what is to come that frightens me.

I'm in intensive care. He's sleeping. One lonely brown shoe lies on the floor next to the commode.

"He's had a restless night. He's still confused," the nurse says.

The monitor pulls my eyes to the screen and the pale blue line changes drastically. What does it mean?

The specialist comes in. I move to the back of the room as she checks all signs. I watch her reaction.

"Get in touch with the neurosurgeon in New Westminster," she tells the nurse.

We're in a waiting game. I see this fiercely independent man reduced to bed guard rails and tubes connected all over, restrained from doing what he wants. Strange how nurses discuss his condition as if I can't hear. You could understand if they were speaking while the patient is out of it, but I'm very much aware.

I hear them working on the fellow in the next bed, draining his lungs.

"It's the colour of coffee with creamo in it," says the nurse.

He was found in Miracle Valley — the place for recovering alcoholics.

Should I phone Willy's brother in Sweden? Or should I wait until he's got results from New Westminster?

He's awake now.

"What time is it? he asks.

"Ten in the morning."

He lurches to get out of bed but I push him back.

"Got to get up," he says.

Two minutes later, "What time is it?"

"Early in the morning, go back to sleep."

"You go back to sleep too" he says.

I sit here writing, not doing much good. He's sleeping. They've got him doped up. Willy, who won't even take an aspirin!

Arrangements are being made for the ambulance to take him for access to special machinery. They also will check for brain damage. If it's clear, they will return him to Mission. I am to go home and wait to hear results.

Driving home, I try to think positive. What else to do?

Back at the hospital, room #306. Results of the tests were good. "I've got to go pee-pee," he says. "You've got a catheter," I say. "What's that?"

"It's a tube so you don't have to go to the toilet." He struggles to get over the bars. "Got to go pee-pee."

He's pulling at the catheter tube and throwing off the covers.

"Give me my shorts, got to go pee-pee."

He remembers his shorts, that's good.

"You're exposing yourself to the visitors," I tell him.

I go to the nursing station. Telling them, my eyes watering, "I seem to set him off. He thinks he can make me get him out of here."

"He's like that when you're not here," she says, calming me. "It's good if he has someone familiar around. I'll come with you."

He's less agitated this time.

"I want to pee-pee, give me my pants."

"They cut your pants from you, Willy."

"Why?"

"You've had an accident, Willy."

"I want to go pee-pee."

He falls back on the pillow, closes his eyes to sleep.

All the fire doors are closing automatically. No announcement, just this silence shutting out the world, locked in by an invisible force. A man walks near our room and I ask him why.

"I heard they did that when someone dies," he says.

The third day I find Willy sitting in a lounge chair outside his room.

I gently kiss his swollen lips.

He faintly returns the kiss and says, "Don't you think you're overdoing it?"

He thinks I am his nurse!

He seems to have more awareness today but refuses to believe he's had an accident. I hold up my purse mirror so he can see his face.

"I guess I had an accident," he says. "I must have made a mess of the car."

He sleeps again and when he wakes, tells me, "You don't have to stay."

"It's the same whether I write here or at home," I say.

Every few minutes, his eyes open and flick over to my chair.

"I guess I'm the weak one now," he says.

I feel pressured and worn. Last night's visit was a battering ram of demands that he come home.

"Take me with you home," he repeated over and over, reminding me of E.T.

"Take me with you home."

Physically he's getting better but his mind is not. According to him, he's in a hotel in Victoria and he wants money to pay the bill.

"Rosa was in the other room. She only had to pay six dollars for the room but she skipped out," he told me.

Always we're rushing to catch a ferry. We're going to be late, hurry, hurry. Or we're in Whistler or Squamish and why do I question that we are there? He gets angry with me when I won't accept what he is saying.

I need some help. Do I play along with his ideas or do I correct him? He gets livid if I do. Why don't they have a few guidelines for caregivers like me?

I have told his brother about the accident and working through the language difficulty, assured the three nieces from Sweden that they will be met at Seattle airport regardless if Willy is up to it or not. They will arrive in two weeks.

When I visit Willy, there is this lady in a wheelchair in the hall. She dresses in pastel colours and beige pants, silver-grey hair and childlike face. She can move the chair *slowly, slowly*. Her eyes always find mine and bore into me.

Like two laser beams from outer space. Even if I turn away, I feel their rays. When I sit in Willy's room, she positions the chair so it's facing towards us. I squirm, wanting to escape the scrutiny.

As I go towards the elevator, she puts the chair in my path. I press the button and wait. Her stare never lets up.

Willy phones from the hospital.

"The doctor says I can come home."

I see the doctor and check with him.

"It will help him to be in familiar surroundings," he says. "He's not used to taking drugs, and it's better if he's home."

The suitcase is on the bed and Willy keeps putting hospital stuff in it.

"That doesn't belong to us," I tell him as he puts a medical manual in it.

"Sure it does. It's been here all the time."

I turn my back and he's slipped the support collar in there. It's not going to be easy.

"Got to pay for the other two rooms we rented," he says.

He's always on and on about three rooms in a hotel. But he isn't so crazy, he's been in three different rooms, ICU, New Westminster room and room 306.

Thankfully he hasn't taken off his hospital identity tag. He shuffles back and forth when he walks. If he goes out, people will think he's drunk. The band on his wrist will help.

We arrive home and he semi-staggers to the back garden to check his beans. He comes indoors and goes to his potted plants, sticking his large fingers tenderly into the soil to see if it is damp enough, then lies down on the chesterfield to rest.

6.

April 1995

Is it possible to enter Willy's world of thoughts and knowledge? To step out of my fairy tale view of people and to see the underbelly? I try not to get downhearted when I hear him talk about the greed and meanness of human beings.

This morning, sitting on the side of the bed, he starts.

"People shouldn't interfere. Do-gooders often aren't needed and can create more trouble."

My antennae quiver and off we go in an argument. I'm trying to solve this and want to understand where he comes from with these set ideas.

For me, I'll step in Willy-Nilly (pun), anytime I can.

Yesterday a lady in front of me was twenty-five cents short to pay for her developed film. She said she would have to walk home and back to get the money. I gave the money to the cashier: what's twenty-five cents for heaven's sake? After that I saw a lady trying to retrieve her coin from one of those male engineered shopping carts. I held her bags and tried to help. Willy was forced, like it or not, to make the thing work.

To get back to this morning...He told me what happened when he had his morning coffee at McDonald's.

"I had moved my newspaper," he said, "and spilled my coffee on the floor. I was ready to wipe it up when a young man appeared with paper towels and did it for me. He went to the counter and paid for a fresh cup. Then he hands me a card saying "Jesus Saves.""

"He embarrassed me," he told me. "He wasted his money because I could have got one free for seniors. And the crunch was, he wanted to get a message across that was neither wanted or needed. Always, people do good so they can get something in return."

There was an anonymous fellow who handed him a five dollar bill in a Christmas card last year.

"But," says Willy, "it was just a nuisance, because I had to find someone who really needed it. I didn't want the guilt of taking it from someone who did."

I told him that I heard a volunteer in an organization saying she was feeling badly because she was benefiting emotionally from her job. The answer was, "It is natural. If good comes back to you from volunteering, accept it. Meanwhile you have helped the world be a better place."

I hang on to my belief, even though the media often prove I am wrong.

I wonder if we can compromise, Willy and me? Sometimes people are self-serving, but I will keep believing that not all human beings are out to have repayment for their kindness.

7.

Buying a car

My brother and his wife from Australia are to visit us for three weeks. They ask us to rent a car and meet them at the airport.

Willy owns a baby blue Nissan truck, which is his joy, equal to the love for his bike. It has a manual gear shift, which I am too nervous to deal with. It doesn't have a radio or any useless trimmings but is reliable and economical. It has hauled much in our time together, including my paintings. Without that truck, I would have given up entering shows.

Two days before the guests arrive, we arrange for a rental. The hours are not compatible with the arrival plans.

Willy veers around to the European car sales place, drives up to where two Westfalias stand, with their price label of thirty thousand dollars and asks me, "Which one do you want?"

There has been no discussion prior to this, except for my fairy tale dream of owning a Westfalia, purely for the feeling of a carefree vacation. I know Willy thinks this is frivolous and my brain turns quickly. Could I live with his constant disapproval? What if it broke down? It was only a dream after all. When a dream comes flying, smack into your face, you have to wonder, will it be a nightmare?

He's waiting for an answer. "Well?"

"I can't accept that Willy, but thank you all the same." My dream takes wing and flies away.

He drives to a car mart. Looks at this one and that one and asks me what I think. My brain is still addled with what are we doing here when we only agreed to rent one? And what about his truck?

He sees a demonstrator Tercel. The salesman suggests a drive in it. Willy wants to be sure I can handle it. I haven't driven for nine years and then, only old clunkers.

It is an automatic and it has a radio. It has power steering and room for paintings in the back when the seats are down. It is white.

And that is how we bought a car.

My life changed. I could drive again and our visitors could be accommodated. Willy sold his truck and now the car would be mine.

The condo

1.

May visit to Kelowna

Strange how trips get writing juices surging. We're on a jaunt now and there's the urge to record.

There's no planned repertoire for us going on trips. My antennae are finely tuned so I can pick up vibes from Willy that it is time to go! It must be a Scandinavian tradition to take several vacations during the year. Other Scandinavians can report this to their fellow countrymen in Canada. It apparently means, (a) that he can still afford it and (b) that he's not too old to partake of life! When restlessness gathers in Willy's wirey frame, it needs to be calmed by excursions.

I have everything in my neighbourhood. I don't want to travel anymore. I compromise, and when I'm in the experience, enjoy learning and absorbing. But I ache to return to my own territory.

I had made that remark that I haven't seen Ann for a while. Ann and I shared a studio in Winnipeg. She and her husband built their dream house overlooking the lake in Kelowna. He always called it "Ann's House."

Anyway, Willy says, "How about we leave early next week for Kelowna?"

I find a write-up about a side trip around Princeton, cut from a newspaper years ago. The paper is brittle and ochre coloured with age. I get out a map about this area and present it to him, thinking at least it's off the highway. He makes that hateful, spitting noise in his throat. A dismissal.

"Why does the noise bother you?" he asks.

"The sound is demeaning, banishing my idea," I tell him.

He said, "In Denmark, no one takes any notice of that. It's a way of saying Uh! Huh!"

"In England, we say, we will knock you up in the morning, which means we will wake you up. In Canada, that means you will have sexual intercourse with the person. So we don't say it here."

Why didn't I think of that before? He seems to understand that explanation!

He suggests I drive to Hope. He wants me to be self-sufficient. It goes smoothly until the confusing interlocking roads.

"Which one? Which one?" I cry out.

And he says, "You know the way."

My hands strangle the wheel.

"Which way? Tell me now!"

"How come you don't know?" he asks. "It's you who wanted to see your friend."

Speeding up, I take the wrong turn. I pull over.

"You never discussed with me where we are going. I figured you would tell me what you had in mind. How do I know what you want?"

He's surprised. Figures I should have read his mind.

We stop for gas in Princeton, finding some shade under a tree marked "Pets." A plaid shirted man with red, wattled cheeks, limps awkwardly from his large older car towards us. He flicks his head to one side, indicating we've left the parking lights on.

"You might have trouble with the battery," he says.

He takes out a long cigar and sits on the buffer log, telling us his wife has gone to the hospital and they can't find out what the trouble is. They won't let him visit until an hour's time. He drags at the cigar. Tells us about his previous car.

"That motor gave out in two weeks," he says, "so I refused to make payments. Two huge, burly men came to my door. They had to go through my field to get there, I told them, 'I can sue you for trespassing. Get out!' I never saw them again. One day, the car disappeared from my driveway and that was that!"

Willy goes to sit in the driver's seat but I tell him I'm going to keep on driving.

He shrugs his shoulders and tells the man, "She didn't even want to drive to Hope, but now I can't get her away from the wheel."

We tell the man goodbye and good luck about his wife. He looks lonely, sitting there on the log, waiting for visiting time.

Kelowna nears...

"It might be a good idea to find the motel strip I stayed in when my brother visited Canada in the seventies," Willy says.

It isn't hard to find along the lake and Willy doesn't quibble about the price.

There's a heat wave. In the room a rackety air conditioner rattles away but doesn't make much difference to the temperature.

I phone my friend and tell her we will visit after dinner and she gives me directions.

They have sold "Ann's House," wanting to be closer to town, even though Ann had sworn she would only leave the house feet first and in a box. They looked at many others, but either he liked it and she didn't or vice versa.

Finally Ann said, "Choose anything, I can't stand this anymore!"

So now they live in "His House." He feels badly about it, so she has a new grand piano and new furniture. Where is her studio? She will probably get one later and maybe she doesn't need it as she used to, because she is enjoying other aspects of life.

Other aspects! What's that, I wonder. I am trapped the other way. Blinkers on and two tracks — writing and painting.

When we had the argument about planning a trip, Willy said, "You don't want to talk about anything but painting or writing anyway."

Ann and I get caught up with her life. We arrange to meet at the art gallery tomorrow.

Willy walks around town while I sit in the only shade on the steps of the art gallery, waiting for Ann. The searing heat is impossible to escape. My skin can't take more of it. I look for the cool in the same way fish make for the deep undercover of rocky ledges.

A group of seven- and eight-year-old children hone into this spot, ignoring me. Girl behind me eating a lunch of fruit salad, lording it over the lunchless others.

One says, "Anyway, I don't like pineapple. I like pears."

They recite, "He loves me, he loves me not."

The boys run here and run there. Now they examine an ant.

"If it has a red back, it's a fire ant."

They push it and blow on it. They squish the dry earth making a mess on the steps. The ant struggles on it. One boy has a toy car and runs it back and forth over the thing, pushing down hard and yelling, "Road Kill!"

There's no hope for a future without violence if small boys want to do this.

The girls are chanting as they rhythmically clap their hands.

Now the teacher gathers them together and tells them about the show in the gallery.

Ann calls me from the door and we go in to see what the authorities have given us.

They give us a lot to talk about. The show's about a print maker's repeated workings with limited subject matter to arrive at a perfected print.

We go to a restaurant mainly so we can relax and talk. Our lives have taken different forks in the road but we have a lot in common and laugh easily together.

I'm still driving as we travel on to Kamloops. Long stretches of road with no pulloff points to take a break from fast driving and monotony. Looking in the rear view mirror, the front of the cars take on personalities. Low slung sports models send out aggressive rays as they bear down on my rear fender. Willy sleeps.

Just to make him mad, when he wakes I say, "Had a good nap did you?"

And he says, "This is napping country."

Why are we going to Kamloops? Because I didn't know what he wanted, so I suggested we see a provincial art show there.

It's a mess. The show is over.

We are at the top of the hill overlooking the town and he asks, "Do you really want to go into the town?"

"Yes," I tell him.

I'm tired of going past towns and having no inkling of what they are about. Now, I get to see their town's gallery and they have a Japanese pottery show on.

It's always the same with me. Whenever I sense "real art," it's like a religious experience. I admire the Japanese artists and their dedication to excellence.

Tea bowls are in a case and I want to tell everyone, "This is the spirit of the tea bowl. Rugged and of the earth. Not the refined sophisticated objects that Westerners think they should be."

This gallery is an example of good staff doing their job: Research done on artists who have shown in this gallery and explanations of the works on display. The support from governments and corporate sponsors takes me by surprise. Yet, it is only the basement of an old building, painted white.

Stores are now closed in Kamloops, so no excursions possible there. Wal-Mart is open, so that's permissible. Wandering up and down the aisles, I get stomach cramps and have to keep running to the ladies room. Oh Boy! (My sons hate when I say that. They think I should say Oh Girl! the odd time.) Always something with me on trips. Willy goes through them undisturbed, but me, it's the beds too hard, my back hurts, or I have to eat now! (Diabetes!). I like being home. The bed is finely tuned to my body. My back can be eased without being subjected to unsympathetic chairs, and meal routine is just that — routine.

Another thing about Scandinavians taking a holiday. I think, and it's just me thinking, that it is permission time for them to relax rules on drinking and sex. Anyway, knowing that, it works in reverse on me, which means a dilemma. As some people have said: "Poor Willy!"

Next day, as we're pulling out of town, Willy says we should stop at a restaurant for lunch.

We have cheese and peanut butter in the car, so I say, "Why not just stop for a loaf of bread and we'll have a sandwich in the car?"

He's angry. Can't understand why we shouldn't eat at a restaurant.

He says, "We'll never find a place that sells bread around here. You treat me like a coolie."

A coolie? A coolie? What has a coolie got to do with a loaf of bread? I can't figure it out. We call in three places, but no bread. He's right. Backtracking, we finally find a loaf and he begins a slow descent to normal colour in his face.

"There won't be anywhere out of the sun to eat," he says.

He's right there too.

And so it's more of endless dry landscapes, the sage brush clawing at the raw sienna dirt hills. It would be great to be a painter in this country because the territory is stamped with its character. Simplicity and strength. But I couldn't take the relentless heat. Memories of Mission's clouds and shady trees soothe my brain.

At last...a turnoff and a few pine trees. I don't notice a cow-crossing grate until the tires are grinding over the ruddy thing.

Willy says, "Next time, look for the two tracks on it that are smooth and aim your tires there."

I'm learning.

Willy gets out the lounge chair from the trunk and I have a jolly picnic with the coolie and the celebrated bread.

There's the Indian paintbrush plant right at our feet and wild strawberry plants in bloom. It's similar to the prairies, where one has to really look for the spring crocus amongst the thaw of winter.

As I get back behind the wheel, I venture, "Where are we headed now? Home?"

"Yes," he says.

At Spencer's Bridge there is a sign that warns of road closure on the way to Hope. They are blasting rocks. A lady tells us it should open at 2 p.m.

"I'd like to see what Spencer's Bridge is like," I tell Willy.

"There's nothing there," he snorts.

But we cross the old bridge and see the heritage country store that's being renovated. The inn next door offers white river rafting.

Onto the highway again.

I say, "I want to call into Gold Pan Park."

"There's no gold panning," says Willy.

"I want to go anyway. Maybe I can see some gold."

It occurs to me, since I'm in the driver's seat, I can turn off if I want. I'm starting to like driving.

The picnic tables stand empty. Crows evaluate our looks. Are we careless eaters? They fly closer and closer, ebony wings flashing thalo blue in the sun, daring with their need. I go down to the stony shore, looking for gold nuggets. Nothing. But when I get back to the parking lot, I find a dime! I flash it in front of Willy's face. It's usually him who finds money.

"I might not have found gold, but I have silver!" I flaunt.

East of Hope, we were held up for two hours on a metal bridge in blazing sunshine. We turned around to find a place with some semblance of shade. Willy got the chair out; I was comfortable until I remembered, Bears!

We are in the Bonanza restaurant in Chilliwack. It would have been great to have taken our big family here once a week.

The last leg of the journey seems endless. I am getting tired. Wonder what the mail has brought?

For the first time in my life, I have driven twelve hundred miles and lived to tell about it.

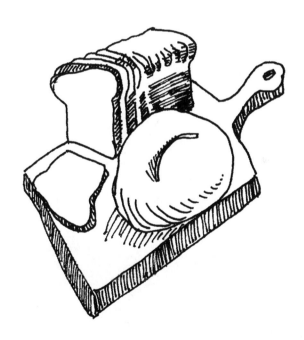

2.

David

The logger's axe smashes into the willow stump. I go out on the deck to watch. Seventy-two year old Willy swings the handle in a wide arc. The weight of the axe head delivers power! And he's been complaining about his shoulders for weeks.

He climbs wild cherry trees to eat ripe fruit.

"God gave this bounty, it *behooves* us to eat it," he says.

Well, he fell. Rolling down a bramble covered bank. When he told me, I fretted. How would we find him if he had a broken leg?

I could hardly tell a search party, "Look around every cherry tree in the area."

He's able to swing an axe and carry pails of dirt or water; he just can't sleep on that side anymore. This presents a problem. I can't sleep on the side facing him because of an arthritic neck. There's a gulf between us as we turn our backs to each other in bed. We used to sleep with his arms around me. Now, we are two lonely aliens in what used to be our coming together time.

After I read him the nightly story, (we're reading *Sense and Sensibility),* he reaches to kiss me and cries out in pain.

He makes smacking noises with his lips and says, "I'm faxing you a kiss."

3.

Powell River

"I'd like to see what the end of the road looks like. The one that passes through Powell River and ends — just like — that at Lund."

I'm talking about where we should take a trip now that the weather's warmer, the veggies are harvested and the lawn doesn't need haircuts for a while.

He's been asking where I want to go. I did tell him I'd like to spend a couple of nights in a Vancouver hotel and do all the things I've wanted to do. And I could visit the children. That idea was crossed off the list in no uncertain way, that's when I asked about Powell River.

"Good God!" he says. "When we worked up there we could hardly wait to get out. No one goes to Powell River!"

A week passes and he comes into the studio and asks, "Would you like to see the Grand Coulee Dam?"

"It depends what's there."

"It's an engineering masterpiece. People go from all over the world to see it."

When there was no response from me, he said, "It's a massive dam."

To ask me if I want to see a dam is like asking if I want to see a cement wall!

"No thanks," I said and his face went the colour of red cabbage with the veins protruding.

The other day he came into the bedroom.

"How about going to Powell River?" he asked.

Jumping at the chance, I tell him "sure" without reminding him of his harangues before.

"Are you going to let me look in the shops?"

"Shops! No one buys in Powell River! The people go to Vancouver to buy."

Silence...then he says, "If you want to shop, it's fine with me."

"I don't want to buy. I just want to look. So I'm allowed to look under duress?"

We set off on one of those beautiful B.C. September days, air crisp and sun shining. He times it dead on to reach the ferry at Horseshoe Bay. The other line-up for the ferry to Nanaimo is long. Some will have another sailing wait.

I figured I'll go to the ladies room when we get on the ferry, but the sailing departure is delayed.

"Go over there," says Willy, pointing to a restroom across the parking lot.

"They might get you to move while I'm in there," I say, but can't wait any longer and run across the tarmac.

Pushing the door open, I'm surprised to see they're putting urinals in the ladies' toilets. I'd better check this. Sure enough, because of my hurry, I'm in the men's room.

I get back to the truck just in time, because we are told to board. These ferries give me a holiday feeling. This one is smaller than the big runs.

First we skirt around Bowen Island. I think of my friend who lives there now with her new husband. Like me, she had a new life. Unlike me, she had years of looking after her former husband who had Alzheimer's.

Willy remembers boating here in the old days with his girlfriend and her daughter. When the ferries came within five miles of them, the daughter screamed because she thought they would be crushed. He laughs, remembering.

I'm talking to him but he can't hear me properly.

"Sneeze?" he asks.

"No! Freeze!"

"Wheeze?"

"Freeze!" My teeth are clamped as I have to repeat myself again.

"Seize?"

"Oh! For Pete's Sake Willy, admit that you can't hear."

But he says, "The hearing doctor said I was fine. I didn't need a hearing apparatus. If I wanted to wear one for decoration, that was fine with him, but my hearing was okay."

"Well," I tell him, "the next time you go to the doctor, I'm going with you so I will know what's really going on."

"I don't know what you can do more," he says. "I told him, I can't understand what my woman is saying, and he says, 'but that's very common — nothing to do with hearing'."

Laughter.

I found out he has a system to camouflage the deafness. I ask him a question and he will say, "No." I tell him something, this time he will say, "Yes."

Half the time, it will be the right answer and the other half of the time, he thinks I am just "yapping" as he calls it. Another thing he doesn't hear is the Bing!

Bing! Bing! of the turn indicator on the truck. Sometimes it goes on and on and the guy behind is waiting for him turn and he doesn't.

So I say, "Willy, your flicker is on."

Well he didn't want to be told. Now we play a game to see if he can go a whole trip without me telling him his flicker is on. I point out other cars who have the same problem. He now calls me The Flicker Inspector!

Part of the time, misunderstanding comes because even though he has done a lot of reading, pronouncing words is another matter and sometimes, I have difficulty in interpreting what he says.

We reach Gibsons, a small town perched on a hill overlooking islands. Film companies come here to do films for television.

It's not as picturesque as I thought (Willy says that word as *picture-squew*). Guess that's what happens when people have over praised a place. I imagined a more rocky coast and not so built up with houses.

On we go to Sechelt and we try to find the arts centre. We see a log building which includes a theatre but the place isn't open.

We go to Rockwood where they hold writers' festivals. There is an oriental garden. I walk through it, imagining how great it would be to spend a whole week here with other writers.

Sechelt is a small town. Seniors much in evidence. So-called galleries seem to be commercial, selling pretty reproductions.

The highway out to Powell River has so many curves.

Willy says, "The engineer must have got an "A" for every curve he could make in the road."

Rocks are different here, more structural and colourful. Arbutus trees. I have missed their molten red trunks and graceful branches. They are artist's trees.

Here comes Powell River. Houses along the waterfront, as it is hilly beyond that point. Most houses overlook the sea and Texada Island. This island is supposed to be the place to gather flower stones, light grey stones with markings of black flowerlike patterns.

We drive through the shopping district and through the old town area. No one can miss McMillan Bloedell's paper mill and the white columns of smoke pushing from the high chimneys.

Willy is reminded of the years he worked here and talks about them.

We see a large motel. All the others have "No Vacancy" signs. I suggest we book in now.

He gives that spitting noise in his throat that makes my insides churn, and he says, "There'll be lots of places."

We drive to Lund. Willy points out, "That's the end of the highway."

I can't believe it, it's a regular road that comes to an abrupt end at the water's edge and one feels as if you can drop off the end of the world.

Two men are bringing up a basket of crabs and I ask, "Where's the end of the highway?"

He points across the water to Vancouver Island.

"Over there," he says, but grins and tells me, "This is it."

There's a motel, but we have trouble finding anyone who wants to rent us a room. A silver-haired man in the lobby tells us to wait, his buddy will come soon. His breath whooshes over my face. Overpowering liquor smell. I look over to his wife hovering in the background. How can she sleep with a man so drenched in the stuff? Her dark hair is permed in precise small waves and her horn-rimmed glasses give her the look of a religious teacher. But one can never tell from looks. She could be a stripper under guise. Maybe she doesn't mind the booze. Maybe she even likes it too. But I know she is miserable being with him.

We drive back to Powell River and of course the motel is full. I am a fool to expect Willy to be contrite. He had noticed a bed and breakfast place. We go there.

It is now getting dark. The lady comes out to the truck and sizes me up and down, looking at our tacky belongings in the back of the truck. Her house is full but there's someone down the road who will take us. She will phone ahead and tell them we will be there after we have something to eat. She draws us a map.

We eat in the restaurant where windows look out on the islands and see the small ferries chug across to Texada. There is a mine there, cottages but little else. I wonder at the expense of these ferries, however they do look pretty at night with their lights reflecting in the midnight blue water.

The soup is good, tasting of vegetables and long cooking. The colour of pumpkin. The menu lists this as "Yesterday's Soup — we say yesterday's because we're cooking tomorrow's today."

It's dark as we start looking for the address of the bed and breakfast place. Finally, after back tracking, we get to a log house amongst tall cedar trees.

The lady greets us and is friendly but is so nervous, she makes me nervous. She wants to be sure she is giving enough service to warrant her money. It gets embarrassing. She shows us an eight-minute video about the district, then bids us goodnight.

I go to have a bath. There isn't a shower and the bath is far too large to fill. A Home and Garden bath mat is draped over the edge, bottle green velour. I swear no one has stepped on it. I decide to forget about it and so does Willy.

Noise seems to reverberate through the house, so we whisper "goodnight" after having an argument whether the bed is king or queen sized.

Outside there is absolute quiet. No dog barking, no rustle of leaves, no movements of any kind. It's like sensory deprivation. It's eerie.

Early morning and I have to go to the bathroom and I see that the lady is reading close by.

When I crawl back in the covers, Willy is in Romantic Mode.

I hiss at him, "No! The lady's outside the door."

But he doesn't give up.

I tell him, "There's no use you thinking up Plan B because the answer is No!"

And we start to laugh and can't stop.

She has baked some scones for breakfast.

She tells us, "The only reason I got into this bed and breakfast was because my two grownup girls were forever coming home, staying months at a time. I figured if I had visitors all the time, I wouldn't have to deal with them."

She tells me she only buys original art, but when I look at them, I find they're reproductions.

We leave the house for our return journey. It's nearly lunch time and Willy spies a picnic spot called Paradise Beach.

What a find! An arc of sand, diamonds sparkling on the sea under the sun. Soothing lapping waves, small multicoloured pebbles and an outcropping of rocks on the headland.

The sun is bright, but not piercing, the breeze is gentle. I take off socks and shoes and wade in the clear water which is spikey cold. I see circular black objects on the edge of the tide mark. To my sadness, I find they are sand dollars, black with oil or tar. There are hundreds soiled with this sickly stuff.

I've always thought each sand dollar is like a small, holy world. They're usually pristine white with a lovely inscribed symbol on their lids. They have little dove shapes inside their pockets. We saw them in the Oregon Aquarium and I was surprised that they stand on their edges in the ocean. They're so clever, they swallow heavy sand to act as ballast and to keep upright.

As the sun cuts through the water, I see myriads of particles of fool's gold. I try to scoop some into my hand but it's futile. I'll just have to enjoy looking at them.

I walk over to where Willy is sitting on a bleached log. Sitting beside him, I show him my feet, which are glistening.

"I've got diamonds on my feet!" I say.

"It's only the dry salt from the water," he says.

He goes off rambling along the bush. A young woman comes down to the beach on a bike. On the main path that leads to the sand, she strips the clothes above her waist and lays face (and other things) up. She isn't considering other people.

When Willy returns I complain about her.

He says, "That's okay, she isn't hurting anyone."

But I'm not so sure. She has altered the mood of the place. I hate her making me feel uncomfortable.

Willy ambles, in a roundabout way, over to where he can stare at her. He just couldn't resist could he? He has no couth! I hate this situation.

We go back to the truck and he makes tuna salad and he's actually bought some tins — we never buy tins — of fruit salad. Then it's time to leave. Time was suspended while we were alone on the beach before "that woman" came.

"She shouldn't have done that so openly," I say. "She should have found a more private place."

It's like when I do nude paintings. I don't go putting them in the public's face. They belong in a gallery environment. But a naked woman on a public beach is imposing her guidelines on others without consideration.

We line up in lane B for the six-thirty ferry and I tell Willy, "It's been a good two days."

He never praises anything but now surprises me with, "Yes, beautiful weather, good sleeping, good roads and lovely scenery" ... pause ... "especially the woman on the beach!"

AAAAGH!

In the lane in front of us a Beetle car with two youths who seem to be in difficulty. One fellow is rummaging for tools. Their interim license expired two days ago. When they get the signal to board, it all but suffocates us with noxious fumes and with a blast, charges up the ramp onto the ferry.

We eat in the cafeteria. Plasticine food but the French fries are good. There's a B.C. invention of a machine that makes a bag of French fries in three minutes after you put a coin in. I like that idea and told Willy, who is always after me to invest in stocks. If I did, I would back that. Did he ever laugh, and laugh. I hate when he does that. He can keep his stocks!

Time to leave. The men with their fluorescent orange jackets, move the ramp down but we're stopped from going off the ferry. A flag comes down and it says "Pin Out." This safety procedure was put in place after the recent accident in the Nanaimo ferry.

Men scuttle around and fix whatever was wrong and we're allowed to go.

Masses of cars on the mainland but it's plain sailing (pun) all the way home.

Mail in our box from my sister with photos of when I was in England. I bring up some bags and sort out paraphernalia that I picked up on the journey.

Willy starts a fire and makes some hot chocolate. He does his *exerceeses* and comes for the night's story to be read.

He says, "It was a good holiday, but it's good to be home too!"

And that, coming from him, is really something.

4.

Common-law

Willy is in the dining room, around the corner from where I sit on the couch in the living room. I am quilting my Hawaiian quilt cushion and he is going through our income tax forms.

"I can save $750 if we were married. So will we get married?" I hear him say.

I ignore his words. He comes into the living room, sits next to me on the couch and says, "Shall we enter as a married couple?"

"I don't think saving $750 on income tax is a good reason for getting married," I say in a sharp voice.

"This is the first year we can transfer money to a spouse," he says.

I ease up a bit and say, "We *are* a common-law couple and I've always considered us to be."

He shows me the fine print. It will mean I will pay my own medical. At least our relationship is acknowledged, out in the open, not fumbled over.

The strangest thing is he gets out the wine and two glasses. His smile is as wide as a canyon. We clink our glasses.

"Here's to income tax," he says.

I correct him, "Here's to common-law spouses," I say.

Signed,

"Officially Willy's Girl"

5.

The move

I told him, "I will keep this bed. The day it goes, will be the day I make a final commitment to you."

My talisman, the lumpy, comforting, single bed with the pale green plywood headboard and suit-my-back mattress. It came with the house I bought when I moved to B.C. It went into Willy's dog house room and he liked it for his snoozes.

There was no ritual with the burning. Taking a deep breath, I acknowledged the episode was in lieu of marriage vows.

We would lose the space of three rooms in the move from house to the new apartment.

It was the accident that made Willy worry about owning a house. His energy was flagging.

"What would you do if I died? It would be too much for you to manage," he said.

We put the house on the market. Willy thought it would take ages to sell, so he absolutely refused to look at the other end of moving.

All he would say was, "It was not to be a small house or a townhouse. It has to be an apartment."

I had already decided that Mission was my home. The realtor found an apartment, which I pray will be my last home. Willy was not enamoured.

"Too costly to heat with electricity, no gas fireplace, and worse, no elevator! I'm too old to pack you up the stairs if you get sick," he said.

I told him, "It may be me who has to pack *you* up."

He couldn't complain about the roof. It has red ceramic tile. Since I went to Europe, I always wanted a roof with red ceramic tiles. The colour warms the landscape.

There is a Japanese type garden in front of the building. I wanted one like that since I was in Japan. And since coming to B.C., I've wanted an enclosed sun porch, just like the one we have now.

There are only fifteen suites in the block. It is well built and quiet. I work in the master bedroom which has two closets and bathroom big enough to store more art gear. A bit cluttered, but I have more walls to hang work. There's even a skylight in the hallway, so one doesn't feel "apartmentalized."

We sold the house right away and Willy went on a cleaning frenzy, scrubbing the deck, dousing the bricks with ammonia, shampooing the carpets. There was no peace. At this time, a publisher from Winnipeg was thinking of publishing *The Life Series,* as a book and to have a travelling show of thirty-four of my paintings. So it is understandable I must protect these never-to-be-repeated images. I wrapped them and put them under the bed.

"I'm getting a metal undercarriage for the bed," said Willy. "We can't arrive at the new place with the two-by-four contraption. And I'm cleaning the carpet there."

I moved the packet to the studio closet.

"I need to get in the closet to disconnect the light," he said.

He had cleaned the carpet by the wall in the studio and washed the wall; I put them there. He decided to paint the skylight trim so I rescued the work once more, praying they would survive the move.

As well as my old bed, out went the bed-chesterfield which had seen us through our first years, until we got the thousand dollar mattress.

Willy was afraid the movers would cost a fortune, so we hauled our stuff downstairs and into the garage to make the loading faster. But they were quiet and efficient and Willy was happy with relief.

There was a garburator here. I say *was* because Willy lost the dishcloth in it and gummed up the works.

We have a sunken living room, two steps down. The other night Willy got up to pee. There was this awful crash. When he got back into bed, I asked what the noise was.

"I forgot I couldn't walk on air!" he said.

Our walks are varied now and Willy's cycle trips have a mile less mountain to climb. After what seemed an eternity — actually ten days — I did some painting and some writing in this new space.

Good fortune seems to have come with us to this new haven. *The Life Series* work survived and has now travelled to Winnipeg.

And so far, Willy hasn't had to pack me up the stairs!

6.

Sense

I am reading Jane Austen's *Sense and Sensibility* to Willy, in installments.

"It's such a soothing story," he says. "Nothing happens."

"You can go to sleep without trouble on your mind."

"Things *do* happen," I say. "They have dances."

In the story, Edward turns up on his horse. He leaves the house early next morning.

"Ah, hah!" says Willy.   "He's a wise one. He's going off before he's trapped."

I am nettled. "What makes you think he's going to be trapped? If he worried about that, he shouldn't have gone to the women's house."

"His horse needed a rest."

"He could have found another house."

"No! No!" Willy says. "There wasn't another house around."

Aaaagh!

Why does he always talk of women trapping men? Seems to me, there's no sense or sensibility to his thinking!

7.

71st birthday

Today, I am seventy-one, the age my sister died. Could this be my final year?

At that moment I let Willy know I'm ready for coffee. Lately these waking noises have to be louder due to either Willy's hearing problem or his reluctance to tear himself away from the stock channel.

Lying here, I remember our decision to not buy presents anymore. A few days ago he decided it wouldn't matter if he bought me something he thought I wanted, a stock pot, one of those large pots to boil the blackberries in.

Usually level headed, I actually felt my blood drumming.

"Don't ever buy pots for my birthday!" I raged.

Willy backed into the nearest chair, face red, eyes startled. He didn't know in my previous marriage that pots were taboo! I felt like a kitchen maid, but never had the nerve to say so.

I was depressed about the overdue birth of our fourth child. My husband presented me with this extravagantly wrapped large box. Inside was a Dutch oven. I had needed some affirmation that I was still an attractive woman, apart from mother and housewife. I cried and cried.

Now Willy opens the door and he has a bouquet of pale pink roses. Good! Reminders of the first roses he gave me, "When we were young," as he says.

He gives me a fuchsia coloured plastic thing with lots of handles on it.

"What is it?" I ask.

"It's called a tropical tote," he says. "It's a bonus gift because I bought this."

He hands me a box with Oscar de la Renta perfume in it. I stretch my mouth into a semblance of a smile. I still have a bottle from Christmas.

"Thank you Willy," I say as I try to pull out the stopper.

It is stuck. I give it a hearty tug. The glass stopper frees suddenly as it is jerked loose and the seventy-five dollar perfume spills all over the bed! We are engulfed with the heady gas of seduction.

Willy is not the least deterred and climbs into bed with me.

Does becoming seventy-one make one jaded? Everything a repetition of what has been before? Or is it because I don't want to pretend anymore? Lately, I am confused. My daughter said she would meet us at the Vietnamese restaurant for a birthday dinner. I had thought it was on my birthday, but when she phoned from the restaurant, I realized I had made a mistake.

I sense the children are saying to each other, "Mother's slipping. Did you hear about...?"

Reminds me when I was sixty-five and burned a pot on the stove. A young person can do that and everyone understands, but for an older person, it's a sign they are getting forgetful. In other words, senile.

There's another thing that makes me dread birthdays.

Willy and others will ask, "How many of your children phoned?"

Of course, some never do and I feel like a failure as a mother all over again. I didn't bring them up to "honor your mother."

One son phoned and apologized for not sending a card.

"Really doesn't matter," says I. "Nowadays cards, letters and gifts are almost a thing of the past except for your immediate family."

Then I realized, what the heck is your mother, if she's not your immediate family?

My daughter arranges to have a dinner the following weekend. My friend comes with a flower arrangement. Another friend of forty year's standing sends a card playing happy birthday. Over half my children phone, send gifts or cards.

Willy takes me to the ABC Family Restaurant for a two-for-one dinner.

Perhaps I should count my blessings and embrace my senior years living with the bicycle man.

Bed making

If proof were needed
to know how different
Willy is to me,
one would only have to see
us making the bed in the morning.
Eight forty-five, I roll out of bed
and we start the ritual.
Our mattress is covered with two foams,
the dividing line made obvious.
I smooth my side of the bottom sheet,
he leaves his crumpled.
I pull the top sheet down
so my toes will be covered.
He pulls the top higher
so his head can go under.
He wants me to have yards of comforter
on my side,
whereas I can't stand the thing.
He likes three comforters
because he is so slim.
I like cool
because I'm built otherwise.
I turn to open the window
and he waits, sentry-like
at the door.

He gives me a pat on the bottom
and a kiss on the lips
as I pass through.
We do the same thing every day,
our differences are obvious,
but we connect
in spite of them.

9.

Clinic

I'm sitting in the waiting room of the orthopedic surgeon's office. The crunch has come. My hip bone is worn. Base of my spine is sore. Walking wears at the whole area and it feels inflamed. So many times I've had scares, but maybe this time it will be bad news.

Thoughts wander when you sit in this atmosphere, and you hone in on others in the room. A young woman at the receptionist's desk has her back to me. Her shorts are like a second skin. I wonder if young women will have trouble in their later years after wearing some of today's fashions. Those aerobic pull-up tunics, tight panty hose and pointed shoes.

I check out the art on the walls. Nice photo of rhododendron. Mass produced style oil painting of mountains, obviously made by someone who hasn't seen B.C.

I'm in the x-ray division of the hospital. Nice thing about smaller towns, one is admitted quickly. The doctor ordered hip and spine x-rays.

"Can you feel anything when you swing your leg?" the x-ray technician asked.

"Yes."

"Can you put your finger on the point of hurt?"

"Yes." Is he thinking hip-joint?

I told him about collapsing fourteen years ago because of spine trauma. What a feeling to have paralyzed legs!

Willy hasn't known how much pain I had during our walks. This may come as a shock to him.

The x-ray technician seemed to concentrate on my right-hand side.

"You do know it's the left-hand side don't you?" I asked.

"Good job you said that," he said.

He changed the camera angle.

I'm now in the small cubicle, waiting to be discharged. I can see an examination table with stirrups. So many times I've stretched out on those.

Raising and bending my knees, feet in those stirrups, seizing up stomach muscles as a doctor says, "Now relax, I can't examine you if you don't relax."

This, as he pushed down hard while thrusting his fingers higher into me. How would he have reacted if we switched places?

The X-ray technician tells me I can leave. To check with my doctor in three days. I must brace myself.

Outside the hospital, Willy waits for me. His eyes scan my face for bad news. "I won't know for three days," I tell him.

Meanwhile, I hope whatever the results, there will be a medical solution.

10.

Married or not

"Did you marry the Dane you were going out with?" I was asked.

"Well, yes and no," I replied. "I consider myself married but we haven't gone through legal or religious rites to put an official stamp on our relationship."

The answer to that was a slap of disapproval.

"It's like being pregnant. You either are or you're not. In other words, you are not married."

I'm seventy-one and my man, partner, spouse or whatever he's supposed to be called, is seventy-five. He's never been married and has no compunction to oblige establishment. I have been a wife, mother and the kind who obeys rules of the land.

I blush to say when my older children wanted to stay overnight with their unmarried partner, I was adamant. "No way!" But it seems fine for me to cohabitate. True, I had to get over initial guilt, but I argued, there's no assurance wedding ceremonies would make long lasting bonds.

Unless I'm due for the Guinness book of records, I'm not going to have children. I have enough money for living expenses, so why do I have to go through legalities?

The government is slowly acknowledging arrangements such as ours exist. They are leaving a space on forms for common-law couples.

When Willy had the accident, he was out of it mentally. The hospital registry clerk asked me to sign for his admittance.

She asked, "You are his wife, aren't you?"

She tapped her pen on the side of the form.

"You are able to register him," she said, "but in the case of him requiring an operation, you cannot sign consent as you are not legally married."

"Who would sign then?"

"His brother, sister or one of his children."

I was upset enough with his condition, let along being faced with the fact five years of living and caring for each other has been eradicated.

"He has no one in this country. Only a brother in Sweden. What happens if he needs an operation now?" I asked, "Who's going to sign permission?"

She didn't know. Only that it could not be me.

We are dismissed as a unit.

I asked some people in the health field, was it so? And nobody knew for sure. I phoned the government health office and they told me they were in the process of recognizing common-law rights as regards to hospitalization. It will take a while yet.

Others in the same relationship can take heart. One day we will be counted legitimate!

The condo
11.

Vancouver Island

We were early in the lineup for the ferry at Horseshoe Bay. We paid $21.75 for the car; weekdays, seniors themselves travel free.

Willy gets out the thermos of coffee and I attack the *Mists of Avalon*. Eight hundred and fifty-two pages! I've been told it's a must read because it has to do with subjects of my paintings, the Holy Grail, goddesses, churches gaining power in England...Morgaine (the protagonist) sounds like me sometimes.

The triple deck, pristine white ferry docks silently. Cars and foot passengers are let off with efficiency and we drive up the ramp and park.

On the main deck, some people stretch out on soft cushioned chairs, snoozing. I attack my eight hundred and fifty-two pages. Willy does what he always does, wanders off. I never ask where, I know he will reappear when needed.

We drive off the ferry at Nanaimo, miss the motel. Willy is good about it and finds the way to the Bluebird Motel. The purpose of this trip is to reconnect with the founding members of *Art 10 Gallery*. I reluctantly part with ten, twenty dollar bills for two nights stay.

We have a kitchenette. Willy has brought along the basics of eating. One of the endearing pictures I have of him is when he fills plastic containers and zip-lock bags for our outings.

I am to show slides of my work and tell my friends about the miracle of *Portage & Main Press* publishing a book about my art and my life.

Being on the Island brings memories with a force. The little house which had looked adorable but cost more money than I had. The college courses, trouble with teenagers and the desperation to get my life on track.

Gerd comes to the motel for me. She comes from Norway and is, as a friend should be, solid and true. We go to her house and have dinner and visit. She has tamed her garden. Many women artists are passionate about their gardens. They pour their creativity into flowers and shrubs. No critics in that sphere. No hauling framed work to galleries.

"I need to put my hands in the dirt," Gerd says.

I reserve my art news for the next day; I've brought copies of my work to let the group see the progress since I left Nanaimo.

The next day I have a bit of time to go with Willy to Newcastle Island, a provincial park, a fifteen minute boat ride away. The small paddle boat is docked by the sea walk. Willy was not too keen.

"How much?" he asked the man on the quay.

"Oh! We wait until we get half way. We turn off the engine and then tell you about the increase in fares," he said.

I fish in my purse.

"Never mind, I'll pay," said Willy.

We disembark on the island and I see the flat, champagne coloured rocks with pockmarks. I have missed them being in my locale. I go looking for tidal pools. I love being close to the sea, it replenishes my energy. Willy sits on the edge of the beach in the shade of a bush, watching and waiting for me. I look back at him. He reminds me of a deer, blending in with his surroundings.

When I get back, we follow a trail, intending to walk around some of the island. We pass a coffee house; I feel him stiffen.

"They always have to spoil nature. They have no brains!" he says.

But I was glad it was there, I had forgotten to bring something to eat. Walking can disrupt my diabetes.

We start towards the pine studded bush, A sign confronts us. "COUGAR SIGHTING! Do not run! If you see one, look at it eye to eye and walk backwards." I can't move. I sense cougars all around us.

"They're only big cats," Willy says.

"You can go on, but I'm beating a fast retreat," I tell him.

No worry about the beach though. The island was like Avalon, a place where one takes on a different persona. A quiet, peaceful, less stressed persona. I was sorry to leave.

In the evening, we gathered at Edna's place. We started *Art 10 Gallery* fourteen years ago.

These ladies belong to Avalon. Gentle, giving, timeless…each painting in her own style. Ethel is over ninety and can't climb stairs now. Two of the ladies drove her and carried her up the steps.

Other people experience life's tender moments in school reunions and such, but I have not had such roots in my lifetime. In Nanaimo though, with those women, I felt a reconnectedness. We had a dream, fourteen years ago. I had been teaching the art group and realized these ladies had some good paintings.

"Where do you show them?" I had asked.

"Nowhere," they said.

Their works were under beds and in their garages. These women were the core group to start the gallery. They work out sitting schedules, arrange for feature artists, keep a diary of events and they have become a family.

When we returned, we saw the Tercel in McDonald's parking lot.

Gerd said, "Where's Willy?"

Everyone asks that!

"He will appear when I get out of your car," I say.

And sure enough, he did.

I wish Gerd lived closer to me. I said goodbye with sadness in my chest.

Willy heard traffic was held up from Horseshoe Bay, we took the Tswassen ferry. It was smooth sailing.

"Where would you like to eat supper?" Willy asked on the drive home.

"I know you won't approve, but we are passing George's restaurant. If I pay, can we eat there?"

"Okay," he said.

I ignored his struggle to drown his I-don't-need-six-waiters-to-hover-over-me lectures. Or his don't-want-to-pay-for-the-ambiance-I-only-want-good-food.

But it *was* good food and I tried not to reel with shock at the bill. At least we know a good place to recommend now.

Our apartment feels calm and reassuring, as though welcoming us home. And the silken thread connecting me with my friends remains strong.

12.

Christmas Eve in a seniors' condo

From my window, I see ebony crows,
black spirits
before ghostly white trees.
Snow comes
twisting and curling with the wind.

Old men walking
to their mobile home park
struggle with plastic Save-On bags,
making tracks across the street.

In the gnarled tree
a stellar jay flashes
his iridescent wings.
Small birds dart
in shriveled rhododendrons
gathering morsels before all is hard.

Snow piles higher.
Older women rethink Christmas visits
give up expecting companionship.
But Willy is out
Shoveling our pathway.
His leather face and hands
seem not to heed this bitter weather.

Sometimes things aren't happy

1.

Gifts

Willy has never had a Christmas stocking. In his day, in Denmark, they had nissermen visit instead of Santa Claus. The children left rice in a bowl for these gnomes. They wore red toques, were mischievous and left presents, but no stockings were hung.

"Why are you hanging that?" Willy asked after I bought him a Scandinavian stocking and a striped one for me. "I think you're asking for presents," he said.

I took them down because I was humiliated.

But this year, he made me hang them up. Trying to jump into the swing of the season, he came home one day with a large bag.

"I've got stocking stuffers," he said.

"So many?" I queried.

And he said, "If you buy in bulk, you get a discount."

Bulk? Bulk? Did he mean some kind of food? He put the things in my stocking.

"I suppose you're going to look?" he said.

"No," I tell him. "You can feel for size and flexibility, but you can't look."

I did feel them and I'm sure they are ten deodorants! I know I have difficulty finding my brand, but really!

"I'll take you to Abbotsford today to buy your real present," he said. "You told me you wanted a special nightgown."

He gives me $150.

I go to the best lingerie store and try on a peach-coloured crushed-cotton nightie.

The clerk says, "You will feel like a princess in it."

I did. The yoke was overlaid with cobwebby lace, long puffy sleeves were caught at the wrist with more lace. I looked like an older version of a Christmas fairy.

I got thinking it was really too beautiful to wear and Willy may get bothered by the ruffles and lace, so I bought a cheap alternate in another store.

When I told him, Willy laughed and laughed.

And I remembered my mother. After she died they found a chest full of silk and handmade underwear and nighties she was keeping "for best." Am I to do the same?

I put it against me so he can see how lovely it is. The corners of his mouth crinkle, and he says, "Looks to me like No-No Nannette."

I told Willy I would wear the new nightie on Christmas Eve.

He is making remarks, such as, "I can hardly wait for the Chemise parade."

I love when he uses old fashioned or European phrases; atelier for studio; hose for socks; and Chemise is cute.

I seem to write a lot about favourite dresses or coats. They meant a lot to me and the nightgown will join the list.

Christmas morning and I empty my stocking. It isn't deodorant; it is small jars of spices!

Well at least he has a bit of the idea about Christmas stockings.

2.

Visit to Victoria

Guilt! Other older women are such great mothers and grandmothers; I don't measure up. Willy pokes at me with reminders that there's more to life than painting and writing.

"Okay, okay," I tell myself.

For starters, I'll make a date to visit my youngest son. He and his wife manage a bakery in Victoria and have bought a house there. He wants me to share his accomplishments.

"What about next weekend?" I ask my son.

"That's busy. How about the following?" he suggests.

"No. I'm doing a show."

And so on.

We will meet on June 14th, a month away.

"Are you coming with me, Willy, or do I go alone?"

"I guess I'll come. How long will we be there?"

"Two days."

"Why would anyone want to be in Victoria for two days? It's nothing but a tourist trap."

He's thinking he'll be without his bike for two days!

"If we make the journey, we may as well make it worthwhile," I say. "We've been invited out for dinner on Saturday night. How can it be enjoyable if we have to rush for the ferry?"

I know better than to expect Willy to stay in someone else's home.

"This is my idea, so I'm paying for the ferry and the hotel," I say.

"We'll have to pay more for the parking than for the hotel," he says, "and the *tieves,* lots of *tieves* there."

I call to mind Deepak Chopra's law: Do Not Defend.

"Will we go by bus?" I ask.

"No, we'll drive," he says.

Driving! It's just that his reactions and manners are opposite to mine. When nearing warning lights he slows a half mile before and creeps along. My entrails tighten, forming a solid core as I sympathize with the cars behind us. Are they thinking we're running out of gas?

"Only worry about yourself, don't think of others," Willy says.

But I need to be aware of everything. The windshield fogs up. A button clears it but Willy's face gets red if I turn it on.

"Wears the battery down," he says.

If I turn on the fan, he waits until I'm not looking and turns it off. We drive wrapped in a shroud of mist, and him flapping an old towel at the windshield.

My stomach writhes into a knot at the thought of what's ahead and we still have a month to go!

On the 12th, Willy brings out his knapsacks and starts packaging peanut butter, jam, coffee, rolled oats. Fussing, checking, ordering all ingredients for a buy-free holiday. I imagine him with a wig and he takes on his mother's persona. He's also checked the car.

I buy a map of Victoria, this is a forbidden purchase. I get tired of driving in a maze with no idea if we're close to the sea or other landmarks. I remove the price sticker before I put it on his chair-side table.

No use saying, "Here is a map Willy and the street is so-and-so." I've learned to be subtle.

I pack my case a week in advance, too. My main concern is enough clean underpants and my medicine. Make-up; an eyebrow pencil for my straggly white eyebrows and lipstick to brighten my pale complexion. Willy is wrong when he says I take a long time to "decorate your eyeballs."

Camera. Why? When hundreds of slides and prints lie in boxes unused, unlooked at?

Sweater and jacket. Brolly. Always my brolly, after all, it is B.C.

We're only going over night. Why can't I just go with clean underpants and medi?

The day has arrived and we get in the car, map safely slipped into a side pocket.

Swartz Bay terminal. Long, long wharf, cars lined up all the way.

"No room on this sailing, you'll get on the next," says the ticket girl.

An hour and a half to wait.

It's hot, the sun blazes down. I wear my long sleeved fuchsia blouse, wrap-around sunglasses and Willy's find, a baseball type hat with an eye shading peak. It has some sports insignia on the front. Apparently, it's the "in" thing; young people see me and say "Hey! Real neat!"

"I'll take a walk," I tell Willy, "and buy Saturday's newspapers."

"Too expensive here," he says.

I charge ahead, buy two papers and pay a dollar for coffee, even though he has a thermos in the car.

He sees me on the way back. He's found a seat for me in the shade amongst the wild rose bushes. He takes out the advertisement pages to make a cushion for my bottom and leaves me to catch up on the latest in art reviews and book critiques.

A man walks past smiling at me says, "How lovely, sitting amongst the roses!"

Later, when I tell Willy, he says, "He's looking for a punch in the mouth."

On board, I go to the newspaper shop and see the cards on display, reproductions from my paintings. I casually switch them to front and centre.

Tugging at a lady's sleeve, I say, "I have to tell someone, these are taken from my paintings."

"Oh, yes dear!" she says.

Does she think I'm unbalanced? I don't care, I feel proud knowing my artwork is out there for many to see.

Off the ferry, to find the hotel my son recommended. I squirm as we pass the Empress Hotel; we were told to turn there.

Willy finds the place, draws into the parking lot and frets, "The *tieves* will steal everything."

No elevator. Creaky stairs. Oh, no! There's a pub. I envision a raucous night. The room is on the cool northside and has a large window.

My son and his wife pick us up and take us to the bakery. How interesting to have my children show me their businesses! They all have a creative bent and are original thinkers.

We go to the house they have bought. My heart jolts. It looks like the house I used to own on Vancouver Island. Small pane windows, cove ceilings, friendly kitchen.

We watch the hour long video of their Hawaiian wedding. It feels good to know the children are putting down roots. Their friends invite us for an outdoor dinner. Lovely evening, talking about business ventures and family stories.

Early goodnights. They have a busy schedule and can't spare any more time to visit. Willy and I walk in the quiet Victoria street, then have a good night's sleep.

Willy has promised to enter the spirit of vacation; we head for the museum. We cut through the Legislative Buildings. We see the splendid horse drawn carriages filled with Japanese tourists. New York, Montreal, and Victoria; I've seen these in all those cities and wished, just once, to travel on one, clop-clopping down the road. But I'm always with an unromantic partner. Small matter! I aim the camera while Willy studies the different species of horses. He tells me the chestnut one is a thorough-bred.

"Compare his build," he says, but I can't see the difference.

He rarely resists stroking creatures like this, rubbing their noses and clucking at them. They never fail to turn lovingly towards him. Basic communication I guess.

Willy pays museum admission. I enjoy the energy of the Native masks and artifacts.

"There's another section," I say.

"No, no, that's all there is," he says.

But we find the other section, a replica of logging and mining in the old days. Willy perks a little.

It's time for lunch. "It's close to our parked car, we'll lunch at the James Bay Cafe," says Willy.

The holiday visit turns light-hearted as I taste true Welsh rarebit for the first time since leaving England. Royalty photos adorn the walls and hand knitted tea cosies warm teapots. Willy pays the bill.

Time to catch the early ferry; we don't want to run into rush hour traffic. No line-ups, we board in ten minutes.

This ferry has my cards on display as well. I move them to the front, but this time, I don't tell anyone they're mine.

The drive home is painless, and Willy did well. It was a good trip after all.

3.

January 1, 1997

Willy is delighted to demonstrate his superiority by correcting me and adding, "my dear!" in an ingratiating tone as if talking to a wayward child.

For example...I say, "The sky is blue today."

He will say, "There are clouds in the distance and they will bring rain my dear!"

I ask him to desist. "It's bad enough you correct every flipping thing I say, let alone adding that extra spike."

But he hasn't given up. I can almost see him rise from the floor with glee when he says it.

Sometimes I feel like giving up. It's hard slugging to make him understand or to change him.

This morning I say, "Today I take down the Christmas decorations. I need some good boxes."

Willy: "Why do you need other boxes? They were in boxes and they can go back in the same ones. We didn't buy new decorations so there shouldn't be extra."

Doris: "We have new angels and the wreath that Puck gave us. We didn't buy them, they were given to us."

Always, I have to defend my reason for doing things. For once, why can't he say, "That's fine Doris."

If I taped our conversations, some female audiences would say, "It's too tough to retain your confidence. Forget it."

4.

Whidbey Island: August 1996

Whidbey Island, or more precise, Coupeville on Whidbey Island was relaxing. Willy drove. I wouldn't have gone otherwise. Dorothy gave us a detailed map, but Willy refused to look at it until we were at the point of the crucial interchange. He has a gut knowledge and we were on track.

Past Desolation Sound and onto Whidbey Island, one feels the peace soothe the senses. The English type farmlands were orderly and the orange-gold wheat fields were being harvested in the afternoon sun.

I had asked Willy which hotel he would choose; I should have known he would choose this cheaper one. That was before he gave me $500 American for the expenses.

It was on the list of accommodations from the art group.

"Where is it? Where is it?" he asked, looking left and right.

But I couldn't tell him; I was in shock. Forty motorbikes sat in the parking lot of the motel, the noise from the beer garden was deafening.

I had to register in the bar.

The large, heavy set men and women were watching the loudest baseball game and I had to yell over the TV ball game to state my business. But the room was fine and neighbours orderly. I even tolerated hearing their TV.

And the bikers didn't stay overnight!

We were in Whidbey Island so I could attend Katherine Chang Lui's week-long workshop. She is revered as one of the best jurors in the States, has an analytical mind, as well as being a painter "with soul."

I expected the week to be akin to visiting an art psychologist. It would be my absolute last workshop. I would attend the workshop from 9:00 a.m. until 4:30 p.m. each day. Willy would explore the island on his bike and I promised I would be his alone after 4:30 p.m.

Willy met me for "early bird" dinners. We walked afterwards and entered the *tranqueel* feelings of that small historic village. We walked on the beach; I found a collection of pebbles.

"Coupeville used to be known for its pebble beach before a lady visited from Mission. Now the beach is bare," Willy said.

But he carried the bulging plastic bag.

On our last day, I still hadn't spent my "expense" money.

Katherine closed the workshop at 4:00 p.m. I had one hour without Willy and 120 US dollars in my purse! I ran down to the main street where I'd seen a silk, dusky blue top and slacks. It fit. The saleslady gave me twenty percent off, which meant I could buy it...so I did.

It was my birthday money!

The highway home seemed like New York traffic. My head was trying to sort out the past week.

What was to come?

What would I do without a mentor?

There was a line-up at customs.

"How much did you spend?" the customs man asked.

In his low voice, Willy quoted the bill, "One hundred and ten dollars."

"Ten dollars? You're free to go," he said and before I could correct him, we were across the border!

5.

The vacuum cleaner

I know now,
how a man feels
when his wife gets out
the vacuum cleaner.

Willy does this job in our house.
Decks are cleared
and nose down,
he turns on that awful motor.
Charging forward and onward,
nothing will stop him.
Even if I'm talking
to a visitor.
We have to shout
above the racket.

Chairs are pushed away,
plants moved.
The worst
is when that monster
enters my studio.

Framed work stacked on the floor
gets put in another place.
Files and "things to be attended to"

get moved around.
Carefully placed reproductions
stored under furniture
will have their position changed,
while I clench my jaws
waiting for their ruin.

"Don't be ungrateful,"
friends tell me.
"We'd love to have a Willy
look after that for us."
But it remains an ordeal
knowing the noise-decibel-breaker
will invade my space again!

November 22, 1996

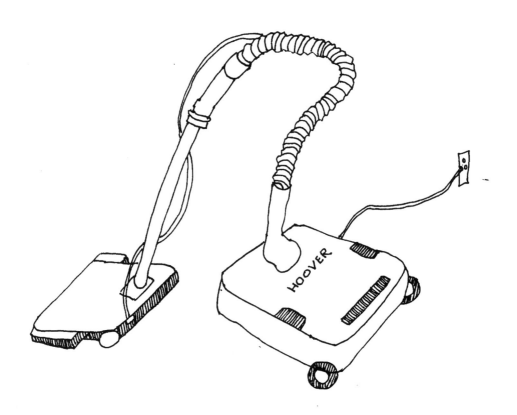

Sometimes things aren't happy

6.

Flying home

It's all very pleasant,
this visiting.
Especially when one connects
to the family.
But it's good
to be going home.

Going home to Willy
waiting to hold me
in his knobbly arms.
And I'll find Willy's
picked up all the newspapers
he likes to strew
around his chair
to make an island
so he can sit like a king
in the middle of it all.

Home to my
hallowed studio
tubes of paint ready,
paper primed.
The word-pro mute,
until,

I bring it to life with
words.

Going home to the
answering machine
playing friends' voices.
Home, with rain and brollies,
temperate weather.
Our apartment,
my paintings
smiling down on me.
Home to our thousand dollar mattress
Oh! My grateful back!

In the morning,
he'll bring
my wake-up cup of coffee,
creep under the covers
we'll talk, argue
and maybe make love.

But most of all,
home to my guy
who makes me mad,
makes me laugh,
and makes me realize,
I AM HOME.

7.

The facts

"My original man kicked me out when I was in my sixties," she told me. "Got himself a younger model. I wouldn't want to take on a man again. Too many compromises are necessary and the woman always has to do the changing. It's okay for you because you've got this special man. I don't think there is another Willy. Oh! When I think about someone taking me in his arms with love, I ache. Then I remember what you have to do for it and forget it!"

I want to tell her, "No! No! Our situation isn't perfect, haven't you read the book?"

Then a friend tells me, "I'm always quoting you and Willy. You are my ideal couple."

Am I giving the impression we live a fairy tale romance? Well I must guard against that because there's no such thing.

He just came into the studio. "Think we'll get a car. Automatic so you can drive it." This, with his truck having no problems and him against automatics.

He is writing and asks, "Does a 'J' go to the left or the right? I can never remember. I'm sorry if I'm not perfect."

He's referring to his second language and he even speaks a third!

Signed: Grateful Doris

8.

Restaurant quarrel

"Two nonsmoking. In a booth," I tell the young hostess.

It's the same request I make every Monday night when we go for the senior's special at the local place. Today's special includes soup, bun, and tapioca pudding with a scoop of strawberry preserves at the bottom.

"He will have a glass of red house wine and I will have water," I tell her as she seats me in the aqua booth.

Willy is still studying the blackboard specials in case there is a new development.

On the way here, I exploded. I think he *likes* it when I explode.

It all started when I returned from Vancouver at 5 p.m. I had gone with the executive of the art group to buy a printing press. Until now, the club was not keen to divert to other directions. We had called into the print place on Granville Island and were shown what could be done with linoleum. We priced the presses.

When I came home, I told Willy, "It was so much fun. The art group is going to buy a press."

"What in heaven's name is a press good for?" he says. "Waste of money. No one makes prints now when we have copiers and you'd be better off spending your time on your own stuff."

That's why I blew, but have now calmed down.

"No one will use the press. It's a waste of money," he says, as he sits opposite me.

I have been reading Deepak Chopra's *Seven Spiritual Laws of Success*. It becomes a blur when I have to remember so many lessons, but *one,* the most useful to me, I can handle: Do Not Defend.

It makes a lot of sense; you can't have fights if you don't defend. Actually, it was Jesus who said it first. In our case, friction resulted when I took the bait. Willy figures this makes life interesting. *Stir up the pot,* he calls it.

But my nerves can't take it. I'm a woman and an artist; so I'm sensitive to everything.

For the past nine months when he creeps under my hide, I repeat to myself over and over, Do Not Defend. It works. But there are times, like now, when good old Deepak can't help at all.

I hiss at Willy over the table, "You are a miserable man. You take away my joy and you see black in everything."

My eyes are fogged with tears and my chest is solid rock.

"Don't cry here," he says.

He might as well have said, "Don't you dare cry here."

The customers and the waitress will gawk, don't you see.

Never mind me and what I am feeling. I have a sudden flashback, to the time I knelt on the floor wailing.

My marriage was over and my then-husband stood over me saying, "Don't make that noise, you'll frighten the children."

Willy pushes the wine glass towards me.

"Have a sniff," he says.

A walk with Willy

*We hold hands and
with the slightest tug
on his fingers,
he senses the way I want to go.*

*There is no use talking to him
as we trudge
the hilly sidewalks of Mission.
If I say, "Willy, see the daffodils,"
he'll look straight ahead and reply,
"It's common."
If I say, "the dewdrops
each have their own rainbow,"
he will say,
"It's supposed to be that way."
If I say, "Mount Baker is glorious
in the peach sunset,"
he will say,
"Everyone knows that."*

*If he carries on about unions, NDP
nurses, doctors, universities
or people who are corrupt,
I will purse my mouth and refuse to
make excuses for them because*

it only fuels the lectures.

So we walk in silence
broken by the safe topic
of weather.
"Wind is cold," or
"Sun is hot."

Once in a while
he'll stop for something like
a copper coloured caterpillar
trying to cross the sidewalk.
I know he sees these things,
he just doesn't want ME
to be the one to point them out.

We repeat the walking ritual every day.
We understand the rules.
Our minds in separate worlds,
our fingers connected.

10.

Lament

In my studio
I sit opposite
glassed paintings.
 A window reflection
obliterates the work
I see only cerulean sky,
puffy clouds, and
bare boned tree branches.

It is a world
I'd like to enter.
Serene and calm
like the land of Meditation.

But here, on the chesterfield
a pall of sorrow
hovers over me,
my man and I
are at a danger zone.

Respect and affection
are eroding.
Something has to give.

"You're like a detective," he says,

"always looking for some transgression."
I said I don't like it
when I watch my
T. V. program
and he sits, sighing
those massive sighs
of disapproval,
then getting up
to sit in an unlit
kitchen corner.
Waves of reproach
work their way to me.

He wants us
to just sit on the chesterfield
and stare into space!

His answers to my utterances
are dismissive
as if I were no account.
If my talking dries up
what is left of our conversing,
But nothing?
He doesn't give of himself.
Silence is his mistress.

Sex used to bring us close
but now
the doctor says, "No more."
I feel it has robbed
my man of the chance
to enjoy (prove) his prowess.

He talks of the days
he travelled by bus
meeting different people.
Observing others in their ways of life.
Not beholden to anyone.
"Why don't you travel then?"
I ask.

"Maybe I will," he says,
"for a couple of months."

We walked yesterday
and for the first time,
our fingers
didn't connect.
A bad sign
coupled with
my sense of being tolerated
but no longer loved
Can I love
this intolerant man?

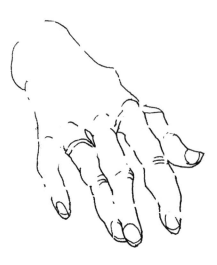

A black cloud
covers our dear apartment.
I don't want it!
He's closing the door
and
I think I'm helping him.

I want him to ease the sadness
in me, because
I can't allow sex.
He will not talk about it.
Can he know that I feel less a woman?

This has been a dark time.
Three women came today.
Two wanted words of wisdom.
They didn't know
that even at seventy-two
and seeming to be in the best
of situations,
my heart listened to them
but cries for myself
at the same time.

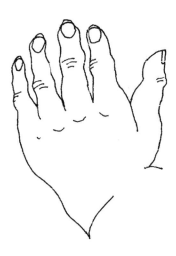

Further to lament

He called from the intercom downstairs,
"Are you coming for a walk?"
"Yes, just give me time to get dressed."
This time,
his hand reached
for mine
and later,
we stop at Save-On
and he buys me
daffodils.

12.

Hospital

Willy took it well enough. I have to have a repair operation for a prolapsed bladder.

I bring knitting, art supplies, books, and some crossword puzzles.

"Hospital stays are holiday times," someone told me.

There are two other ladies in my room. One with a heart condition and asthma. She chokes and I rub her back until she breathes easier. I ring for the nurse who comes with medication. The room fills with sympathy. There is a kindred spirit between the three of us.

In the bed opposite to mine, the lady called Ruth hasn't seen her doctor since she had her operation four days ago, but she doesn't complain. She reassures me about my upcoming operation, having had the same procedure.

"Time for a bath!" an aide sings. She hands me a face cloth and towel.

"Bathroom to the left, around the corner."

The bathroom is massive. No plug. Lots of taps. I'm scared to touch anything. The aide produces a plug and tells me the taps control the temperature.

After the bath, there's a form on my bed to fill out. "Do you use drugs?...alcohol?...cigarettes? Yes or No." I wrote a paragraph answering. "Well yes, I have a glass of wine in the evening but I don't intend to be lumped in with drug addicts."

Willy visits. It's good to see him.

Night time. A nurse asks the "Asthma lady" across the way, "You have to count your urine output for the next twenty-four hours. When did you void last?"

"Five p.m."

"So, you will count twenty-four hours from six p.m."

"No. Five p.m."

"Six p.m."

Is it any wonder instructions are misunderstood?

Ruth comes over to my bed. She is crocheting with fine pink wool.

"I crochet things for Mother's church bazaar," she says. "Last year I made toilet paper roll hangers. I accent them with ribbons and lace and embroider roses around the trim. They sold for eight dollars apiece. I had to make more of the peach colored ones because everyone loved that color."

The *"Asthma lady"* calls over, "My doctor is the same as yours."

"Oh! Do you like him?"

"My husband says I tell the doctor what's wrong with me and he agrees."

Nurse comes with a sleeping pill.

"I see you sleep with your feet out of the covers. My mother does too. When we go tenting we have to cut a hole in her sleeping bag, otherwise she panics."

I drift off to sleep.

In the morning I'm hauled onto a cart and pushed to the operating room. I hear my favorite music.

"Who's tape is that?" I ask.

"It's mine," says the anesthetist and while I tell him about knowing Kitaro and how I love his music, I'm off to other worlds.

Three days later and I'm not feeling too bad. An aide comes cleaning and tidying the room. She is so efficient, I am impressed and ask what her name is. She doesn't answer and leaves.

Ruth says, "Her name is Burton, the same as mine. She was my best friend. She couldn't have children and had always wanted daughters. She was like an aunt to my daughter. Then she took off with my husband!"

Willy comes to take me home. We park the truck in the underground parkade and take the elevator to his apartment. I remember I left my pretty slippers in the truck.

"Will you please bring up my slippers," I ask Willy.

"I'll get them later," he says.

"Someone might steal them."

"Well," he laughs, "we have gas *tieves* and tape deck *tieves* but I'm sure there aren't any slipper *tieves*.

He gets them anyway. He's glad I'm home and I'm glad he's there for me to come home to.

Section 11.

Small stories

Small stories

1.

Waiting in emergency

Waiting in emergency —
how ominous it sounds.
How many emergencies have I had
yet have overcome the traumas
to pick up normal life again?
Reminds me of Willy's accident.
So easy to forget
the fine balance we live in.

Easy to forget
how scared I get
that this time
it will turn out to be
the beginning of a downward trend.

Being seventy-one
puts a different perspective
on simple things.
A burned saucepan
can start suspicions of Alzheimer's.
A slight fall can break bones
signifying an orthopedic future.
I'm here because of a strange infection
that flared up on my right leg.
I'm diabetic and must be on guard.

Visions of amputations.
How would I manage?
But thinking of Douglas Bader
who flew aircraft with
two artificial legs,
figure, if he could do it — I can.
Only trouble is
he was young
and young makes a difference.

Out of emergency now.
Willy waits for me.
"Tell me. Tell me," he says.
He too, braces to expect bad news.
"They think it's shingles.
Think I've been under stress.
You'd better be good to me."
He grins.
Once again we've survived
a visit to the emergency ward!

April 13, 1996

2.

The Wedding: August 19, 1997

I will be staying at Laura's house for most of the week. It is central, quiet and close to the river. I feel good in my designated room, even though there's a new futon bed. Will my back take it? Willy phones to see if everything's all right.

"Keep your chins up!" he says.

Next day, Mary Dixon, the publisher, picks me up and takes me to my solo show, opening thirty miles away.

The paintings suit the space. In the middle of the room a long, slim table sits laden with ethnic goodies. A throne-like chair with carved wooden arms and wine velvet upholstery, sits in a corner. "Reserved for Doris Paterson" a sign states.

I change into a long flowered pale pink dress, loose and cool. Then I meet people, smile a lot and answer questions. Once underway, I let down my reserve and enjoy the process.

Six seniors in wheelchairs come.

"How nice they've brought the seniors," I say.

There's laughter of course; I am a senior.

Mary introduces me. Tells when it all began three and a half years ago when she visited me in Mission and saw the paintings and prose for *The Life Series*. How she published a book about it, also the *Willy and Me* book and how the show travelled for a year.

Has it really happened to me?

I read from *Willy and Me* when we came together, a midterm piece, and a recent poem.

Some ask questions; I get fired up with answers. A journalist from the paper digs for answers to other questions.

I sit on the throne seat and people bring books for me to sign. One by one, they tell how they were affected by the show and how a certain painting triggered pain or pleasure memories of their lives. They share their private struggles, trusting that I will understand.

A senior couple tell me they were married in November and his name is Willy. What a hoot!

Driving back to Winnipeg with Mary, I realize this is the last stop for the show. It feels like when the children left home. But the books will live on and for that, I am thankful.

Laura's house is rustle and bustle. Her son has just leased a studio for his jewellery making. There is to be a barbecue at my former husband's place and there's salad making and bread roll fixing and getting decorations. The phone rings constantly and Laura chauffeurs her daughter to soccer, her son to his work, her husband to his job, and me to the mall to see about a wedding cake for Saturday. The bakery at the mall showcases a three-tier wedding cake. It looks perfect.

"I'll order one of those," I tell the clerk.

"That's a styrofoam cake," she looks at me as if I should have known. "They pretend to cut that for photos. They have a real cake to share with the guests."

Oh my! Does everything have to be phoney these days?

"I'll have one like that only in fruit cake," I say.

"Three tiers in fruit cake would cost you $650," she says. "How about a white cake?"

"$650? No way. But a white cake would collapse under the weight of the tiers."

"No. We have boards supported by pillars and these have spikes through them so each layer is supported."

"Can you be sure of that?" I ask.

"Absolutely," she assures me. "$153 for the cake, decorating and the topping of a couple joined in plastic matrimony."

"We'll pick it up Saturday morning."

Son Ted, the groom, picks me up for a visit with Debbie, the bride-to-be.

"We're going to move all the furniture upstairs," Debbie says. "We'll have the arch at the bottom of the staircase, decorated with tulle and flowers. Only thing we haven't figured out is refreshments."

"I've ordered the wedding cake, why don't you just serve simple sandwiches?" I ask. "It would be easy to serve."

Ted drives me to Laura's house. Thank goodness Suzie, the dog, knows me and doesn't bark. It's very late.

I have made arrangements to go to Mary's for dinner. Laura drives me. I take pictures of Mary's garden. Wildflowers and annuals burst with joy.

Inside, there are many paintings; some of them mine from long ago. Four other women join us for dinner. Even the most delicate of these ladies has a strong viewpoint and the evening slips away with vibrant interaction.

Next day, Barbara, my eldest daughter, picks me up. She and her husband George, live in a small town thirty miles from Winnipeg. George is newly ordained as minister of the United Church.

Barbara's kitchen is filled with food. She has offered to take charge of the refreshments for the wedding. Not only make, but organize, serve, and clean up afterwards.

We sit at the dining table doing the womanly thing of preparing for a celebration. One thousand meatballs, chicken wings, pasta salad, etc. She puts a chicken in the oven for tonight's dinner and suggests George show me the church.

Manitoba and small country towns are his milieu. I think *Jesus* would like his church, simple, warm and friendly. A plain wood cross, haloed with light, hangs above the altar.

George takes me to his office. An Asian marionette hangs from the bookshelf. She has a magenta cloak, bangles and a yellow crown.

George says, "I kept seeing a pile of dust on the crown and found out it was termites."

"How did you get rid of them?" I ask.

"I left it in the freezer for a few weeks."

There's a photograph of Barbara and him walking down a path. They cast long shadows and I think of walks with Willy.

We return to Barbara, who is making up plates of pickles.

My paintings are on the walls in each of my children's homes. Paintings from my beginning as an artist. I'm grateful they bought my work; it helped me keep the faith. Barbara has an oil painting of a mother and child, clothed in winter parkas. The child sleeps while the mother sits patiently. I call it *Bus Stop Madonna*. When I painted that, I had just made a giant step by renting my first studio! My own space! That was also the time when the marriage started to tear at the edges. What makes a painting have a life of it's own, as this one does? Everyone reacts to its indefinable magic.

Dinner is great; chicken with stuffing, new potatoes, yellow and green beans from the local farmer's market, salad, apple and banana cream pies. All my children are great cooks. Their father's mother and my mother excelled in that way too.

I feel badly they have to drive me thirty miles and then thirty miles home again. I long for the comfort of being with Willy.

Saturday, today is the wedding.

Laura's husband goes to pick up the cake. They return with three separate packages. "Did they show you how to put it together?" I ask. "Yes. Everything will be fine," he says.

Everyone scurries to dress. Laura brings out extra food. Buns are her specialty.

The cake is reloaded into the car and we leave for the ceremony.

Barbara is there already, filling platters. Debbie wears a cream coloured silk pant suit. She looks lovely. The groom is most handsome. George will officiate. My other son will take photos with my camera.

The wedding cake is placed on a large table in the dining room. Spikes go through the pillars, a board goes on top, then the next layer. No one breathes as the top layer goes on, then the plastic pair. We all feel relieved until the whole thing starts to weave and wobble like a nervous bride.

"Quick," I say, "get Debbie! We'll start taking photos of cutting the cake now!"

It holds just long enough. George removes the middle layer and we all laugh.

About thirty-five people have arrived. The ceremony is sixteen minutes late. The best man still hasn't arrived nor called.

Barbara tell the groom, "Enough! Decision time."

He asks his brother to take the position of best man. He was the designated photographer! I will have to take the photos.

As I record with the camera, I feel proud of my two sons standing there.

Debbie's sister cries so much, she can't read what she has prepared. George talks about sharing in a relationship.

Later, the groom asks me to dance. I haven't danced in years! He tells me, he loves me. The tears cascade down my face. When I return to my chair they don't stop. Why am I crying? I honestly don't know. Is it because I pulled myself away from half of the family when I moved to B.C.? All I am sure of, is my heart hurts and I can't make these tears behave. Am I making a spectacle of myself?

Debbie comes over to take my hands in hers, "I'm going to look after him, don't worry."

The cake is cut. It's delicious and there's plenty. Barbara's refreshments are perfect and served with quiet efficiency. I command my tears to dry and get on with socializing.

Time to go back to Laura's. Barbara comes with us while George visits someone in the hospital.

She says, "One of the wedding presents was a night in a theme hotel."

"What is the theme of their room?" Laura asks.

"Well," Barbara says, "there was only one theme available."

"What is it?" we want to know.

"It's football!"

Jokes fly around the car until all of us are laughing uncontrollably.

There's a message from Willy on the answering machine to say that Mark and Lorna will pick me up at Vancouver airport.

Early morning and Laura drives me to the airport. I've borrowed an extra suit case for the books and bits that I picked up. No seat partner. I read and sometimes close my eyes to let last week flash by again.

I look out the window. It is the clearest of days. Farmers tilling; not in straight lines but great curves like half a spiral. I reach in my purse for pen and paper and outline the patterns. It resembles a quilted hanging. Maybe I'll do one like that.

I think of my studio...my dreams are born there. I think of Willy and how stalwart he is. He will never understand my art but his ears pick up my distress note and he's there for me.

Families are families in many varied forms. This past week I have connected with mine and I hope the wedding will be the start of a bright future for Debbie and my son.

3.

Fortune cookie

When I read diary entries dated three years ago, I can see some of our clashes were serious. But we are still together.

Apartment living has been an advantage for us at this age. My studio is separate. I control the thermostat and windows. There is room to entertain my visitors.

I drive the Tercel now, unless we go out of town. We walk to the stores, bank and post office. He waits outside when I go into a store; no more arguing.

We had joint ownership of the apartment but, for his own reasons, he signed it over to me. I felt uneasy at first, but have accepted it.

Willy is now seventy-seven and is as fit as when we met. He bikes every day all day and plays chess with a friend one afternoon a week. A time for Danish pastries and Schnapps.

My art has changed yet again. It is mature work, matching my years. It feels good. When I went to a course on fiction writing, I was told my short stories should be a novel. So off I go with this new trend.

Coming back on the Christmas train from Vancouver, I felt a jolt of appreciation when I found Willy was at Mission station, waiting for me.

"Let's go for your favourite combination dinner at the Chinese restaurant," he said.

My fortune cookie reads, "Life just gets better!"

4.

Cat

A neighbour asked Willy to feed their cat while they were away.
"It's a shame they don't give it a name," I said. "They just call it Cat"
Willy said, "Nothing wrong with that."
"How would you like to be called *Man?*" I said.
"I wouldn't mind," he replies, "especially if people would bow when they said it."

5.

Nosebleed

"Your nose has been bleeding, Willy. There's blood on the sheets," I say.

"It's just because I have weak blood vessels in my nose," he says. "It's only a small amount so don't worry. Not like when I was *joung*. It would bleed and bleed all over the place. When I was twenty-four, I worked and lived on a farm. The farmer's wife saw the mess the bed was in and she was very cross."

Shaking her finger at me, she screamed, "Don't do that anymore!"

"And I never did."

Fireplaces

"Willy," I said, "I heard the fellow on the radio talking about fireplaces. He said having a fireplace in the living room reacts positively on the people who live with them. If you observe those around a fireplace, you will find they don't feel awkward if there isn't any conversation. Everyone is comfortable as long as they are looking at the flickering flames."

"Well," he said, "we have a fire every night and it's true we don't talk very much."

"It is comforting," I say.

Willy says, "And we can donate our voice boxes for transplants. We can label them, 'Good As New. Hardly Used'."

7.

Pigs

He told me about a job he had at a pig farm, manning the weighing scales. He was sixteen.

Danes and Germans liked their pigs fat, so they were no problem. English butchers, however, insisted on pigs weighing exactly 168 pounds.

"Lean and mean," Willy said.

This category of pig fetched a higher price. The weight was exacting to the point where the scale registered this poundage without undigested food.

Willy had to make sure the pigs reached this specific weight. To weigh them, one man would pull the ears and Willy, pushing with his body and hanging onto the tail, with the animal "kicking and squealing and shitting all over you," pushed the pig into a caged scale.

If the pig was underweight, it went in a pen for extra feeding, until the next collection time, hopefully it would have gained enough. The overweight pigs went into other pens to be starved.

"Don't they complain about not getting food?" I asked.

"Sure! They never stop hollering. They hollered when they were happy and they hollered when they were mad anyway."

"Didn't it get on your nerves to hear the racket?"

"Nerves? What nerves? Did you ever hear of a chicken catcher who had nerves? You just got on with it. And the smell! All animals have a smell, but I swear pigs are worst of all. You'd come back from all that slithering around, to have breakfast. To this day, I never eat bacon!"

Willy's story telling

"It's easy to write a story," Willy says.
"Then let me hear *you* tell one!" I challenged. And so he began...

It was a dark, miserable, rainy night. Foggy and clammy on a California graveyard. A headstone quivered with the unbearable climate.

Den, the smallest gravestone, said, "Let us all sing to cheer each other up. Soon there will be more gravestones. Gravestones anonymous."

Out of nowhere, there appeared what seemed to be a Nebraskan dude.

With his typical southern drawl, he said, "Howdy partners!"

All misery was forgotten. The rain had stopped. The fork had stopped forking. It was another world.

This light-hearted fellow had, by the touch of his tongue, changed a seemingly hopeless situation!

9.

The fly

"I kill all the flies in my apartment," Willy says, "I can't stand them buzzing away, knowing they will lay thousands of eggs. One time, I was in a motel, while I worked on a month-long job. This big fly came in, big as this around. I figured it didn't matter if he laid a thousand eggs because I'd be gone by the time they hatched. Everyday, he'd sit on a shelf and look at me and I'd look at him. I couldn't believe he could live for the whole month, but I know he was the same one, that's for sure. And we got used to each other."

Bursting of the bubble

He tells me people are mean
and greedy.
He tells me they clamour
for spotlight and power.

"They only do good," he says,
"so they benefit
themselves."

My chest surges
with rolled-up-in-a-ball
resentment
at his way of looking at people.

It cannot be true
that humans are mostly
base creatures.
I fight against
his negative dirge.

But in spite of this stance
my skin is pricked
I hear a friend
voice vengeance and hate
without room for compassion.

I experience being pushed down
as someone scrambles
to undermine
my position.

I press hands over my ears
to shut out proof
of his sad views.
But voices inside me
cite more examples
which validate his words.

I was a Pollyanna
living in a fairy tale bubble.
At seventy-one,
the pin pricks rent
the rainbow surface
and I am bereft
with knowledge.

Pillows

I like to arrange pillows on the chesterfield to support my back when I read or watch TV. It's never quite comfortable enough, so I add more and more cushions. Watching me, Willy says, "Are you the Pea Princess?"

Souvenir drawer

As his birthday nears, I get bothered about presents. We have agreed only cards on birthdays and Christmas, but it's not working. "I buy anything I need," he said.

The fleece T-shirt with a picture of his Nissan truck. $400 binoculars. Leather address book. Two gold watches. Gold cufflinks. All are in his souvenir drawer; not used.

What else to give him? I've bought him sweaters and he does occasionally wear them, but daily he pulls on this thrift shop one of twenty years standing.

He never accepts gifts graciously. I am subjected to a lecture on the stupidity of spending. If I buy anything for him, it has to lay for six months before he will even put it in the infamous drawer; an added rap on the knuckles!

Over the years, however, he has mentioned that homes in Denmark have Grandfather clocks. It must be important. He will be seventy-seven this birthday. Grandfather clocks cost in the thousands and we haven't room for one. I take a chance and buy a smaller version which can hang on the wall, hoping the next apartment won't hear the chimes.

I buy it two days before his birthday and the darn thing won't stop chiming. Wrapped in towels in my bathroom, the sound travels through the apartment. May as well let him have it now.

"Oh!" he says, "you couldn't wait for the right day!"

But I forgive his bad manners as I see he *loves* it. He hangs it on the wall above his desk, checking it constantly.

The Westminster chimes peal every quarter of an hour.

Willy makes reference to it all the time. "He's singing his own Christmas greetings! He's a modern grandfather, that one: He runs on tape!"

Small stories
13.

Willy's sourdough bread

The smell of Willy's bread was like a siren call for me when I first met him. I marvelled how his large hands kneaded the dough until it surrendered into silky submission.

Willy learned bread making by reading library books and simplifying the recipe for baking sourdough bread:

Recipe Starter:

| 1 cup water | 1 tsp. sugar |
| 1 cup flour | 1 tbsp. yeast |

Mix together & let stand in fridge in container with hole in the lid for 24 hrs
.

In a bowl:

| 1 cup water | 2 tbsp. salt |
| 1 cup starter | 3 tbsp. molasses |

Leave for 8 hours (up to 24). Have two well-greased bread pans ready.

Put mixture in large bowl and add:
2 cups warm water 2 cups rye flour 2 tbsp. wheat germ

Add white flour while kneading into a firm ball, about 10 minutes.

Bake 45 minutes in 325 degree oven.
Switch off oven and leave in for another fifteen minutes.

Thinking 'curved'

1.

Getting the book out: 1990

I remember when I first put together the *The Willy Stories*.

Thanks to editor Karen and a printer who honored the deadline, Karen and I picked up two hundred books from the printer and headed for the bar to celebrate.

It's like having a baby, printing your very own story. You wonder what it will look like and if anyone besides you will love it.

I'm the mother of a large family, a stay-at-home mother of the old persuasion. It doesn't set you up with confidence to be a writer of any consequence. But of course, it's Willy who makes the stories interesting.

Karen and I had agreed on a price for the stories to be camera ready. She put the whole shamoz together and it was printed in large print so people would be able to read it with ease.

I had a poster made for the book signing. It read, "An amusing story of two older, disparate people." Had to take it down because too many thought it said "two *desperate* people."

Someone gave me a ten-dollar bill for a book before it was even printed. I was going to frame it as evidence of my first ever book sale, but Willy said, "Frame a zerox copy of it — no use tying up money when you can use it!"

Willy has never read the stories — says it's all fabrication anyway.

A lot of books went to seniors for Christmas presents. Maybe there are older people who are nervous to start another relationship, but if Willy and I, who are so opposite in almost everything, if we can make it — it's worth the risk!

Journal writing

I came across pages of journal writing which were done while we lived in the house on Rose Avenue. I'd been reading books about writing your thoughts — just pouring it out. They said you would have a better understanding of yourself if you did this. I don't know if the exercise accomplished this goal but when I looked through it recently, there were a lot of truths; Truths which should be included in the stories of Willy and me,

It's obvious now that we wouldn't have lasted much longer as a couple if we had stayed on Rose avenue. I could get the bus into town but I couldn't carry my paintings or participate in gallery functions when the buses weren't running in the evenings. His truck had manual gear shift and I was too nervous to drive it in this hilly town. Conversations would go like this:

Doris. "Will you take me to Abbotsford this afternoon? I've made the decision to print another hundred Willy stories. I need to go to the printer's."

W "Why don't you go on Monday?"

Me. "This is a busy time for printers. The sooner I get it in the better."

W "Next week will be all right."

Me (resentment brewing, but accepting.) "Can we go to the Town Stationer with my paintings. I promised them."

W "They didn't get in touch with you, so why bother?"

Me. "I promised them three paintings this week."

W. "If it's business, like you say it is, that's not the way to deal with it. Let them come to you."

Me. (Resentment now at boiling point.) "It's my business and I'll deal with it my way. Sometimes I ask your advice and weigh your answer against my ideas.

Sometimes I take your advice, but in this case, I want to make the decision. I should have my own car then I wouldn't have to ask for rides when I have to carry things."

W "I don't understand how you can call your painting a business when you don't behave in a business-like way."

And that's how it goes.

If I have any suggestion, it always has to be counteracted to put me in a lesser place.

He's always calling me Number One Person because we put my name on the census form as being number 1, but in reality, he's making sure I'll never be in that category. I don't want to be above or below I just want to be equal. But he has the standard-gear truck and there's no way I'm going to drive it.

I debate whether to catch the bus, the paintings aren't too heavy, only awkward.

By the time I'd finished my daily chores, I let it be. He tries to explain his way of seeing things. "We should do two things at the same time instead of running off for one thing at a time. Anyway, you think crooked and I think straight!"

"I don't think crooked," I say, "I think *curved*."

He took me down at 2 p.m.

Once home, I was changing pictures in frames and decided to put the painting of him and I hugging, in a wooden gold frame. When he came near I said, "Look Willy, I have you in a gold frame."

And he said, "Think of that! This morning I was in shit. And now I'm in a gold frame."

I've got to admit, he *is* funny.

October 14th, 1993

I wanted to phone Carole yesterday. Carole, who taught me this new way with acrylics. You paint shapes and colors until the piece 'speaks to you'. For two weeks now, this piece refuses to surrender its meaning. I don't want to be so dark but there's nothing for it but to overlay more color. The thing sits confused with itself and frustrates me.

So I'm reading a book which says have faith, stick to it, what you want *will* happen. I remember Willy's joke about one man telling another that an ax will float on water. All you have to do is to keep saying, "I believe. I believe it will float, and it will float."

Well the man throws the ax into a lake, saying, "I believe. I believe." At this point the ax is going underwater and he continues, "I believe. I believe — it will sink!"

So it is with this painting. I have lost faith. The last application of paint yields a Buddha-like face.

Next day. What do you know? The Buddha turns out to be a story teller; A large lady reading to children. I write the words "Once upon a time" around her head and it's good.

Willy just came in to say he's back and I tell him I didn't even know he had left. "You thought I'd disappeared into *tin air,*" he said and then he goes on, "the only stock that's doing well right now is the undertakers. If they have people like me disappearing into *tin air,* their stock would go way down!"

There was a film on TV last night about this young whippersnapper of an artist. He buys things like a plastic blow-up bunny and has a forge create them in stainless steel. He gets one million smackers for it. It's the forge that makes the thing, he just directs and pays for it to be done. He married the porn star who made it into the government in Italy. He simulates sexual positions with her in the nude and the porcelain people make a china tableau from the pose. Quite lovely really, if only he wouldn't make remarks such as, "Instead of Michelangelo's God touching (to create) man — I am touching Hilda's ass!"

October 22nd, 1993.

It's raining hard. Willy will be half drowned. He doesn't care though — through sleet and snow he gets on his trusty steed (which isn't as trusty anymore). He goes to McDonald's for free coffee, free newspaper and free look at the young girls. He says I'm wrong about the last one but I defy anyone to be with him in those places and not be embarrassed. Which is wrong really because other men are doing the same thing but have perfected an unobtrusive way of doing it. In other words it's all right if you do these acts, just do them undercover.

I heard a man say, "It's fine if you sleep with other women, just don't let your regular girl-friend or your mother know about it."

November 5th, 1993.

I've had a vaginal infection. Willy will have to wait for any sexual contact.

He asks, "How's your bottom?"

"It isn't my bottom," I say.

"How's your sitting apparatus?"

I'll have to see the doctor on Monday if it hasn't improved. I'm going to walk more and measure my food intake. Maybe it's the blood sugar, maybe it's this and maybe it's that.

November 7th, 1993.

Well, I've had my cry. It's getting close to the day of the big show, I'm up tight and this vaginal thing doesn't clear up. Willy says. "Are you all set for the show?" and I say, "No, I need to get power bars for the lights." He goes red in the face and his voice booms (strange how he can articulate when he's angry.)

"What the hell do you need power bars for?"

Off we go again. I try to explain how much it upsets me when he gets angry at me wanting to buy something. I tell him I've resorted to hiding things from him, like getting my friend to buy the lights for our paintings. "I don't want anything to do with people who pay double the price for things," he says. That's when I cry. I remember the time I wanted to buy sun screen in the States and he said "You don't need it." And my face peeled the next day. "Let me make my own decisions," I tell him. But he says he only wants to help.

He told me he was used to being on the job-site and he did things the most reasonable way. "Well," I said, "you're not the foreman here — I'm a woman who lives with you."

The porridge boiled over in the micro oven and I felt like bawling again. We're reaching a dangerous state. Each of us entrenched in our different ways. In a few days, this time will have passed but right now I'm digging in my heels to not accept the non-acceptable.

Willy took off for his sojourns on his bike saying, "When I come back, you'll be your normal self." He thinks it's only a temporary upset. I feel like saying, "It's been the same explosive business ever since we first came together."

Must tend to the stew.

Signed: Stewed Doris.

3.

November 1, 1993

Willy figured the treats for Halloween right this time. He counted forty-eight trick or treaters and had enough for all.

I don't know if he counted the last one. On the spur of the moment, I draped an old, heavy dark tablecloth over me, took a flashlight and aimed the light under my chin, crept out of the back of the house to reach our front door. In a cracked, high-pitched voice, I cried out, "Trick or treat," never suspecting I could really fool Willy.

He was taken aback and nervous as I pushed the door and went into the house. He tried to lift the cloth. I burst out laughing and the tablecloth fell to the floor. We held onto each other, rocking back and forth, laughing because he was absolutely taken in.

"You didn't give me a treat," I said.

"Well," he said," I knew you were too big for candy but I thought of offering you a glass of wine."

The kids had behaved well, stopped calling at a decent hour and said thank you. Most had their parents with them. Life isn't as bad as the Province newspaper makes out.

Signed: "Life can be beautiful" Doris.

4.

November 3, 1993

What a storm we had last night! The power went off. I took the flashlight and went down to my bathroom. Something outside the bathroom window went a-knocking and clambering around, enough to stop my heart. The trees were swaying like never before and I thought some on top of our backyard hill would surely snap. I ran upstairs to Willy and bed.

This morning I tell Willy, "I'm glad I have you when there's a storm." He said, "I don't know what I can do about anything." So I thought about it and said, "Well, you might be the first one to get clobbered with a tree, so I would feel better."

"There'd be a race to get under the bed first," he said.

We laugh and once again I wonder why I think it's something to laugh at. I must stop trying to analyze that to death and just enjoy the fact that ever since I've known him he's made me laugh about simple things. That's his treasure trove, his witty way.

Sometimes when we've had a to-do I yearn for him to ease the tension with his funniness. But that's putting pressure on him. As for me, I can't seem to think quickly enough to get over trouble with a clever saying.

I'm sitting at my desk as the sunbeams pour through the window — yes, the storm has gone. The sun rays exaggerate the puckered skin on my arms. They're also pockmarked with brown spots — I'm getting old.

Yesterday Willy went to his doghouse room for a nap. He had the door closed and was there for two hours. I was getting nervous and told him so later.

"You were thinking you were going to find a corpse in there eh?" he said. The thought gave me a jolt because it could happen.

Willy comes in to say he's on his way biking,

"May the sun follow you," I say.

And he says, "Don't you want any for yourself?"

I'm getting up earlier these days at eight o'clock. Willy boasts that he gets up at six. I call him Father Superior and he calls me Mother Inferior. I let him be superior in that regard for a few hours in the morning. But after that... .

5.

December 18, 1993

Today Willy is seventy-three years old. Vern phoned to wish him a happy birthday at seven forty-five this morning. He knew it was Willy's birthday because it was in the book, which he's read three times.

When Willy came with my wake-up coffee, he was wearing his pointy birthday hat. Is it possible that he's learning to play?

He's strung some small lights outside for Christmas. They hang in a crazy drunken fashion but I quiet my tongue. Better we have them in an awkward display rather than as it was before for me, with only my lonely little tree.

Mission library said they'll buy two *The Willy Stories* books. I can't believe it. Willy and me in the library!

I insisted that he come with me to get his present — a waterproof jacket. I also treated him to dinner at Joseph's. He said he felt like a kept man. Later my friend asked him what it felt like to be a kept man and he said, "Pretty good: I could do with more of the same."

Thinking "curved"

6.

Silence

How do I get used to it? Will I ever get used to it? It can hang so heavy. Without a radio or conversation in the truck, there's a vacuum and we seem to be worlds apart. Doesn't he know how unhappy it makes me?

Am I being unfair? He always had silence before he took up with me. He said he was never lonely and perfectly happy with his own company. He has an aversion to idle chit-chat. But I think idle chit-chat has a place. It keeps the wires humming and it oils the wheels of humanity.

There are different kinds of silence of course. Some are spiritual and there's wonder in that. Silence is not a bad thing in itself, but if it goes on for hours and repeated every day and night, it gets hard to bear.

I wonder if he really isn't monk-like, craving the world to be shut out and needing to hold onto his own thoughts. I'd like to ask monks if they really want absolute silence. Maybe they use it as a penance. They do chant their prayers. I know Willy doesn't hold with that business. Figures it's not doing the world any good, chanting by themselves.

Silence. I longed for it when our house was always so busy with children. But when I was on my own I couldn't stand the nothingness, had to have the radio on for company.

Willy's hearing isn't good and it's too wearing to get people to repeat words over and over. Perhaps this has contributed to his preference for silence.

Protein.

W. "They've discovered there is more protein in the blood of people with Alzheimer's disease."

D. "Is it because they eat more meat than usual?"

W. "They don't know. They forgot if they did eat a lot of protein. I'd better not eat it so I can remember what I forgot!"

Unknown territory

I've been talking to him about a documentary on TV about the sloth. He's obviously not listening.

D. "I bet you don't know what I've been talking about."

W. "I don't understand what you're saying."

D. "What an excuse! You just don't want to listen to me."

W. "No. No. I just can't get my brain around unknown territory."

7.

Energy efficiency dragon

Yes, that's what he is — a blasted dragon about turning the thermostat down or lights off.

This lady was coming to buy five *The Willy Stories* books. Her mother in Calgary had snitched her copy. She belonged to a book club. Kind of neat because they discussed books of authors they hadn't heard of before.

I told her on the phone, she'd distinguish our house by the outside light being on. I heard Willy come in and I stood at the top of the stairs because I KNEW he'd reach for the light switch to turn it off. I shouted down, "I'm leaving it on because someone is coming." And he says, "You can't see it on in the sunlight."

I get agitated because I can sense his vibes needing to switch the thing off. We've had this out so many times. When I turn up the thermostat (in extreme frost bite circumstances) I tell him to allow me the decision to turn it low or not. I confess sometimes I do forget and feel I've let myself down, so to speak. But I hate when he follows me around turning these things off.

It sounds as if I'm complaining about a small condition, but an artist senses what another person feels. I know the steam rises in his head when matters are not according to his mandate.

8.

April 27, 1995

Two crated works arrive back from the Taos juried show. Large parcel broken and wood slats missing. I'm mad at the man who made these fragile excuses for crates. The Plexiglas on the smaller painting is cracked. So be it. What a business it is sending these entries to shows. What a lot of money for crating and sending, returning and paying for the entry fee and the dissembling fee at the other end.

I see there's a catalogue enclosed and sit down on the studio couch to read it, checking on other artists who were chosen. As I read, I feel my chest fill with pride. Such illustrious company! Dorothy is in the list too. This is great. Such a reputable show. Juror writes of being tired of same old landscapes — wants to see "fresh and meaningful work" says watercolor has had the stigma of inoffensive paintings. He wants a show of strength.

Hooray! Hooray! I feel good and go to tell Willy who's eating his breakfast.

D. "It's an excellent catalogue Willy."

W. "Did they sell any?"

D. "I don't know. That isn't the point anyway."

W. "What's the use to go to all that expense and trouble if they don't sell."

D. "It doesn't matter if they sell. The main thing is that it's on my resume for my reputation. Don't you see that I need to have proof that even though I didn't go through all the right channels and even though I had ten children, I can stand with the best in the USA."

W "What best? There are millions in the USA. Only a small percentage entered."

D. (chest now in fighting stance.) "Why don't I learn? It doesn't matter what you say, you can't detract from this moment of pride. I've received affirmation that my work can stand with the best. I wouldn't be proud if it was conservative jurying with routine work, but this show is extremely professional."

W. "What good does it do you: you didn't sell."

D. "Why don't you understand. Selling is a by-product. In the art world there aren't certificates to say you've reached a higher standard, only the acceptance into these acknowledged top juried shows. So this stamp of approval is as good as it gets."

I guess this is the day — April 27th, 1995, that I allow myself to know I really am a good artist.

in order.

I can take the car out without him saying, "You'll wear it out if you beep using it!"

I can walk to Gardenworks and sit there for a while, drinking in the colors of the flowers and seeing doo-dads which the gardeners use to enhance their gardens. Arbors, fountains and wrought iron seats.

I'll probably try out new recipes and stay up really late. Buy a cordless phone to have next to my bed at night and watch what I want on TV without those massive whale sighs of disapproval. I'll have my classic music tuned up louder and I'll stay in the library for hours.

I won't walk as far as we usually go.

But I'll miss him. I realize we're bonded now.

9.

Christmas letter to my friends 1995

We moved into this senior complex last February and we like it fine. I've got lots of bright space to work in with double closets and my own bathroom (always a priority with me). Everything's looked after in the building so Willy is off the hook.

We're overlooking the highway so it's noisy in summer. On the other hand, we have a good view of Mount Baker, can walk to the stores and the glassed-in balcony separates the activity somewhat.

The Willy Stories, which I self-published a few years ago, is now to be published by Portage & Main Press in Winnipeg. It will be called *Willy and Me.*

The Life series book is being worked on by the publisher and the contract states it will be done by September 1996. There'll be a traveling show of the paintings and reproductions for sale.

I've recently discovered that I can write fiction - thanks to Paul St. Pierre who ran a course here. And I've written some poetry.

Willy and I chug along - he making me furious one minute then warming to his sweetness the next. Ah well! Isn't that reality in life?

Won't write more because I'm squeezed for time, like everyone else on this planet (except for Willy of course -the stinker).

10.

Willy: May 5, 1997, California

This morning Willy left for parts unknown and California. He caught the six-thirty morning train to Vancouver where he will board a Greyhound bus. It is one hundred and fifteen dollars return.

This is how he vacationed when he was single, committed to no man or woman; talking to strangers, hearing their stories and observing — always observing.

He has this Danish friend in southern California, he has known him since they were at logging camps or oil sites together. Bert lives close to a simulated Danish town called Soulvagne. Willy loves the authentic smorgasbord and the true Danish bakery items they have there. It brings back memories of his homeland . Bert and Willy spend many hours playing chess, being on the same level of proficiency.

Porridge was waiting for me when I got up this morning, in the same bowl he has served to me for the seven years we have been together. I will have to make my own until he returns. When is that? I don't know. I bit back the questions because I wanted him to feel free. I did, however, tell him, "If I don't hear from you after a week, I will alert a posse."

He told me to rotate the plant pots every week, so I figure it will be two weeks. I think I should be congratulated for not pushing the point. Funny. If I go anywhere, he has to know the exact minute when I will return.

And how do I feel with him not here? It helps there's an art show in Mission which I'm involved in. My son is coming tomorrow and a friend comes Thursday. I can get on with art work until nine at night without feeling I'm neglecting Willy.

For some strange reason, I feel like cleaning up generally and putting things in order.

I can take the car out without him saying, "You'll wear it out if you beep using it!"

I can walk to Gardenworks and sit there for a while, drinking in the colors of the flowers and seeing doo-dads which the gardeners use to enhance their gardens. Arbors, fountains and wrought iron seats.

I'll probably try out new recipes and stay up really late. Buy a cordless phone to have next to my bed at night and watch what I want on TV without those massive whale sighs of disapproval. I'll have my classic music tuned up louder and I'll stay in the library for hours.

I won't walk as far as we usually go.

But I'll miss him. I realize we're bonded now.

11.

A different Willy 1998

A few years ago one of my children was in financial trouble.

A parent gets torn apart in these cases. People say, "Let them find their own way out. It doesn't help to rescue them." But I fret and vacillate from wanting to relieve their suffering to thinking of myself, now I'm in my seventies.

I had sleepless nights and paced the floor and Willy knew I was much troubled

I've written about Willy saving on all he buys and I may have given the impression he is a tight-wad. But it's just that he wants good value for his money. Unbeknown to me, he sent two thousand dollars to the one in question. It solved the problem.

Many times he has been generous. Sending me to England or on a painting course in the States. Other times, giving quietly where he thinks it will help.

When I found out what he had done, I was so moved, I wanted to do something to show that I loved him. What to do? Should I suggest we get married? That took some chewing over and I didn't really want to do it. I may have felt soft and loving at the time but I can get plenty mad at him. I might regret it — or he might.

I finally went to him and said, "If you want to visit Denmark, I'll come with you. I'll take some money from the term deposit and pay my own way. You can visit where you lived as a boy. We could visit your mother's grave, then go to your brother in Sweden."

"My *mudder* doesn't have a gravestone, they burned her," he said.

Two years have passed since my suggestion. Our relationship has been dicey, maybe helped by me buying a computer, at which I spend hours every day.

I bring up the idea again.

"I haven't got a passport and they cost sixty dollars," he says.

"We can start by getting one."

"I'd have to get geared up to pay sixty dollars."

"If we're going, I need to know how much it will all add up to and what time of the year so I don't make commitments ahead. How long would we stay and where would we sleep?"

"Everything over there is a horrendous price."

"It's once in a lifetime thing and we could make it fun. I'd like to see Tivoli Gardens in Copenhagen as well."

I figure the trip would do many things. He'll use his language, which changes his conversation into an exuberance not obvious when he speaks English.

He'll relive his roots and we'll share this.

He'll be showing me everything and I'll be on the receiving end.

He'll see his family again.

And I'll try desperately hard not to be always seeking out art galleries.

"Well?" I ask in an effort to pin him down, "what time of the year?"

"May would be best," he says.

Good! At last we have something definite. It's now August 1998 and I can look forward to this treat. And maybe it will pull us closer together.

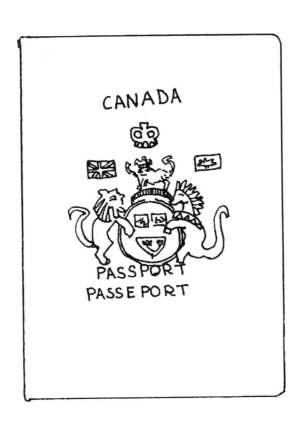

12.

Christmas letter to my friends 1998

We're off to Hawaii again, so I'm getting Christmas mail done early. Looking forward to the holiday but not the drive to get to Vancouver airport.

The sequel to *Willy and Me* is now complete ($14.95 if you want one) and now my autobiographical stories are almost ready to go to the publishers. It won't be wasted because, if nothing else, Mission Archives is collecting all my documents.

Willy and I have been together almost ten years now. He hasn't altered in appearance since I first met him. He has all his teeth (except four front teeth which were perfectly good but he was told he'd look better with them taken out). What remains of his hair is still dark brown. He has bulging muscles and legs like a robot, not feeling stress even after he cycled eight hundred kilometers to Kamloops and back this summer. He's still contrary and is now seventy-eight years old.

We have a commuter train, which goes to Vancouver early morning returning early evening. At Christmastime I go on what they call a Santa train with all the children and Santa, singing carols. I can visit all the big city shops and get a feeling of Christmas.

I took some time to adapt to a computer. I have an e-mail address.

I will be showing my paintings in a Whistler gallery.

Merry Christmas from Doris and Willy.

Section 13.

New millennium

1.

Willy's father

He died when Willy was seven years old. "What kind of father was he?" I ask, "did he get angry with you?"

He laughs, remembering. "We were dressed in the fad of the day, in our Sunday clothes and we went for a walk in the bush with father. There was a big puddle and we fell in it. Our pants, boots and socks were all wet. My father took them off and dried them as well as he could because he could never let *mudder* know he hadn't taken good care of us."

He remembered his father holding his arms and swinging him around and around. And that his father had curly hair.

Comic life.

Coffee time in the morning and we're talking about strokes.

D. "If you or I have a stroke, make sure you remember a code for communication. Sometimes people can't speak but they can blink their eye-lids. So, we'll have one blink for 'yes' and two blinks for 'no'."

W. "I don't want to be learning all that. I think its easier to concentrate on prevention."

2.

The same old ...

I feel I must warn him about my knees. I don't want to, because it's just adding to the list of my body breakdowns! Makes me feel I'm coming to the end of being independent. I must gird up to accept needing Willy's help. Both knees are acting "loose" and out of control and there's a burning ache.

It helps to live in this senior's condo where some women have replacements for their joints and recover with alacrity and good nature.

It was on our morning walk when I introduced the topic.

"Willy, I'm afraid my knees are giving me trouble."

The response is as expected. It is as it always is.

"It's your own fault. You don't take care of yourself. I know how you should behave, but you don't take any notice of what I tell you."

Blood rushes to my temples and the familiar chunk of iron materializes in my chest.

"Can't you, just for once, respond in a better way?" I hear my voice gain volume. "Don't you realize I feel badly about becoming a trial to you? Can't you stop using these confessions of mine to expound how perfect you are. You lecture me every time I am vulnerable. I want you to say 'I'm sorry about it Doris.' I'd feel better if you showed compassion. To my mind, you can't love me if you can turn my sorrow into a platform for your preaching."

"Nobody's told me that before. I don't do no harm to anyone."

"Again I'll tell you, you haven't lived with anyone. Anyone else can just walk away. And I'm a woman, we think differently from males."

And I tell him the joke.

A man had been very saintly. God, wishing to reward him, came to him and said, "My son, you have lived according to my word. I would like to grant you a wish. What will you wish for?"

The man thought for a while and said, "I don't want to go to the airport and wait for flights every time I want to go to Hawaii. How about making a bridge from the US to Hawaii?"

And God replied, "My son, we don't have enough concrete to make a bridge that long. The currents are too strong and there isn't an engineer to work it out. No, your wish is impossible. Choose another one."

The man said, "Well, I've been having trouble trying to understand what my wife is on about. I wish to be able to understand her."

And God thought for a while, then said, "Er. How soon do you want that bridge built?"

Willy laughed. But did he really hear it all? (His hearing is often in question.) If he did, did he understand? This is the thing! He blanks me out.

And it's the old recording of our arguments. Same old incriminations. Same old, "it seems you'd be happier on your own," from me.

One day, he's going to take that idea and go. As I type this, panic quivers around me.

I had enough sense to tell him I've had good years with him in the past while. But I had to be clear that these put-downs gather like needles in my pincushion heart until there's no room for any more and I have to clear them out.

"They're not put-downs, they're just facts," he says. "I do everything I can."

So I quote once more — it's always once more — the man I knew who came to me with these words: "I gave her everything," he told me, "I gave her a lovely house, jewelry and a car. I did all her errands and did the grocery shopping, I even made wonderful dinners for her. I don't understand why she left me!"

Can one possibly explain to a practical man that a woman needs things money can't buy? Especially compassion and tenderness when you might have to have two knee replacements.

3.

Shrimp-colored roses: January 2000

He'd bought five pink tulips only a few days ago. Why was he presenting me with a dozen shrimp-colored roses?

He lowered his eyes and pushed the bouquet towards me. A label fixed into a transparent three-pronged holder read, "Happy Anniversary. To dear Doris with all my love."

And I didn't know what it was an anniversary of. We've never had a wedding ceremony and we met in September. I know I have bemoaned the fact that we have no date to celebrate like other couples. So I stood holding the flowers, trying to figure it out.

"It's been ten years," he said.

And then I twigged. Ten years since the first time we had sex!

We went on our walk and came to Superstore. As I too wanted to acknowledge our "anniversary," I bought a fancy Hazelnut torte cake. As I was going through the cashier desk with it, a young boy, about seven years of age, standing in line behind me said, "Is that for a birthday?"

"No," I said, it's for a wedding anniversary." I hesitated. "Well, it's really not...."

I suddenly realized what I was going to say and shut up.

"Congratulations," said the seven year old, "I hope you will be happy."

How sweet of one so young, in these inconsiderate times, to want to join in one of life's celebrations - even if it is marriage in disguise.

4.

Christmas shopping with Willy

Christmas shopping with Willy doesn't mean *he* will do any shopping and this is our procedure.

Two nights ago he said, "I will be giving you a stipend for your Christmas gift." A stipend? What is a stipend? I look it up in the dictionary and it says, "Wages given in return for services rendered." How big is a stipend, I wonder?

"We will go to Abbotsford so you can have a better selection," he said.

I didn't need anything and couldn't figure out what I could get that I haven't got already. He smiled that knowing, crooked smile of his and told me he had no qualms that between then and shopping time, I would think of something. Well, it's true; I could do with a leather purse. I got one recently from the Thrift store but the lining was torn. After I fixed that, the clasp broke.

Then there's the matter of a nice brooch. Women don't seem to wear them like they used to. From the bottom reaches of my mind, there surfaces the digital camera for $1,400 I saw the other day. I try to suppress images of the salesclerk demonstrating all the new things you can do with it. Maybe I could use it to find and record abstract shapes for use in my painting?

This morning, after he had put his bread in the oven and I set the timer for the required baking period, he handed me a bunch of paper money. When I counted the stipend it came to $600. Wowee! I turned him to face me and said, "Do you give this with love? Because if you don't, I don't want it."

"Yes, I do," he said and brushed my lips which could be construed as a kiss.

Having had my breakfast of ground flaxseed, soy flour and rolled oats, and taken the sweet smelling bread from the oven, we take off for Abbotsford with me driving. I'm a nervous driver but feel better if Willy sits next to me.

"Why is that?" he asks and I tell him, "If I'm going to have an accident, I'd feel better if you're with me." He rolls his eyes.

"You said you want a purse," he says after we get to the mall, "here is a purse store. So choose one."

"But I want to see other stores. They may have better ones." I say.

He doesn't understand. He relieves me of my bulky winter coat, then charges down to the end of the mall, me behind, trying to keep up with him.

"There's a jewelry store," he says, "look in there for your *broooch*."

There's only three in the whole place. One had gold circles and cost a hundred dollars, but I wasn't enthused. The sad-looking, red-haired saleslady shook her head from side to side and apologized for only having three examples. "Cycles come and go," she said in a hopeless voice, "and you're just not in the right cycle, wanting a brooch."

"Well?" said Willy sitting on a bench outside the store.

"I'm not in the right cycle," I tell him.

We return to the purse shop and I find a black leather one with umpteen pockets and zippers for fifty dollars. I buy it and think, oh boy! I can put more towards the digital camera. Yes, guilt about some families starving while I buy a camera, is receding from my brain.

I look in a large store in case they have a buyer of women's clothes who relates to my taste. But no. I remember Willy needs slippers. I don't know where he got the ones he wears at home but I'm ashamed of them. They're made of something resembling corduroy. The color was dark blue but has been washed to an ashy hue, complicated by splashes of bleached spots. (Willy has a fondness for bleach.) The heels are flattened and the fronts have stretched beyond anything resembling a slipper. I buy him a pair because his eightieth birthday is on the 18th December.

He's pacing back and forth at the front entrance of the store so I do the sensible thing and suggest he try them on. I brace for a lecture not to buy him anything, but he is compliant. The slippers are too tight. We go to change them and the situation turns out well because he says he would prefer the other style and to my greatest surprise, he appears pleased. Now that is not to say he will ever wear them, but at least I'll feel better, knowing he has a decent pair.

"Your *broooch*, you've got to get a *broooch*," he says.

We go down to Sears. Everyone's chatting and laughing and discussing presents together and here I am, chasing after him as he charges down to Sears. I pass a kiosk laden with Asian embroidered tablecloths. How many hours have hands worked to make these intricate designs? Wonder if they involved children? I think of the TV documentaries where youngsters sit in hovels packing cigarettes or weaving rugs. I should part with some of my stipend to buy a tablecloth. But I don't and hurry to catch up with Willy. I call to him to sit on a bench while I buy calendars from the bookstore. I'd love to browse through the books, but mustn't expect everything. I buy one on angels, mostly derivative of paintings through the ages. Then I see one with the pictures of Maud Lewis. I can't get her out of my heart.

She was a disabled woman and nobody wanted her.

Eventually she married a mentally retarded man and lived with him in a double-garage-sized cottage in Digby county, Nova Scotia. Her mother had shown her how to paint.

Maud would sit by the window and recapture on canvas, scenes she had grown up with. Even the walls and ceiling of the cottage had flowers, birds and butterflies painted on them. She sold the canvases for two dollars and fifty cents each. These works were light-hearted and made you smile. Her husband collected the money. But never mind, she did what she loved to do.

I wish I could have a purity of spirit such as Maud had. But I haven't and that's that. I buy one calendar for my friend who does have her spirit and one for me.

Sears has some brooches in boxes with the name Anne Klein on it. While I look for one that's not too garish, Willy spies a watch strap for my ten dollar watch. It's $4.99, and I say "okay" when he suggests the saleslady attach it for me.

The brooch is silver colored with rhinestones. It'll do for over the Christmas season, so this is bagged as well.

I want to look at the ladieswear here. Willy faces me with the look that says, "now pay attention." He will sit at the entrance to the store. Am I sure I know which door that is? Am I sure I won't go through another exit? My blood-sugar is warning me it's low and I'll have to eat. There's a coffee shop and lots of people having coffee and treats. Willy says, "We'll drive home." In all the years I've been diabetic he still doesn't understand, if I say I need to eat now, I mean now.

So I get coffee and a cream-cheese bagel and sit at a little metal table. Willy will not buy a coffee. Christmas shopping doesn't mean one will be lax and buy a coffee other than at McDonald's. He comes to sit opposite me. He has found this excursion very wearing.

We drive home through the valley, the blueberry fields glow with bushes in their winter mantles of magenta. The distant mountains are navy blue, iced with a white as pure as Maud's spirit.

The smell of Willy's bread greets us as we open the apartment door. I transfer the contents of my old purse into the new, count the money I came home with and turn my thoughts to digital fun!

5.

Christmas letter 2000

I'm now an abstractionist in my paintings. Never thought I would be but we change and grow beyond where we thought we would be.

The past year has brought about a new understanding of — as Willy terms it — "the downward stretch." I was living with stress and my blood pressure confirmed this. I'm trying to go slow and to not feel guilty when I don't do the things I used to do.

High point of the year was traveling to the red rocks in Utah and Arizona with a fellow painter. I wanted to see what Sedona's vortexes were all about. Instead we found Zion park with its incredible energy and power. Everywhere I looked in the rocks, people and faces were formed by the crevasses of the rocks. I painted small paintings of them and the outcome was a book titled *Stories of the red rock people.*

I got an evaluation of last year's memoir book, *You do it whichever way you can,* from American Writers' Digest. We got top marks except in the marketing category. They said we could have a book about a war bride and mother *or* an artist but not both together. Book sellers don't know where to slot it!

Willy is still Willy and cycles every day, sometimes to Nanaimo and back. Someone asked him, "Don't you get tired?" and he said, "How can you get tired if you're sitting down?" He'll be eighty in December. I'm going to throw him a party.

I think of my friends throughout the year but at this time, you are closer than ever to me. Merry Christmas.

New millennium: 2000

I'm in the doctor's office again. What a way to welcome the new millennium! Same old recurring cough but this time bringing up blood. I know the response will be the same, "Blood is only due to coughing so much. You'll just have to wait until it gets better."

I cough so hard I wet my pants. Does this mean I have to have the operation, which has been pending for years? When I told Willy, he said, "So they're going to stuff you shut!" Oh dear! I don't want to think about myself like that.

Well, we've had ten years. He's still going strong at seventy-nine years of age while I'm definitely the lame duck. I joked one day, telling him "You can trade me in." Yesterday he directed the same phrase to me and it didn't seem funny when he said it.

Other seniors deal with these events, then why do I find it so hard? I try to find a safe cave where I can sort these things out and tend to my wounds. Can I with gracious spirit, knowingly allow Willy to find sex elsewhere?

He didn't link up with me to play nurse. As I'm three and a half years younger than him and having had many children, I'm sure he thought I was open (pun) to constant sex.

My once luscious hair, now clogs the comb with hundreds of spider web silver threads. My stomach muscles refuse to do as they're told. And now — will I have to rely on Depends?

Making matters worse, my paintings are disappointing. After all these years, instead of becoming easier to accomplish what I want from them, they thumb their nose at me and drag themselves into murkiness. And always people are telling me to go back to the way I was painting before. There is no reception for my murky work. I feel I'm sinking in quicksand with no one to extend a hand to help me out of it.

I read all these articles and books on how it's good to go through rough periods. "You'll come through stronger," they say. "You need these agonizing times to appreciate the upbeat ones. It is a learning experience," they say.

Well, I feel I'm due to see a rainbow anytime now. I want to stop coughing and hope the new millennium will send my rainbow soon.

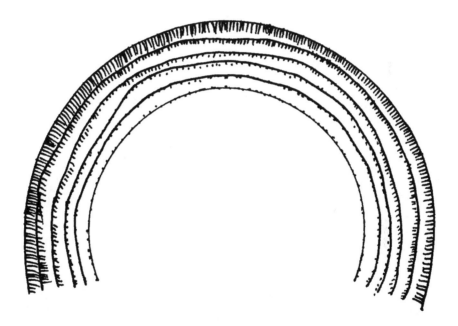

7.

Willy is eighty years old

Ten years ago today I had a combined house-warming party and birthday party for Willy when we moved into Rose Avenue house. And today I have invited the sixteen people in our complex to celebrate with him, his eightieth birthday.

He hasn't changed in that time. Still the Spartan. Still cycles all day, every day. Still hasn't an ounce of fat on him. Well, maybe he's mellowed a bit in our relationship. I never cry anymore. There was one point when it was getting to be a habit with him to make cutting remarks towards me. I was feeling unhappy, unloved and tearful. He came to me one day when I was crying in the bedroom and said he'd better go to live somewhere else. "I've never knowingly hurt anyone," he said, "and I can't bear it that I'm hurting you. This situation isn't good."

Panic. What was I doing being overly sensitive to what he says. Oh God! I must take stock of what a gift we have. I held him close and begged him to listen to me. "We're so lucky with everything. We've both got to try harder to overcome this one problem. I will try not to take your remarks so personally."

"And I'll curb my tongue, I promise," he said.

He came to lie beside me and we felt it was a new beginning. Yes, it worked but he's so careful with what he says now, I think he lives in fear of that happening again. He's always preferred if I get mad at him, rather than see my tears. Told me, it tears him apart.

Yes it's been ten years since the Danish lady cooked the Danish specialties for him and all the people came and it was wonderful.

For this birthday I've ordered the traditional Danish celebratory cake. It's made with almond paste. There are about twenty rings of this cake graduating from dinner plate size to the smallest knob. It stands about two and a half feet tall. Willy will go to the Danish bakery to get it and I pray there won't be any snow on the roads.

Well he's just so proud of it when he comes through the door with the cake in three separate boxes and he puts it all together, inserting tiny Canadian and Danish flags in the layers. I've made small sandwiches, sun-dried-tomato squares, cheese balls and apricot squares. He readies the wine and I get the coffee and tea going.

Willy's brother and family phone from Sweden and send flowers. "They paid good money for those," he says. My children send him flowers.

Everyone comes in the apartment now and even though the chairs are close together, everyone finds a place and they're giving Willy cards and hugs and there's a very warm feeling. Eventually I read the story of his birthday, ten years ago and the visitors love it. The highlight of the party is his Danish cake.

The party's over and all have left the apartment. His cheeks are flushed, whether from the wine and schnapps or the good feeling, I don't know, but it's one of those times when everything has gone right. When he kisses me, I know he was pleased with it all.

8.

Schnappes

It's close to Christmas and we call in to the liquor store for my sherry. In England, it's a tradition to have sherry for Christmas.

I figure I'll buy Willy some Schnappes for a surprise Christmas gift. He's at the other end of the store so I think it's safe to ask the sales clerk with a whisper, "Where is the Schnappes?"

"You mean peppermint schnappes?" she asks.

"No. No. The Danish kind."

"You mean Acquavit?"

"Yes, that's it."

She leans over the counter, cups her hands to her mouth and yells to a cashier, "Where's the Acquavit?"

The cashier yells back, "You want Acquavit?"

I put my finger to my lips and say "Shhh!"

The clerk turns to the cashier and says "Shhh!"

The cashier responds with a loud "Shhh!"

Now the audience in the store has come to a halt. Bottles stop clinking, cashiers stop serving, customers hold their breaths for the next outcome. All get the message — it's a Christmas present. Willy is immersed in reading beer-bottle labels and doesn't notice a thing. The clerk takes me to the place where the bottles are and the customers resume their business.

Acquavit is twenty-seven-fifty. Of course, after Christmas he'll go to check what I paid for it and think I'm stupid, but hey, it's Christmas and that is that.

Siamese twins

We're on the chesterfield. Willy says, "Do you want to go for a walk?" and I tell him, "No thanks, I've gone far enough today."

"We have a split relationship," he says.

"How do you mean?"

"One walks one way and the other the other," he says.

"But we touch bases," I say.

But I think he means he wants a Siamese twin arrangement and I've been operated on for that.

Needing Willy

"I respect you but
want to be separated
till I sort myself out."
I read the note on
the Christmas card
from my daughter.
Where is Willy?
He's later than usual.
doesn't he sense
I have need of him?
Even if it IS his birthday,
I need him to listen
to my pain.
Oh! What if something
happened to him?
Without him, how could I bear
these arrows
that pierce the bullseye
in my heart?
If I couldn't tell him about
my failure as a mother,
how could I survive?
But failure?
How did I fail?
By being compassionate

during a family crusade?
I only know
how to be me.
I only know
how my inner voice
directs me to behave.
The door opens.
It's hard to wait until
he washes his hands,
he's had another flat tire
in his bike.
I point to the wording
on the card and he says,
"It's all right, she just
needs time, that's all."

Willy anecdotes

Night noises

"How was your night?" Willy asks as he brings coffee at eight-twenty in the morning. Not eight nineteen nor eight twenty-one but on the needle point of eight-twenty.

This question starts something going, explosive or entertaining, I never know which it will be. Examples:

Doris." I heard this continuous noise last night. Something like a train in middle distance only it didn't fade away, it went on for hours and I couldn't figure out what it was."

Willy. "We should have a phone line for mysterious noises, "dial nine one two and say, "Hello. I hear this strange noise." They will reply, "It is nothing; go back to sleep. Go back to sleep."

Cold or uplifting?

Doris. "Can you see Mount Baker today?"

Willy. "I never look there. Why would I want to look at something so cold and miserable?"

I rise to defend my spiritual icon.

Doris. "How can you say it's miserable? It gives pleasure and means a lot to people like me."

Willy. "Ha! I never hear anyone talk about Mount Baker."

Doris. "That shows the difference in the type of people we associate with. My kind feel it's important in their lives; pure and uplifting, almost holy. It makes a difference to my days and I never tire of its moods and colours."

Liking a job
Doris. "What job did you like the best in your working days?"
Willy. "Like? There's nothing to like about a job. You worked to support the belly that's all!"

Repeats
W. "The ice-*cycles* are melting.

On his own
Walks with himself.

Surprises
I cannot take the heat in June and July. Because it's cooler in the morning, I get up earlier and after breakfast, we go for our walk.

This morning there is an English-style drizzle of rain and we put on our rain jackets.

I have been having trouble with diarrhea. We are close to the hospital where I know I can pop in to a washroom if necessary. As we come close to it, I say to Willy, "I have to go to the bathroom."

"What already?"

"What do you mean, already?"

"We've only just left home!"

My mouth draws to a tight line. "Do you want me to go into details? Why do you question me? The other day you had to call into Superstore to go. Did I question you?" Oh! he gets my blood pressure pulsing!

I made it in time. We continue our walk past where a large shaggy golden-haired dog is usually chained to a long rope.

"I haven't seen the dog for a long while," I say to Willy.

"Somebody probably shot him," he says.

Negative. Always negative, I think to myself. How do I stand it?

We come to our little park next to the old people's care home. A bird sings, just about busting his chest with the joy of it. I don't even know if Willy can hear it. But he surprises me.

"That bird is singing his morning song because of the rain. He's happy because he's got a belly full of worms!" he says.

Naming paintings
A painting sits in front of me, featuring a dinner-plate sized circle and I don't know what title to put on it. I call Willy to come.

"What will I call this Willy?"

"Why do you worry after you've painted it. Why don't you figure out a title first, then paint to fit?"

"Be serious. What does it convey to you?"

"Colors. Call it Colors."

"That's no use, it's too general."

"Call it *Couleurs* — that sounds elegant."

"No. No! What is round?"

"Just call it *Round series #1*. Then you can do a square series and then a triangle series."

"No. Think what is round besides the earth and the moon."

"Cookies."

"You can't call a painting *Cookies*.

"Then call it *Oreos*."

Opinion of my latest painting

My abstract painting is propped against the wall and I ask him, "What do you think?"

W. "There isn't a market for that kind of thing."

D. "Leaving that aspect out of it, do you like it?"

W. "I don't know what to make of it."

D. "Can't you just enjoy the peaceful feeling it gives out?"

W. "I want to see a painting which shows something real. I've never seen anything like this and I have nothing to relate it to. It's created from nothing — just your brain."

I smile. Without intending, he's given me a compliment."

Spider

We take a short cut to Superstore on our walk. We go down the slope of a small hill with bushes growing on it to reach the parking lot.

I'm halfway down when Willy yanks me backwards. In front of my face, a spider has spun his web connecting two branches. Its occupant is in the middle, his bronze back gleaming, dew decorates the silk threads. The tableau is backlit with the sun. I clamber around it as Willy says. "You have to watch out for these things. That was a *web-site!*"

More surprises

It's usually me who points out interesting items on our walks. He never allows himself to acknowledge them. He's perfected this utterance which could be interpreted as either yes or no as he keeps his head down all the while. But the other day he surprised me as we cut through a gravel parking lot. Struggling clumps of grass push through the small stones and I've never seen anything of account there. But this day, he pulled me to stop to look down. "It is a wild-strawberry plant," he said.

Just when I'm ready to despair of him communicating, he shows me how in tune with nature he is and all my pointing out to him is as familiar to him as his stock channels on TV.

Finding things

His "finds" in ditches and roadside bushes are legendary. It appalls me to know items, which are hardly worn, are pitched with carelessness and wastefulness. The other day he came home with a good pair of gloves and said, "It's not often you find such quality in the ditch. But it's non-negotiable and you can't exchange them."

It's all in how you look at it

Doris. "Today is the longest day of the year."
Willy. "Or the shortest night — as the Frenchmen say!"

Different words

He calls glow worms *Lighting flies*. I love it.

Humour

Mosquito bites balloon up with swelling on his skin. I'm sympathetic when I see yet another on the back of his large hand.

"Don't concern yourself," he says, "this one is only small, it must have been by an apprentice mosquito."

Supposition

Willy is back from his overnight cycle trip to Chilliwack with a black plastic bag to sleep on.

"Did you enjoy the trip? What did you see?" I ask.

"McDonald's have a nice new building and it has three washrooms. One for *womans* and one for men." The other, he tells me, "must be for gay people!"

Grace bestowed

We see a shimmering colored hummingbird. Willy says, "He has bestowed us with his grace."

Dinner at the Wee Chippie

Willy has coupons for the Wee Chippie restaurant. Two for one. Full meals are more than we can eat, so we order seniors servings. I tell him I will ask for a doggie bag for what we can't finish.

He says, "No. I've got it all figured out." He's attached the handle of a plastic bag to a button on his shirt. The bag hangs around his waist, similar to a horse's oat-bag.

We have our dinner and when the waitress is occupied and no one is looking, I get a signal from him, to scoop my excess french fries onto his plate. He then opens his jacket to sweep them into the plastic bag. He does up his jacket and now he can walk out of the restaurant without having lowered himself to ask for a doggie bag!

April 20th, 2001

On our walk to the doctor's office I see a garden with a giant splash of tulips. Fire red, salmon, and dusty-mauve colored specimens. "Look Willy," I say, "isn't that a beautiful sight."

"It's their last exclamation for Spring," he says.

When I come from my appointment (renewing prescription), he tells me while I was in there, he used his talents to find three pennies by the side of the road!

Down the home stretch

Third Hawaii

We go to sit in the aqua booth of ABC family restaurant. After I take off my jacket, he says, "We'll go to Hawaii for a holiday. How is that with you?"

"This is a surprise. When were you thinking of going?"

"The beginning of December. We could stay for two weeks this time but we wouldn't know what to do with ourselves for that long. What do you think?"

"Whatever you want Willy, it's your money so you should decide."

"Is the first of December okay with you?"

"It would be nice if we could go in January when it gets cold here."

"Well I'd like to get it over with. We'll go beginning of December."

And that's how we plan a holiday!

He gets an up-to-date Fodor's book on Hawaii from the library, another concise one on Oahu. He gets accommodation books from two different travel agents. Good for him, he has the patience to read the fine print and discovers bonuses or restrictions which I hadn't seen.

Finally he decides Outrigger Surf, three blocks from *Waikickie*. A warning flashes as I read, "for extra payment you can get upper floors to escape noise from busy street." But I don't mind street noise, it's the loud TVs, wild parties or domestic fighting which turns vacations into nightmares for me.

Instead of reading our nightly short stories, I read information on Hawaii from the library books and the spirit of their land comes back to me.

Recently I've had a longing ache to sit in a small Japanese garden and absorb the vibes away from my busyness. The Japanese have elegant taste in their dress, gardens and sacred places. I hope to find such a place in Hawaii.

But first, we have to get there and it is an obstacle course to reach the airport from Mission if one doesn't drive.

We agree to, get the local bus to the Greyhound bus stop, take the Greyhound to the Vancouver bus stop, and then catch the airport bus from there, hopefully in time for the plane to leave.

I have sworn to myself I will not panic. Willy, bless him, says if we miss the plane, we'll lose the money and that's that!

I am to have two hundred American dollars to spend. One hundred is my Christmas present, he doesn't want to be bothered anymore trying to think what to get for me.

November 2nd I get passport photo taken (it's awful), a money order for sixty dollars, and mail off the form. Willy goes on the Westcoast Express train to Vancouver to apply for his passport (his photo is beautiful) and returns a week later to pick it up. November 20th rolls around and I have not received mine. Willy pressures me to research the reason.

Meanwhile, I prepare small sheets of heavy watercolor paper, ready some paints and an artist's pen. No new luggage. Passport finally arrives.

Hurrah! Special friends insist on driving us to the airport on the day and we sail on roads, which thankfully are not snow covered.

On the plane I go to the toilet and wash my hands with the liquid soap in a bottle on the sink. It doesn't produce lather, stings my hands and feels sticky, there's a sharp smell of lemon. I don't have my glasses to read the label. I tell Willy, "What could it have been and why was it there if it wasn't soap?"

"Go rinse it off well," he said.

I return with my glasses and can see the label reads "Air purifier. Deodorant." The stewardess assures me there are no harmful chemicals in it.

When we arrive at Hawaii airport, Willy knows he will have to go to the luggage carousel for a greeting with a kiss and a lei. I laugh when it is a young man instead of an enticing female.

We recover from lack of sleep and are now waiting for the #4 bus from the University of Hawaii. I'm sitting on a cement seat while Willy paces back and forth on the sidewalk.

I had it in mind to visit the Japanese garden mentioned in the small travel book we have brought with us from the library. We've walked tens of miles around the campus, asking students for directions and getting into so many arguments, I've lost count of them.

"Why do you go running ahead while I'm checking the map? He had said.

"Because you take it in your head to stand in the blazing sun with no seat for me to sit on, while you peer forever at the thing!" I said, "You don't say, 'Let's sit in the shade and I'll try to figure things out,' like any sensible human being."

I had wanted to see art books in the University library but the receptionist told me this was the Sinclair library and I needed the Hamilton library. She drew a circle around the place on the campus map in red ink to make it clear.

It was worth the hike. While I devoured as many of the contemporary art books as I could within an hour, Willy sat like the Thinker statue, outside on a bench.

I had seen a cafeteria close to the library and checked the prices, which were reasonable. I relayed this to Willy but he was not going to be shaken from a sign he had seen a mile away advertising a ninety-nine-cent hamburger, so my weary feet plodded there with him.

After an agonizing search, we found the small Japanese garden tucked away behind Krause Hall. It felt so good to be there. I had appreciated all the sculptures and murals around the campus, but this was for me.

Ultramarine and pale pink waterlilies, volcanic stones, tall grasses and bamboo. Seats under an overhang and a fence all around. It was an oasis. Willy left me there to draw for two and a half-hours.

When he returned, I asked him what he had seen.

"Nothing," he said.

"Where did you go?"

"Nowhere."

"You were gone all that time, you must have been somewhere."

"I was sitting just around the corner from you all the time."

"You must contribute something to our holiday Willy," I said, "you can't beep saying "Nothing" and "I've seen it all."

"Well I have."

Our bus, we finally find out, doesn't run from this stop. We take another one to go back to the hotel.

Willy wants to mail cards from Hawaii to Jana, his niece in Sweden. There are many stamp machines but he doesn't want to pay more cents than necessary and if he doesn't put on enough, he says the post office will dump it. It seems there are only two post offices in Waikiki and he finds one in Royal Hawaiian shopping center. He also finds a card with a Santa under the palms and is delighted with it. I don't send any cards.

Willy has bought us bus passes and we take full advantage of them, hopping on and off without having to find the right change. We sit in seats for the elderly to the fore of the bus. It's usually crowded, stacked two and three deep, people hanging on to the rails for security against abrupt stops. Depending on the height of these persons, we have no choice but to stare at their buttocks, bellies or crotches. Willy has a good time. Bus seats are hard and finally I take a small cushion with me to make it easier for my back. The bed in the hotel is good, helped by the foam we brought with us. Willy squeezed it into my suitcase with lots of compression and I had to smile thinking if a security person would undo the zipper of my case, this thing would uncoil and jump out at him like a jack-in-the-box.

The bus trundles around the island and we can get off whenever we want. The sight of the aquamarine sea pounding and crashing, spewing foaming waves, will stay in my memory

We get off at Dole's pineapple plantation. We looked for the free pineapple juice sample, but couldn't find any. We share a Polish sausage bun and coffee and Willy buys a tray of pineapple chunks. We walk to the back garden and take photos of each other in the wooden cutouts, "just to prove we were there," he said.

When we go to return to Waikiki, we have to sit in the scorching sun at the bus stop. It is unusual because most stops are covered with a tile roof for shade. My straw hat is now battered and cracked but it's a necessity and I've given up caring what I look like. The bus comes and as we sit high, I can see the barren hills in the distance with pineapple fields below. I think about the Chinese who came here many years ago and wonder how they felt when they had to harvest those pineapples in unrelenting heat.

We go to the zoo again, me looking for the bleeding-heart dove, but he's behind a dense screen and won't expose his incredible scarlet heart breast for me. Willy gets tired of waiting for it to appear. Of course I spend most of a day in the art gallery and draw with my artist's pen. Also spend time at the library art book collection.

Our last day, riding on the bus, we hear a shout of "Willy! Doris!" and it's six people we know well from Mission. What a laugh. We go with them to Kodak's tourist show and enjoy the fun as we are supposed to do there.

Coming home, the plane is late and we miss our connection by bus to Mission. I phone my son who had offered to drive us home and he comes to pick us up at the train station and bring us home, thank goodness because we are sleep-deprived.

I had read in a library book, that long ago, before white men arrived in Hawaii, some healers had gone to Waikiki.

They spent their time healing and spreading their magic to the people there. Before leaving Oahu, they so loved the place, they dragged four massive boulders to the beach and in a ceremony, installed in the stones, their spirit of healing and magic. The stones are now surrounded with an iron fence and a plaque tells the story, but tourists don't seem to know about them.

Mainly because I've painted a boulder series, I went to take a photograph of these pieces of stone and I saw one had a tremendous face of an old man. When I came home I painted a depiction of this boulder and incorporated healing hands. It will go into my series.

Willy and the meat balls

Our seniors' complex is going to have a luau. Well, it's a fun thing and we're all going to wear muumuus and maybe do the hula dance.

I bought a muumuu on our last trip to Hawaii. Willy had given me American money and it was our last day and I had a hundred dollars left. We landed up in a shopping center with ten minutes before closing time. You'd better believe I was not returning home with extra money in my purse. On the rack of muumuus was one more to my taste and it cost $99.99 so I bought it. It's a lovely cobalt blue with patterns made of gold prints. The skirt has a deep frill at the bottom.

We're all to contribute to the dinner: Perry is making a poi dessert and Hawaiian salad and I volunteered my Hawaiian meatballs. The recipe calls for tiny meatballs, which have chopped almonds in them. I need to write a warning next to the pot, because some people have allergic reactions to nuts.

My son made this recipe when I visited him in Winnipeg. His mother-in-law had just come home from work and not being able to resist the smell of the meatballs cooking, she ate one and then two and then three. The rest of us were talking in the living room when we heard this awful strangling noise coming from the bathroom.

I thought a piece of the meatball must have stuck in her throat. She was turning blue and couldn't breathe. The only thing I knew was to get behind her and with my arms under her ribs, pull hard, release, then pull hard again.

Afterwards she told me she was allergic to almonds. I had used the wrong action for allergy but by luck, the sudden thrusts allowed the airwaves to open enough for her to breathe. "You saved my life," she said, "I have only ten minutes to get to a hospital and I would never have made it." She then turned to my son and yelled, "Who in the world would put almonds in meatballs!"

So as you can imagine, I'm careful about who tastes these morsels.

I have to pan-fry so many. Willy is doing nothing but sitting in his chair in the living room, staring into space, so I ask him if he will turn the first batch over and over to brown, while I prepare the rest.

"Why did you open your mouth to say you'd make them?" he asks while turning the tiny things with one of his large hands wrapped around a fork and the other around a spoon.

"They will enjoy them," I said.

"Make them large, that way we won't have to stand here so long."

"I want to be sure they're cooked through and they make a nicer presentation when they're small," I say.

"Flatten them, they'll cook faster," he says.

"Meatballs are supposed to be round," I say.

"I don't know why you do these things. You're only open for criticism."

"I'm used to criticism with my art."

"You don't eat art!" he says as he keeps turning the little things, "and what about e-coli. You never know about that!"

It's true. I begin to have visions of Mission's hospital overflowing with seniors from our complex suffering from e-coli. Headlines in local paper, "Doris Paterson made the Hawaiian meatballs which sent all the seniors from her complex to hospital. Investigation now proceeding." Willy is nowhere in my visions; he's gone on a bike trip to the Okanagan!

"Taste one Willy, they're good," I say.

He presses his lips together and refuses. But I know him. He'll wait till I'm not looking and pop one into his mouth. He doesn't want to be *told* to do things.

Finally, I'm able to take over his job and eventually the meatballs are secure in the freezer. "I'm sure glad that's over with," Willy says. To be fair to him, he only wants me to have it easy and not have my blood pressure rise.

We're going to have the luau outside on the lawn. How do I keep the recipe hot when I have to bring it from the third floor. And what do I put it in? I've given away all my crockpots. Well, I'll buy one. Did you hear that infamous word? Buy? I will have to use devious means to get one. Yes, I know we have no room to keep these things and I know I have just spent two weeks turfing non-essentials from the apartment because space is limited.

I'm ready to take the flack and I'll find a spot for it. I'm already thinking of reasons to have it. The complex has Christmas dinner and is in need of a crockpot. And it'll be handy if I have people for lunch or dinner the odd time time.

And while I'm at it, I'll buy Willy a jolly Hawaiian shirt, maybe it'll put him in the mood. Here's hoping there will be no allergic reactions and no hospital visits. Maybe even Willy will do the hula!

Painting the balcony floor: August 2001

I don't know why he's so interested in the state of floors and carpets! When he first came into my apartment, he was aghast at the blackened areas on my rug. "I'll rent a rug cleaner and fix this up," he said. The following day he arrived at the door with one of those hulking, noisy machines and set to work to erase every blemish. When he's at the helm of a machine of any kind, his adrenaline rises and he pushes the thing as if he's on the job site of some construction work.

I was forced out of my place while it all dried, remembering someone having told me, "Once you clean a carpet, it gets dirty quicker than before."

On my return, he took me to see places where he had dealt a blow to all black marks, looking for approval on my face.

Well, I can easily live with a few black marks but I stretched my mouth into a smile and didn't offer to pay for the machine because, after all, I hadn't asked for it.

It's been twelve years of using carpet spot remover and if I'm off for a few days, he will have rented that ruddy thing again. And now, it's the enclosed balcony which has gained his attention.

One time I was away he got this rubber paint to paint the floor and make it really waterproof. "It needs a week or so to set up," he said. This, as my shoes made a sucking sound when lifting them from the floor. That was two years ago and it has remained sticky.

Last week he said he was going to go over that rubber paint with some latex stuff. I couldn't help it. "From all my experience with paint," I said, "you can't paint water based over oil based paint. And I'm sure you're just going to make it worse."

But of course he didn't hear and started getting out rags, paint cans and an extended paint roller.

Now my white cupboard has to be moved to the dining room. All my excess wrappings and stuff for my art work will be spilled. He's moving his heavy green trunk to the hot-water tank room. This is the trunk we have lugged from place to place. The trunk which took my paintings to Chilliwack on the back of the truck. The trunk which must have had a fancy girl come out of it for a new year's party. I say that because there's a snow scene painted on the bottom with the words, "Happy New Year!"

He surprises me when he says he'll get rid of it now. Hooray. It's always taken up so much room and looks ugly. He's kept his tools and assorted clothes and shoes in there and I've been a good girl and never opened the lid to investigate as to what other treasures he might have there.

I think I'll beat a retreat to my studio and am glad my friend is taking me out later.

"Come and see how you do a job like this!" he calls.

The balcony floor has large dollops of paint in different areas. I can feel his joy at being back in action on the job site as he swings the pole with the roller on the end of it, dipping into one pile and spreading the paint. Dipping into another and doing the same. Yes. It looks like an efficient way... until... he steps backwards, putting his shoe plonk in the middle of one of these dollops. "Better get me a plastic bag," he said.

He puts his ruined shoe in the bag and pushes on with the designated work.

Later he tells me he threw the bag into the dumpster, then realized the shoe had his favourite inner sole in it. He had to climb into the dumpster to reclaim it.

The balcony looks very nice I must admit. Yes, it's still sticky, but as he tells me, "It takes a few weeks to set up!"

Wedding: November 7, 2001

Eleven years ago, my dentures needed relining and lying back in the long, brown plastic dentist's chair, I waited for the dentist to come in. The cubicle was all white and dental tools placed just so. A framed reproduction picture of Jesus holding a lantern and knocking on a closed door, hung on the wall.

The dentist came in with confident strides, snapping on transparent, disposable rubber gloves over his hands.

"I remember you," he said, maneuvering my mouth open to pop out my dentures, "you were going out with a Danish man. Did you marry him?"

"Well, we live together and consider ourselves married but haven't had the official ceremony," I said, flapping my toothless gums and sounding like a fish underwater.

"Either you're married or you're not," he said his face stern and accusing. "If you haven't participated in the sacrament of marriage, you're living in sin according to the word of the Lord. You're breaking the commandments." He readied the blue stuff to put in my mouth, timed the minutes necessary for it to set and eased it from my mouth.

It was the same old tug-of-war inside my chest. Anger at being lectured to and a nagging feeling from my upbringing that maybe he was right. I told myself, dammit — no. I didn't live by the God of the old testament. I figured if Jesus was living in these times, he'd smile on a couple in their seventies who had found each other. Certainly he wouldn't punish them.

When the dentist was through with me, I met Willy in the parking lot. My chest was hurting and tears fell down my face.

One day, Willy went to New Westminster and returned with a marriage license. He thrust it at me and said, "Now you can be a married woman."

I felt my cheeks flame with anger. How dare he humiliate me that way? Hasn't he heard of asking, "will you marry me?" I didn't expect him to go on his knees, but was he so crass not to recognize this would be a serious step for me? Was there absolutely no romance left in this Spartan example of a man?

I took the license and shoved it back to him. "Not on your life!" I said.

That was four years ago and we've been through some rocky times. However, since living in this apartment, we've solved most of the problems. I have my own section — the master bedroom for a studio with its attached closets and bathroom. I can make decisions in this area, jacking up the heat when I feel cold and putting on lights other than at his designated times.

During the years we've lived here, he transferred ownership to my name. I thought he wanted to have everything in order so he could leave me. I thought he was weary of my prodding him to socialize etc. and etc.

Two things happened simultaneously to make me think of the marriage business. I heard of a common-law partner dying and the other person not being acknowledged in the will. And there was a notice in my credit union's window to say they could issue marriage licenses. I inquire about the price (one hundred dollars) and the clerk gives me a list of marriage facilitators in Mission.

I watch his face when I ask if he thinks we should get married. This time I don't expect romance. There's a flicker of light across his face and then its gone, resuming the look of one ready for anything untoward, expecting the worst.

"Yes, we may as well," he says, "we'll need witnesses."

I tell him Marianne and Bert will come and we can get the license down the street for one hundred dollars.

"I only paid fourteen dollars for it before," he says.

"It's different now Willy."

Two days later.

From his desk drawer, he takes out his purse — like those carried by Victorian ladies, a long rectangle of threadbare damask material. There's a gold colored metal chain and two gold knobs which click together to close the purse.

He takes out two small gold, interwoven circles. "Are they earrings?" he asks me.

"No — they're your gold cufflinks," I tell him. His mother gave them to him.

He takes out a man's ring with a large, oval onyx stone.

"This was my father's wedding ring," he says, "my mother had the stone put in it and gave it to me. I've never worn it."

I tell him a wedding ring should be a plain gold band. I get the idea he'll be looking for sales on wedding rings, so I suggest he can get his and I'll get mine.

I tell him when he wears his ring, the waitresses won't flirt with him anymore because they'll know he's married.

Is there *really* a difference in our relationship or am I imagining it? Is he actually pleased about the whole thing? I'm not telling anyone we're getting married because we don't want a fuss. I don't want my children to have to take time from work and besides, there's a rift in the family. If they show their anger, I'd be hurt and it will spoil everything. It's only between Willy and me. I'll send a note to all after we're married.

Of course, Marianne and Bert know and when they told their visitors from Toronto, they clapped. I wonder why, when nothing has really changed.

A week later:

Willy has just returned from cycling to Nanaimo — about 70 miles one way. He has one of the forms we have to fill out.

First thing it asks for is a vital statistic number. What is that pray?

Then a facsimile number: Oh yes! They mean FAX number.

They talk about *consanguinity* and say see reverse of form, which reads: a man may not marry his grandmother, mother, granddaughter, daughter or sister.

A woman may not marry her grandfather, father, grandson, son or brother.

I wonder about the cousin relationship — is it now lawful for cousins to marry?

October 30th: He's checked for rings at the jewelers in the shopping mall. Said there's nothing under two hundred dollars. I told him our local Gold Bin is cheaper. He said he'd come with me when I get mine.

There's nothing large enough for him so they will order one. He notices it's in fourteen carat gold. "Make it ten carat," he tells them. They will order a smaller size for me in my selection. "What's the total cost?" he asks, getting out his wallet, which bulges with sale coupons and many denominations of dollar bills.

The jeweler totes it up to be one hundred and fifty dollars and tells Willy to pay when he picks them up on Thursday.

Now we've done that, we can phone the commissioner. We know we will have the ceremony in our apartment.

As we walk towards the library, a sour acid rises in my throat. I have to stop to find a Tums in my purse. "I've got heartburn," I tell Willy. Actually it's more than heartburn, it's a case of severe nerves. I feel quivery and agitated combined with an adrenaline rush.

The Commissioner has a sweet voice. She tells us to get the license and have identification with us. She will charge eighty-five dollars of which some goes to the Government. She will arrive at four p.m. I ask her not to wear official robes because I don't want anyone to know until after I've told my children.

1st November: I've got a gift for the witnesses and I wrap a *Willy and Me* book for the commissioner. I ask Willy are we going to have the ceremony in the living room. We can move the chesterfield to make room. He goes into one of his blusters. "We're not moving any furniture," he says, "for goodness sake, it's only a wedding." He points to where his desk is located in the dining room.

The space between the desk and the divider is only two feet. Not enough room for our photographs to be taken.

He's going out the door without a decision on this question. I have to yank at his sleeve to stop him.

"Okay," I say, "we have to compromise. What about in front of the wall in the studio? And it's not 'only' a wedding. It's *our* wedding."

He's shaking me off but I make him come to the spot I have in mind. He agrees and hurries out the door.

Later the phone rings. It's my son from Victoria. "I hear you're coming over," he says. "Don't know where you got that idea Paul. No, we're not coming."

After I put down the phone, Willy says, "You'd better phone him back. We *are* going to the island. If we have a wedding, we have to have a honeymoon."

I put up a dam on any negative reasons for doing such a thing. Play it cool Doris, he's never had a honeymoon. If that's what he wants, let it be — even though I dread driving this time of the year.

"How are we going and where are we staying?" I venture to ask.

He tells me we will drive and stay in motels and with that, he settles down, content with himself.

November 7th, 2001. Dear me! I'm remembering November 10th, 1945, when I married for the first time. The following day was Armistice Day and we stood with the silent, sad crowd in the gray, damp fog by London's cenotaph. The date of this wedding is too close to the other. Don't think about it.

I bought a lemon-filled white cake from Safeway with "Willy and Me' written on top of the white icing. Cost nine-ninety-nine. Willy comes in and sees the cake on the kitchen table. I'm in the bathroom and when he finds me he says, "I thought you'd gone away and I would have to find another 'me'."

The cake for my first wedding was hard to put together because of rationing during the war years. The family had to give up their sugar and butter rations so mother could make a fruit cake with marzipan on each layer, topped with royal icing.

This morning I mailed announcements to all the children at once. I hope they won't feel slighted when they know about the wedding after the fact.

Something always goes haywire at weddings but because this will be simple, there's not much chance of that happening. Willy is fussing. "We've got to have cookies," he says and actually leaves to buy some.

My crepe-de-chine dress is the color of old rose. The overlay is chiffon and has tiny rose-colored pearls scattered over it. My shoes are pale beige leather sandals. I bought them at the thrift shop but they're hand-made and look nice.

Willy is wearing his thrift-shop pants — but they're smart and the same Harris tweed jacket which I wrote about twelve years ago.

Three fifteen and Marianne and Bert come through the door. Oh! They're wonderful. Everything turns into a celebration because they have armfuls of roses and my bouquet is made of old fashioned roses and heather; lovely combination. We have our rings. Willy's is tight over his knuckle but he'll put soap on his finger.

I make a sign 'do not disturb' to put on the apartment door. Turn off the ring of the phone. It would be awful if a telemarketer phoned in the middle of the *cereMonie* as Willy calls it.

Tris Tucker the marriage commissioner arrives right on four o'clock. She's dressed in a nice dark suit instead of her robes.

We stand in the studio in front of my latest blue-gray abstract painting, roses all around us, and we repeat the vows as Tris words them. Willy keeps kissing me between the vows and we laugh because he seems anxious to get to that point. There's a great warmth in the room.

Marianne and Bert take photos and we sign the necessary documents.

We cut the cake and sit in the studio to eat a piece with our wine.

It's over. Willy and I are legally and officially man and wife.

Honeymoon: November 8, 2001

We arrive at Crystal Court Motel in Victoria, which is close to the Empress Hotel and Crystal Gardens; the buildings designed by the famous Rattenburg. We have room # 56 upstairs.

I've brought the library book (700 pages) on Edward Hopper the artist who was known for his portrayals of lonely people and bare rooms that give the viewer a feeling of foreboding. This room reminds me of his paintings. High, cove ceilings and old wooden doors on the clothes closet. Antique icebox inserted in the wall. Guess they used to put a block of ice in it.

We don't waste any time to get to the Victoria Art Gallery, where the Japanese garden is located. Willy knows I need to feel the spirit of the place again. The map says it's twelve blocks from the motel.

The day is crisp and sunny and I breathe in air more pure than that of Mission. I take my cameras and macro lens into the garden. There's a familiar feeling of rightness as if a mantle, just made for me, covers my shoulders.

As usual, Willy waits for me until I've had my fill of the gallery and the garden. He always appears when I step from the door. When I check the settings on the camera, I find I've had it on manual instead of auto. All my focusing will be off.

We meet my sons for dinner just across the road. Lorna, Mark's wife, isn't able to come because she's ill. I bring my bouquet to the table and we tell them we are married.

They seem happy about it. Willy suggests I send the bouquet to Lorna as she wasn't part of the excitement.

Back at the motel, I'm grateful I've brought the foam to relieve my back from the hard mattress. I fall asleep when my eyes get tired of reading about Ed Hopper.

Friday. Willy surprises me by agreeing to visit the museum next door. I would never have purposely gone to see this exhibition of Emily Carr but am profoundly grateful that it is on at this time.

What strikes me most is the amount of work the museum managed to collect to put on display. She was multitalented. I enjoy her pottery. Think she made these pots from local clay, firing them with cedar boughs. They're very earthy looking objects with their rusty-orange and charcoal colors. She made hand-hooked rugs from scraps of material. I loved the one she did of Adam and Eve with serpent. She made it as a present for her sisters and they were disgusted about it. They thought nude figures weren't proper to put on the floor and it was blasphemous to put a story from the bible into something which the dogs could sit on!

There's stacks and stacks of her hand-written pages for her books and revisions and Ira Dilworth's correspondence. Just staggering. There are a number of paintings I hadn't seen before. I felt humbled when I could see the amount of work she had done but disappointed with how few were portrayals of native Indians. Glad when she found her true belonging with the swirling renditions of trees and skies.

The museum had a replica of her "elephant" — the box-like shelter she had towed to the woods so she could be amongst the forest to paint. Yes, she truly worked and struggled all her life. I have a higher regard for her accomplishments because of this exhibit.

The Native section is all subdued lighting. Willy came up behind me and put his hands on my breasts. "Well it's dark," he says, "no one can see." Masks hang from the walls of a sacred cave. Low, eerie lighting against the blackened walls. Feeling the spirit of the cave as I walk towards it, I see a dark shape emerge from the bottom and slide towards me. I let out a scream and step back. Of course, Willy is not perturbed and when my heart stops pounding, I see there's a black mirror at the base of the exhibit and the shape I saw was our feet coming towards it! It takes a while for me to get over the experience.

The other exhibit is of an old-time town. Willy stops suddenly, something interests him. It's an old-time bicycle!

We go down the main streets of Victoria, me calling in book stores small and large. Find an art book which has paintings similar to my doodles. I buy that and then a small book on Hopper. It'll be interesting to see another viewpoint on him. In Munro's Books, I find a book on Dieberkorn. Eighty dollars. I don't care — I'm on my honeymoon. Didn't spend on new clothes, I'll spend it on books. Willy waits outside. When he sees the bags of books he says, "She was on her honeymoon and pretty well cleaned out all the book stores!"

We have lunch at McDonald's. Actually we always find our way by tracing McDonald's everywhere we go.

We find a gallery listed under contemporary art. I desperately need to find other artists who are on the same wavelength as me. Lady who owns the gallery makes the effort to talk about the show. I see some extremely interesting work in the racks at the back. Would my Zen paintings fit in here? The owner asks me to send photos. I'll do that.

As I've been reading Hopper's story, I realize he doesn't miss a beat in trying to sell himself here and trying there, trying this person and that person, never knowing when something will click and lead to a show or publicity. I wish I had a manager.

Son Mark comes to the motel and takes Willy on a dry run to Paul's place so we will know the way to go to dinner tonight.

Everything looks different at night and we get hopelessly lost trying to find the house. I was so thankful to see Mark outside on the road, looking out for us.

Lorna was feeling a bit better and came to dinner. Paul had made two roasted chickens and wonderful veggies. Then we had a lovely cake to celebrate.

6.

Christmas letter to friends 2001

Guess the biggest news of 2001 is that Willy and I were married on November 7th. It was just a quiet ceremony in my studio with two friends as witnesses. We've had nothing but parties and dinners out since. Even the exercise class gave a party and ABC restaurant gave us our dinner free last night! Everyone joins in with such happiness; I've come to the conclusion it's better if one marries late in life.

I was awarded "Woman of the year 2001" for Mission. I accepted on behalf of the arts. It was an honour.

Willy is still the same, biking most of the day and sometimes biking to Nanaimo. He'll be eighty-one in Dec. However, the other day when he was running to catch the train, he fell flat on his face. It's a good job it was *after* the wedding photos because he looked as if he'd been mugged!

People in this complex are getting older. One is near ninety and one ninety-one. Others in their mid-eighties and later seventies. Willy is the only man here when the other man goes to Hawaii for four months.

Had group shows and a larger solo show in Maple Ridge featuring twenty-one years of some of my art during that period. Other solo shows are due in May and October 2002. And so it goes!

All the best from this legally married couple to you!

Letter to Anne

Dear Anne, maybe you've heard by now, Willy and I were officially married on November 7th (so close to the date I married your brother — gave me the Willies, ha ha.)

What an extraordinary thing it is to see people's faces light up when they get the news. They all want to celebrate. Mon Dieu! I'm gaining weight with these dinner parties and wedding cakes! The complex is throwing a "surprise party" and the exercise group is taking me out for lunch; they're so sweet. Must be a reaction to all the bad news we've been having with the terrorist scare. At exercise group we usually begin the session with news. Many of the ladies are older and say so-and-so just died or is in hospital. The instructor gave me the floor to tell of the wedding. Afterwards she said, "Can anyone top that?"

Previous to all this, my brother John visited from Australia. He had been on a tour of Germany and found my mother's birth home and records of her family in the church office. The photo of her stone house is marvelous and you can see the shed where her father made shoes.

Just reading seven-hundred-page book on Edward Hopper. His wife recorded his life and the way he painted.

Sorry you've had the shingles. Did you find any medicine for it?
Love Doris.

8.

Walking with Willy

Okay. Okay. It's good to go for a walk every day, even though he pressures me about it. But isn't it supposed to be a companionable thing sharing conversation and joy in surroundings?

It' more like him taking a dog for a spin around the block. His hands are so large; it's only possible for me to grasp two of his fingers when we hold hands.

In all these years, it's still the same with so-called conversation, unless of course something triggers a condemnation of government or lawyers or unions. Otherwise he is silent.

When we first ever went for a walk, he had a way of closing into my side and matching my steps as if we were Siamese twins. It was quite the feeling: I couldn't get over how he could adapt to my rhythm so quickly. He still matches my pace, which is now slower up Mission's hills, and he adapts to when I want to walk.

I usually have my head up admiring the trees and mountains. He has his head down, eyes shifting this way and that in case he spies money in the gutter or some other treasure. Someone asked him once, "Why are you always looking down? You'll be under there soon enough."

When he finds a penny, which I have just missed, he berates me. "It was right under your nose. You can't be bothered to pick it up." Result is my eyes have to do double duty, flicking them from joyful sights to piles of junk along the way, just so I spot a coin before he does. He's risked life and limb to rescue a penny amongst oncoming traffic. He can find them even when he bikes, half-buried in mud at the center of the bridge. His finds add up to about two hundred dollars a year. "And there's no tax on it," he says.

I used to think he was a real gentleman because he walked on the outside, close to the road. I know now the curb is the prime picking-up place!

The operation: February 2002

"I can't see!" Willy says.

His forehead is crinkled with worry lines and his hands grip the armrests of the chair. He rubs his eyes and cranes his neck forward as if willing himself to see. He can't be having a stroke. I need him now. Oh Lord help us!

He's visiting me after my triple-by-pass surgery. I'm still in a weak state with oxygen connected to my nose, a catheter for my urine and over a hundred staples stuck in my legs, arm and chest.

My mind goes like a racehorse, galloping down the stretch without a barrier in sight. I've been out of the operation four days and haven't been able to stand, walk or even sit in a chair. Any attempt to do so and I faint. And here's Willy, maybe with a stroke and we're far from home in this Vancouver hospital.

He's been worried about my condition, he thinks maybe I won't be able to rise above this helplessness. Maybe I'm not going to recover at all. Maybe I'm slipping downwards and will die.

"What did you just say Willy?" I said in case I hadn't heard him properly.

"I can't see," he said.

Will I press the bell for the nurse or stay quiet and watch him for a while?

He relaxes his hands from the armrest and turns towards me.

"It's getting better now," he says.

What an ordeal it's been! Here I was, going to exercise classes, walking every day, keeping my blood sugar down and in spite of it all, wham! I joined the club of heart surgery people.

Early January, having slight pain while walking, the doctor sent me for tests. He figured maybe it was angina; told me to get nitroglycerin spray and squirt some under my tongue if I had distress.

I gave a speech to an audience at an art show and afterwards the pain became intense. The next evening, as I lifted the pot of potatoes off the stove, It felt as though someone was crushing my chest. I called to Willy "Quick! Forget supper, I have to go to the emergency room."

One is used to sitting a long time in emergency, but this time, doors flew open, blood pressure monitors and drugs were administered within minutes.

Dr. Baillie the heart specialist pulled up a chair beside the bed. He spoke in a calm but serious voice. "It's not angina Doris. You're having a heart attack."

I haven't got time for heart attacks, I told myself. He must have made a mistake — it can't happen to me. I've got too much to do yet!

Whomp! It felt as if a Scotsman had thrown one of those iron balls at my chest. I could hardly get my breath. Maybe it wasn't a mistake after all.

I remembered being taken up to the intensive care unit, but then everything went blank. I came into consciousness, being wheeled on a stretcher cart, vomiting pints of burnt-umber colored liquid, in Vancouver's hospital, 45 miles from Mission. It was morning of the next day. I learned afterwards that Dr. Baillie had come in the ambulance with me because they thought I was dying.

Me, dying? Impossible. I'm a hearty person, running up and down stairs, helping other seniors carry things too heavy for them.

A male nurse, with black hair and dark brown eyes conveying empathy and care, told me his name was Israel. He told me I might only need an angioplasty, explaining they'd take me up to a room to inject a dye through the groin and follow the passage of it through to my heart. If it was a question of only one blockage, they would insert a mesh tube which would keep the artery open.

Not having any more of the squeezing, hurting spasms, I pleaded with Israel to put down the bars of the bed so I could walk to the commode and wash basin. With reluctance, he gave in and I began to wash myself. I bent down to clean my feet. Yipes! I now knew for sure, Dr. Baillie had been right. In terrible pain, I made it to the bedside to ring for help.

Israel was disappointed with me. "I could have been in trouble," he said, "and you promised not to overdo things." I tried to explain I thought it wasn't possible I had a bad heart.

Up I went to this factory type room. Israel told me the worst part of this procedure would be the hard, narrow slab I'd have to lay on. It was like a shadow world in there and two doctors looked down at me, their faces underlit as if a flashlight was under their chins.

There's a policy in hospitals now where they inform you what they're intending to do. "I'm giving you a needle Doris. You'll feel the needle now. We are putting the dye in now. It won't hurt."

Above me, small flying-saucer-looking objects on robotic arms wove down and up and swerved around me, so close at times I thought they'd crush my chest. It was like being invaded by aliens. So intrigued by these things, I forgot why I was under them.

The doctors had decided from pictures delivered by these flying saucers.

"Sorry Doris, angioplasty is out for you. You're blocked solid and will have to have by-pass surgery."

This sounded serious. I wondered if Willy knew what was happening to me.

Did anyone tell him I was here instead of where he left me in the ward at Mission's hospital?

Poor guy. When we first met he didn't ask about my family history. Mother died aged fifty-six. Father at sixty-six. Brother aged sixty. Other brother triple by-pass. If he'd known all this, he might not have ventured into a relationship. With him being three and a half years older, I thought it would be him with health problems before me. But here he was, cycling miles every day and never takes even an aspirin and it was me who landed up in this predicament.

Back down I went to the holding ward or whatever they call it. Israel was waiting with his sympathetic brown eyes. "I'm so sorry Doris. We'll have to wait for the surgeon to give us a time in the operating room." He stroked my forehead. "All your children are phoning. Here's some lovely flowers," he said.

Next morning the surgeon came and introduced herself. A buxom, lovely looking woman with an English complexion and a no nonsense approach. She pulled down the sheet to look at my legs. "These veins aren't any good!" she says as she taps various areas on my legs. "They're non-existent."

"I had them stripped many years ago," I say.

"Absolute nonsense," she says, "why would you do such a thing?"

Well, I wasn't going to explain that after fourteen pregnancies, those unsightly bulging, blue rivulets covering my legs were bearable while I was loved unconditionally by my husband, but I thought improving my appearance might stop the hovering catastrophe of divorce.

"How am I going to do anything with this?" she said, as if I should know

I asked her about artificial arteries. What about pig's arteries? And she just humphed and said I wasn't a good candidate.

Israel told me I may be able to go for the by-pass operation the next day. But it was a two-day wait and fasting until I was able to go.

At one point, the children from Vancouver Island and Vancouver all came to see me. They brought a box of paints and watercolor postcards. As I looked up at them from my bed, they seemed to be ready to get a priest to give me the last rights! They were white-faced and anxious, gearing up to accept this might be the last time they'd see me. It was hard to keep talking because my chest hurt and I finally asked them to leave.

Israel constantly asked, "what level is the pain between one and ten?" I wanted to be sure there was enough room to reach ten if I had a massive assault. So when it wasn't too bad I'd say three-quarters. This amused him because no one's ever given that result.

Trying to be conversational with my children wore me out and my answer to Israel about the pain level crept up to a seven.

Next morning I was given some kind of medication to calm me down before the operation. On the stretcher trolley, I waved goodbye to Israel in imitation of the Queen Mother. In the operating room, someone injected the anesthetic and everything went blank.

I hate to remember the next four days. First thing I recalled was two nurses scrubbing a red dye off my skin and they were trying to stop the bleeding on my leg. They talked between themselves. "It's the skin graft," one said.

As I slipped in and out of consciousness, one of the young women told me my daughter had been waiting outside the recovery room for ages. Apparently the triple-by-pass operation went well, but they had a hard time getting me to regain alertness. Once again, my blood pressure dipped too low.

I pleaded with them to let my daughter come in, so she could see I was all right and she could go home. They refused. Treated me like a child. I told them she teaches nursing and wouldn't be in the way, but they continued to scrub, scrub and ignored my request. I got very upset about it but they hardened their resolve. Another nurse came in to tell me "sorry but your daughter is too tired to wait any longer and has gone home." I couldn't think of anything else. I was so angry with those two, who continued to scrub and talk between themselves.

Low blood pressure got lower. They fitted this contraption in my nostrils. It was like two big plastic cow-horns. And on and on it went with removing neck tubes and patching up the bleeding from my leg. I found out I have over a hundred staples, most of them in my legs and arm where they took out the veins.

I finally get to a private room on a ward. I wasn't allowed to use my arms to lift myself into a sitting position, one had to restrict any strain. My sternum was cut in half and wired together with stainless steel wire. ("Yes, you can go through the x-ray machine at an airport without alarms going off," we're told.) A long rope-like arrangement made of old sheets is fastened to the end of the bed and you're supposed to pull on this to sit up. Half the time the stupid thing is lost in the covers and I haven't any stomach muscles to pull myself up. I constantly slip down in the bed and lay helpless until someone comes to hoist me to the head of the bed again. I was in this ungodly position, panting away, when a visitor from the heart foundation came through the door. I couldn't even voice my name because I couldn't get my breath and my heart was pounding. I hoped she'd call someone to help but she was scared out of her mind and beat a retreat. However, she left me with a small red, heart-shaped pillow with a heart diagram on it. "Hold it to your chest when you exert yourself," she said and hurried out.

My false teeth felt as if they were sitting on shards of glass. I couldn't stand it anymore and took them out of my mouth. The supper tray came with a mound of some awful dark brown looking stuff, which I couldn't bear to look at. Then visitors came through the door and I didn't have the energy or time to put my teeth back in my mouth before they were in the room. I wasn't experienced in these occasions to know what to do. The couple took one look at me and just about fainted. No one had combed my hair and I hadn't looked in a mirror. I must have looked terrible.

I slipped in and out of a drugged sleep, waking when the nurse came to yank out tubes in my chest or to check blood pressure or urine output. Two young women came with a portable x-ray machine, checking for any fluid buildup on my chest.

The ward doctor looked at me every day. She has sleek black hair in pageboy style and wears black and white. Her shoes are pointy toed, stiletto heeled, black patent leather with a checkered design at the tips. You could always tell when she was coming because they tap-tap-tap down the corridor. She was exasperated with me because I kept fainting if they sat me in a chair. "We've checked everything and there's nothing to indicate there's anything wrong. You'll have to admit it's all in your mind," she told me.

So here's poor Willy, worried and stressed with me not recovering the way I should. I take off the oxygen tube and ask him to get my dressing gown and slippers. I tell him if he'll hold on to me, I'll try and get out of bed to walk in the corridor. His dear face lights up and he's relieved I may be able to make some improvement in my condition.

We make a scraggly pair with me carrying my catheter bag, hanging on to him for dear life and him practically carrying me, we shuffle a little way down the corridor. The nurse sees us and she's happy to know I'm able to get out of bed without passing out. Willy lunges me back onto the bed, reminding me of when he carried me over the *threeshold*. I'm exhausted but I did it and Willy can go home in a lighter frame of mind. The turning point has come.

"The only thing we have to worry about now, is if you can make the stairs to our apartment," Willy says, "they tell me you can't go home until you've made fourteen stairs up and down."

When he comes the next time, he brings me a white teddy bear holding a red velvet heart. The white writing on it says, "I can't bear to be without you!"

"I got it from Safeway," he says, "there was a great pile of them but only two had this saying on them." I put it on the bedside table and visitors and nurses laugh and say how cute it is.

He never actually says words such as this but chooses a roundabout way to convey his feelings.

I stayed for seven days in the hospital after the operation, acknowledging the enormity of what has happened to me and feeling gratitude for having another lease on life. Two nurses, one on either side of me, took out the staples with strong tweezers, dropping them one by one into a tray where they form a hill.

It's snowing as Willy drives me home. My son-in-law told him roads were bad and he would drive me instead, but Willy being Willy was not to be deterred. Getting into the car, I feel the cold acutely but am thankful to be out of the stuffy hospital forced air. I huddle down in my sweet little Toyota. Cars are in ditches on the way and wet sloppy flakes of snow splash onto the windshield. But other than slipping a bit here and there, we arrive at our seniors' complex without mishap.

I had practiced stair climbing in the hospital and could easily make our fourteen steps. And oh! how good to be home. Did all that really happen to me? Will I ever believe it?

The apartment is bright and clean and, with a jolt, I see my paintings on the walls with new insight. They are *good!* Better than I thought when I had my nose to the paper and painted every day.

Willy takes on the role of nurse and cook. He never complains or gives me to think I'm a nuisance. He puts me to bed. Wakes me in the morning, put my socks on and lifts me from the bed. He actually entertains the visitors by bringing them coffee or some of his schnapps. He follows me down the corridor when I practice walking, in case I fall. He has nine of my new medicines filled (which came to a hundred and fifty dollars). In short, he's pretty wonderful.

I lay on the chesterfield, still trying to believe I have undergone such a serious operation. A visitor asked, "What have you learned from the experience?" I'm sure of one thing. The flowers and cards with their handwritten notes of encouragement were a source of comfort to me. I hadn't realized so many people cared. Even the exercise group had timed their wonderful fruit basket to arrive at a time when I was recovering my appetite. My neighbor's bran muffins were just what the doctor ordered and another neighbor's wonderful dinners provided an incentive to start eating.

So Willy and I have survived another crisis. Surely that's when you find out if your partner is made of the good stuff! I am one thankful lady for the new life given me and the bicycle man who came my way twelve years ago.

10.

Up to now

We've come to the year 2008. After having three separate books about Willy and me, I'm putting them together as one. It will be called *The artist and the bicycle man* because the bike has featured throughout our time together.

Willy survived another trip to the hospital, he fell in the apartment and we had to get the ambulance. In the hospital he was kicking and screaming to get out of his restraining chair, finally breaking it and then bursting through a straitjacket. "Never seen the like!" a nurse told me. He was delirious from fever but whatever, he will not be constrained. They gave him all kinds of tests but couldn't find out what was wrong. He's back to normal and ignores warnings not to ride his bike. He's now eighty-seven and rides every day.

I'm doing okay and have joined the Federation of Canadian Artists. This year I'll have two solo shows — one from August to early September and the other in the Maple Ridge public gallery mid-December till mid-January. This will be a very large show called "The progession of an artist," and I'm really looking forward to it. However, I've promised Willy that it will be the end of me being aggressive looking for more places to show my work. I'm now eighty four.

It's also the end of writing about Willy: I want to write fiction short stories and I kind of like my poems even though I'm criticized for not being "literary." I'm also going to get off the strata council. My job was maintenance chair. I'm proud of the improvements we made here but now all is in good order.

Willy and I are in order as well, loving in a different way from how we began. But it is a deep, abiding love — a mature love which has understanding and appreciation. A loyalty and supportive connection which surmounts aggravation and difficulties.

I'm glad you journeyed with us. I felt you were with us. Doris.

ISBN 142517650-X

Edwards Brothers Malloy
Oxnard, CA USA
September 23, 2013